Carl Menger's Lectures to Crown Prince Rudolf of Austria

Carl Menger

Crown Prince Rudolf

Carl Menger's Lectures to Crown Prince Rudolf of Austria

---

edited by
Erich W. Streissler
Professor of economics, econometrics and economic history
University of Vienna
and
Monika Streissler

translated by
Monika Streissler
with the assistance of
David F. Good
Professor of history and director of the Center of Austrian Studies
University of Minnesota

with an introduction and footnotes by
Erich W. Streissler

Edward Elgar

Published by
Edward Elgar Publishing Limited
Gower House
Croft Road
Aldershot
Hants GU11 3HR
England

Edward Elgar Publishing Company
Old Post Road
Brookfield
Vermont 05036
USA

British Library Cataloguing in Publication Data
Menger, Carl
Carl Menger's Lectures to Crown Prince
Rudolf
I. Title II. Good, David F.
III. Streissler, Erich W.
IV. Streissler, Monika
330

Library of Congress Cataloguing in Publication Data
Menger, Carl, 1840–1921.
Carl Menger's lectures to Crown Prince Rudolf of Austria/edited by Erich W. Streissler and Monika Streissler; translated by Monika Streissler and David F. Good
p. cm.
Includes bibliographical references and index.
1. Economics. 2. Menger, Carl, 1840–1921. 3. Austrian school of economists. I. Rudolf, Crown Prince of Austria, 1858–1889. II. Streissler, Erich W., 1933– . III. Streissler, Monika. IV. Title. V. Title: Lectures to Crown Prince Rudolf of Austria.
HB175.M446 1994
330.15'7—dc20 94–4584
CIP

ISBN 1 85898 075 5

Printed and Bound in Great Britain by
Hartnolls Limited, Bodmin, Cornwall.

This book is dedicated to the memory of
Helmut H. Haschek (1930–93),
Chairman of the Board of Executive Directors
of Oesterreichische Kontrollbank AG,
financial expert, friend and indefatigable protector
of the social sciences and the fine arts.
His death is a loss to Austria.

Contents

Acknowledgements

In the person of Professor Dr Helmut Haschek, the Oesterreichische Kontrollbank AG had shown serious interest in the publication of the Menger Notebooks of Crown Prince Rudolf ever since their discovery by the historian Brigitte Hamann. It was the Kontrollbank that funded Dr Hamann's initial transcription of the manuscripts; and it was the Kontrollbank – acting through Dr Haschek's successors in office, Dr Johannes Attems and Dr Gerhard Praschak – whose generous contribution towards the printing costs made the publication of the book at all possible.

This support is deeply appreciated.

I am very grateful to Dr Hamann who brought the manuscripts to my attention and who very kindly let me use the typescript of her transcription. At all stages of my wife's work in the State Archives, Frau Hamann was most helpful with advice. Gladly, we take this opportunity to thank her for her kind assistance.

We gratefully acknowledge the help of the officials of the Austrian State Archives (Haus-, Hof- und Staatsarchiv), by courtesy of which the photograph of the notebook page is reproduced here. The photograph of Crown Prince Rudolf, dated 1876 on the print available in these Archives, is reproduced with the permission of the Picture Archives of the Austrian National Library (Bildarchiv der Österreichischen Nationalbibliothek), while the photograph of Carl Menger, the date of which is uncertain, is reproduced by courtesy of the Archives of the Austrian Academy of Sciences.

Erich W. Streissler

Note from translator and editorial assistant

The manuscript of the lectures on Political Economy, as written down by Crown Prince Rudolf after each of Carl Menger's lectures, consists of altogether 17 notebooks, as may be seen from the list on p.1. Each notebook has 8 sheets = 16 pages. In Notebooks I–XIII the sheets are consecutively numbered (on their front pages); in the Notebooks on Public Finance (14 and 15 in the list) sheet numbers start anew from 1. The page numbers as printed here, in the margin of the transcription, therefore refer to sheets and are rendered as recto ('r': right-hand page) and verso ('v': left-hand page). In the manuscript, the sheet numbers are in pencil; they were added later.

The major part of fifteen of the Notebooks is in Rudolf's handwriting: in ink, in Gothic script, interspersed with some words in Latin script, to set them out. The handwriting is well spaced and for the most part easy to read. Rudolf's text was corrected by Menger – partly in Gothic, partly in Latin script, mostly in pencil, occasionally with a coloured pencil. Parts of Notebooks I and II are altogether in Menger's handwriting (in ink), viz. (I), p. 5r to middle of p. 7v, and (II), pp. 9r–15v. On p. 10v is to be found the only word in the entire manuscript which is not unmistakably legible, even though it is written in Latin script. In the German text of this publication, words and passages written by Menger are set in italics. Underlinings in the Notebooks are rendered by black lines.

Occasionally, single words or (parts of) sentences are written in the margins of the Notebooks. These have been transcribed, too, and appear in square brackets. Whenever they are in Menger's writing, this is indicated by 'CM'. Where no name is given, the marginalia were added by Rudolf.

In addition to Rudolf's original Notebooks VIII and IX there exists what is obviously a fair copy of them – in the writing of a third person, as yet unidentified: presumably this was made because a great deal had been altered, deleted or rearranged by Menger in those originals (although certainly not more than in the Notebooks on Public Finance, 14 and 15 in the list, of which no fair copy is available). The present transcription was made from this fair copy, that is, from the Notebooks numbered 16 and 17 in the list. These again are numbered separately. The somewhat odd spacing and sequence of page numbers as indicated in the margin of the transcription of the two Notebooks on Public Finance is to be explained by Menger's changes and longish deletions from Rudolf's original text.

On publication, we had to decide whether to divide up the material by subject matter or by Notebooks. We opted for a division into chapters by Notebooks. Chapter headings correspond to the labels on the Notebooks, with the exception of the fair copy of Notebooks VIII and IX (cf. the titles of nos 16 and 17 of the list on p.1). The respective chapter headings read Political Economy VIII and Political Economy IX, nevertheless. The editor's notes are also numbered by Notebooks, therefore, even though in several cases a topic runs on from one Notebook to the next. We gladly take this opportunity to thank the publisher who allowed the notes to be footnotes instead of cumbersome endnotes; we are sure that every reader will appreciate this generosity.

The historian Brigitte Hamann, who discovered the Notebooks in the Haus-, Hof- und Staatsarchiv in Vienna, also prepared the first transcription of the manuscripts. Having compared this transcription with the originals – with the eyes, as it were, of an economist – I attempted to render the revised version into English.

Professor David F. Good of the Center of Austrian Studies at the University of Minnesota – a specialist in the economic and social history of the Austro-Hungarian Empire – took the great trouble of revising this translation. He would have liked to streamline it somewhat, but I felt that the English version should stay as close as possible to the original German. In this sort of translation, the primary purpose is not to transplant the original so fluently and idiomatically to the target language as to make it look perfectly at home there, but rather to transmit as much of the original trains of thought and expression as at all possible without letting it appear unduly awkward. Therefore I rejected a number of David's suggestions – which is not to say that I did not ponder them seriously. Now, the English version sounds somewhat old-fashioned, but this is as it should be; the German is also old-fashioned (and occasionally a little clumsy). The responsibility for any mistakes is entirely mine, of course.

In her transcription, Dr Hamann changed the German spelling, however, to present-day usage. As the Notebooks are not published because of their literary qualities, there seemed to be no reason not to do that. The original punctuation, though, has been retained; only in a few instances – where this made a sentence easier to understand – I added or deleted a comma. Rudolf uses semicolons very often where nowadays one would use a full stop; these have not been changed, either in the German or – for reasons of easy comparability – in the English version.

The German authors Rau and Roscher, to be frequently encountered in the editor's footnotes, are not quoted from the first editions of their books, but from editions closer to Menger's own day and therefore closer in content to the texts he will have used. Perhaps it should be mentioned that titles and quotations from 19th century published sources in the footnotes are rendered in their original spelling, of course.

I should like to thank our editor, Mrs Julie Leppard, for all the efforts she devoted to this publication; it was always reassuring to know that she was 'at the other end'. Most particularly, I want to thank Mrs Katie Lewis, the copy-editor, for her meticulous and unfailing attention to the manuscript. Apart from a number of welcome improvements to the translation, she raised some 'queries' which showed me that I must have acquired a certain shop-blindness a little prematurely. This made me go over the entire German and English texts once more, to good effect (or so I hope). I am deeply grateful to Mrs Lewis.

Monika Streissler

The notebooks of Crown Prince Rudolf on Carl Menger's lectures

(held in the Austrian State Archives: Haus-, Hof- und Staatsarchiv, "Selekt Kronprinz Rudolf, Karton 11")

	Notebooks[1]	*Sheet numbers*
1	Politische Oeconomie I. 1876. Jänner.	1–8
2	Politische Oekonomie II. 1876. Jänner.	9–16
3	Politische Oeconomie III. 1876. Jänner	17–24
4	Politische Oeconomie IV. 1876. Jänner.	25–32
5	V. Politische Oeconomie. 1876. Februar.	33–40
6	VI. Politische Oeconomie. 1876. Februar. Über den Nutzen der staatlichen Beeinflußung der Volkswirthschaft u. die Grenzen derselben I.	41–49[2]
7	VII. Politische Oeconomie. 1876. Februar. Über den Nutzen der staatlichen Beeinflußung der Volkswirthschaft u.die Grenzen derselben II.	50–57
8	VIII. Politische Oeconomie. 1876. Februar/März.	58–65
9	IX. Politische Oeconomie. 1876. März. Fortsetzung aus Heft VIII. II.	66–68[3]
10	X. Politische Oeconomie. 1876. März.	69–76
11	XI. Politische Oeconomie. 1876. März.	77–84
12	XII. Politische Oeconomie. 1876. März.	85–92
13	XIII. Politische Oeconomie. 1876. April	93–97[4]
14	Finanzwißenschaft. Über Steuern. I. 1876.	1–8
15	Finanzwißenschaft. Über Steuern. II. 1876.	9–12
16	I. Über den Zustand des Papiergeldes in Oesterreich-Ungarn und die Mitteln ihn zu reformiren 1876.	1–8[5]
17	II. Über den Zustand des Papiergeldes in Oesterreich-Ungarn und die Mitteln ihn zu reformiren. 1876	9–12[5]

[1] All Notebooks were labelled by Rudolf. The wording on the covers is given here in the original spelling and punctuation.

[2] In addition to the eight sheets of the Notebook, the inside back cover is numbered as 49.

[3] In this Notebook, only three sheets have been written on; the five blank sheets are unnumbered.

[4] In this Notebook, five sheets have been written on; the three blank sheets are unnumbered.

[5] These Notebooks are a fair copy of Notebooks VIII and IX.

Menger's treatment of economics in the Rudolf lectures

THE RELEVANCE OF THE RUDOLF NOTEBOOKS

The complete set of notes on the course of lectures on 'Political Economy' which Carl Menger gave to Crown Prince Rudolf of Austria in 1876 would be of historical interest if only because of the protagonists. The pupil was a young man of 18 on whom many hopes for the future course of the Habsburg Empire were then centred, but who was to die prematurely, probably by his own hand, in 1889, under circumstances which made headlines in (Austrian) tabloids as late as January 1993. The teacher was to become one of the altogether perhaps twenty greatest economists the world has known, the founder of the long-lived Austrian School of economics and in his day a highly renowned university professor. The 15 Notebooks are mostly in Rudolf's handwriting, corrected by Menger; parts of Notebooks I and II are actually in the handwriting of Menger. Thus, the Notebooks are an authenticated document, as it were, of the whole course as it was actually taught. They were discovered in 1986 by Dr Brigitte Hamann, historian and biographer of Rudolf, in the State Archives of Austria, where they are still kept. They are here published in full – and fully commented – for the first time, both in German and in an English translation.

Surpassing by far the importance of the persons directly concerned, however, the Notebooks are an invaluable document of the history of thought: to a historian of education, they are a fascinating document of how to present a brief course in a difficult subject to a person likely to be of the greatest political consequence, Emperors in Austria then still ruling personally to a very high degree. They are a fascinating document of an intelligent young man's receptivity to what he was taught. For what was taught can be reconstructed almost completely from the texts the teacher must have used, and today's reader can still gauge the learning ability of the pupil. They are implicitly a fascinating document of the political conditions in Austria some 120 years ago, conditions which can be recovered from what Menger thought important to teach and how he went about it. And finally, they are of the greatest importance and relevance for the history of economic thought. Menger, the economic theoretician, founded a school that was to run its course over at least three-quarters of a century. Even in economic theory he wrote relatively little. Rudolf's Notebooks as authenticated by Menger present the theoretician Menger in a rather different light from that on his received picture in the history of economic thought. A Neo-Austrian School, expressly linking itself to Menger's work, is now flourishing in the United States and in Great Britain, offering one of the main paradigms of economic reasoning today. Outsiders, more than insiders, link this theoretical school with a classically liberal position on economic policy. Does such political predilection stem from Carl Menger himself? This question is very difficult to answer because Menger, confined to teaching economic theory (and public finance), published virtually nothing on the fundamental questions of economic policy, his most important work on this topic being a longish newspaper article. The Rudolf Lectures here presented, however, are mainly on economic policy; and they show Menger to have been a classical economic liberal of the purest water, an economist, furthermore, who worked from an intimate knowledge of Adam Smith. This, too, comes as a surprise, because in his published work Menger explains in detail against what and whom he is, but rarely cites the authorities to whom he feels indebted for his ideas and his reasoning. Thus, Rudolf's Notebooks are full of surprises with respect to important questions still very much discussed today.

THE CONDITIONS FOR MENGER'S TEACHING

Menger was a young man and a very junior scholar when he was called upon to teach economics to Crown Prince Rudolf of Austria. Born on 23 February 1840, he was not quite 36 years of age when he delivered the first lectures in early 1876. He had begun the serious study of economics a little more than eight years before, dating the first book he had assigned himself (Rau's *Grundsätze der Volkswirthschaftslehre*) 'September 1867'. His first published work in economics, the magisterial treatise on which his fame mainly rests, the *Principles of Economics (Grundsätze der Volkswirthschaftslehre)*, had been published in the middle of 1871. He had passed his examination as university lecturer (the *Habilitation*) only three and a half years before, in 1872, and had been appointed a full-time professor (in associate rank, at the University of Vienna's Faculty of Law and Political Science) in the autumn of 1873. In other words, he had as yet very little teaching experience, one year of part-time and two and a half years of full-time lecturing. He was still in the insecure and somewhat provisional position of an associate professor, attaining full professorial rank only three and a half years later, in 1879, largely because of his achievement as teacher to the Crown Prince. The chair as Full Professor of Economics at the Vienna Law School was a position not only of great influence and prestige, but also quite remunerative,[1]

[1] See Streissler (1990a), p. 62 f.

and thus a dignity to be much fought over behind the scenes. It was the Emperor, the Crown Prince's father, who had to appoint to this professorial chair; and in the event Menger was actually forced upon the somewhat reluctant faculty, who would have preferred another, outside, candidate, the more conservative Karl Theodor von Inama-Sternegg, professor in Innsbruck[2] (a man who was to remain Menger's often more successful competitor for social status during many years to come). On the other hand, if Menger impressed the Crown Prince, he might, on the latter's presumed accession to the throne, perhaps in ten or twenty years' time, very well reckon with important ministerial office, or, as an outside chance, even with the prime-ministership, which in times of a still very personalized monarchy had – e.g. in France or in England – more than once gone, if only briefly, to the main former educator of the monarch. (Rudolf, of course, was to commit suicide 13 years later, which did not improve Menger's later career chances.) To put it briefly: in 1876, the stakes for Menger were very high.

The position to be taken was certainly also a dangerous one: the question of the ideological principles on which the Crown Prince was to be educated had given cause for continuing disagreement between the conservative advisers of the Emperor and the liberal politicians and intellectuals associated with the Empress.[3] Menger delivered the Rudolf Lectures at the depth of economic depression with its consequent social upheavals. After a brief flirtation with more open-minded and market-oriented economic ideas during the flourishing years of the *Gründerzeit* of 1867–73, which had ended in the great stock-market crash of May 1873, the aristocracy was once again veering towards conservatism. The Liberal Party was still in power, but under heavy attack. Three and a half years later Count Taaffe would embark upon a long stretch of conservative rule in Austria.

Menger was chosen as teacher both because of his liberal views and because he was the up-and-coming young star of economics in Austria of Austrian extraction (Inama-Sternegg, for example had been born in Germany, not Austria). But it was not at all unlikely that a teacher of the Crown Prince might be made to fail and even dismissed in disgrace for mainly political reasons. In fact, Menger did achieve the position of one of the most trusted teachers of the Crown Prince, trusted both by Rudolf himself and by his elders: he was to accompany him later on travels to foreign countries, for example to England, in order to study their economic and social conditions. He was even to work with the Crown Prince on the latter's publications.

[2] Personalakt Carl Menger, Allgemeines Verwaltungsarchiv, Ministerium für Cultus und Unterricht, Letter of the Dean of the Faculty of Law, Lorenz von Stein, dated 31 January 1879, to the Minister. After saying that the faculty would have preferred Inama-Sternegg, nominating him 'in first place', the faculty attempted a curious (and unsuccessful) kind of bargain: if it had to accept Menger, it was only on the condition that Inama-Sternegg be made professor in Prague, the second most important Austrian university, and that the faculty get in addition Emil Sax as associate professor.

[3] See Hamann (1978), pp. 29 f., 32, 77 ff. and *passim* in Chapters 1 and 2.

THE CONTENT OF THE NOTEBOOKS

How did Menger approach the delicate and difficult task of lecturing to the heir presumptive of what was still very much a personal monarchy? He took the politically wise as well as the most economical course: he hardly presented his own ideas at all; he did not teach from his own published work. Instead he taught almost exclusively from already world-famous, i.e. from old, books. He did not even rearrange the material from these books freely, but taught their ideas one after the other nearly in their original order and even sentence by sentence in their exact words. In this way, he guarded himself against possible criticism. Furthermore, he used only a very few books, a fact which is easily reconstructed because he stuck to his texts so closely. This also made his task somewhat easier. His decision may have been influenced by the fact that his lectures to the Crown Prince were, to a considerable extent, to cover topics different from his university lectures: on the whole, he taught him economic policy, while his university lectures were strictly confined to economic theory and public finance, economic policy being the province of his much older professorial colleague Lorenz von Stein.

The main textbook which Menger used was not an Austrian one, but rather the standard German textbook of the preceding quarter century by Karl Heinrich Rau, published in its first volume (on economic theory) in 1826, exactly 50 years before the Rudolf Lectures. This textbook was a four-volume work, the second volume covering economic policy (first published in 1828), while the third and fourth volumes dealt with public finance (first published in 1832 and 1837 respectively). The volume on theory was by then in its eighth (!) edition. In other words: Menger used the German equivalent, as it were, of Paul Samuelson's *Economics*, still used for introductory courses today, 45 years after its first publication, so nearly as old as 'the Rau' was then. In addition, Rau's theory volume was the book on which Menger himself had started his own reading course in economics some eight years earlier. Rau was appropriate also as the highly distinguished former chief economist of perhaps the leading liberal (in the classical sense) German state, the Grand Duchy of Baden: recently deceased, he had been professor in Heidelberg, Privy Counsellor (*Geheimrat*) of Baden and Honorary Member of the Austrian Academy of Sciences.

So far the line chosen by Menger was, by then, 'old-fashioned', but plausibly old-fashioned. The really astonishing decision is this: even Rau is mainly used only for details and case studies. The whole framework of the lectures and most of the arguments are taken from Adam Smith's *An Inquiry into the Nature and Causes of the Wealth of Nations* (1776), by then exactly 100 years old! Was it because someone, for example the supervisor of the Crown Prince's education, Count Latour-Thurmburg, a highly educated and liberal general, had suggested Adam Smith as an appropriate source? Or was it because Menger himself admired Adam Smith so much that he thought one could not better him in essentials? Anyhow, Adam Smith was certainly a classic and could be considered part and parcel of the canon of western civilisation, so that teaching him would be a safe course of action as well.

Still, to stick as closely to Adam Smith as Menger did was quite unnecessary; Rau, who was very strongly influenced by Adam Smith, had not done so. Close study of the Notebooks shows that in fact they follow mainly Book I of Adam Smith's *Wealth of Nations*, with minor variations, and little else. Frequently, the exact idea and the exact course of argument of Smith are presented, so that one can be absolutely sure that Menger consulted and used this work.

After giving the definition of economics, and some of the new German 'fundamental concepts' (goods, economizing) as a kind of preface, Notebook I starts with the division of labour (*Wealth of Nations* I.i.). Then Menger deviates a little from Smith: instead of going on to consider the somewhat forced Smithian idea of the human 'propensity to truck, barter and exchange' (ibid. I.ii.) and the fact 'that the division of labour is limited by the extent of the market' (ibid. I.iii.), Menger discusses private property as the foundation of both exchange and the division of labour (Notebook II) and then the use of machinery, entrepreneurial activity, and the employment of various types of capital as the source of income (Notebook III). But even this deviation stays close to the spirit of Adam Smith, according to whom 'accumulation of stock must ... be previous to the division of labour'; and, in fact, these two Notebooks draw heavily on *Wealth of Nations* II.ii., II.i., and II.iii., in that order. At the end of Notebook III and in Notebook IV we are back in *Wealth of Nations*, Book I, with the discussion of value very much along Smithian lines (ibid. I.iv, end of chapter). Notebook V discusses the origin of money, i.e. exactly the topic announced in the caption to *Wealth of Nations* I.iv, following Smith very closely. Then Menger digresses a second time: Notebooks VI and VII discuss the proper functions of government. This is a quintessentially Smithian topic (ibid. IV); but here Menger relies somewhat more on Rau than on Smith. From Rau, Menger derives a unifying principle: government action is admissible only in cases of market failure due to external effects, a theme which is foreshadowed as one of Smith's proper duties for the 'sovereign', duty number 3 (ibid. IV.ix.51). Market failure, even in this restricted sense, is immediately balanced out by government failure in Notebook VIII and the very short Notebook IX on the evils of the paper currency of Austria. In the whole course of the lectures it is only here that Menger is completely on his own; and here he deals with a topical question of Austrian policy, not with an issue of economic theory. Menger shows his uneasiness about being on his own by heavily editing these two Notebooks. Then we are once more back in *Wealth of Nations* I: Notebook X treats the theory of wages (ibid. I.viii.), but mainly in the differential framework 'Of Wages ... in the different Employments of

Labour' (ibid. I.x.). Notebook XI treats interest (ibid. I.ix.); and Notebook XII the rent of land (ibid. I.xi.), thus following the succession of topics in the *Wealth of Nations* to the letter. Notebook XIII presents the theory of commodity pricing (ibid. I.vii.) after that of factor prices, which is more logical on Smith's own terms, though in conflict with his exposition. The last two Notebooks on a course of lectures given five months later treat taxes, the main topic of *Wealth of Nations*, V. This topic ends Menger's lectures, as it does the *Wealth of Nations*.

The reliance on Adam Smith is stronger than even this enumeration might suggest. For Menger refers to the four volumes of Rau's comprehensive textbook mainly with respect to topics which Smith had at least briefly sketched and Rau had only treated more extensively. It is almost as if Menger checked at every step whether what he taught was mentioned in his 'bible', the *Wealth of Nations*. Such dependence on Smith was quite unusual at the time, even in German-language economics, which relied much more on Smith than did contemporary English economics. Apart from Smith and Rau, Menger used only a sprinkling of other German-language textbooks, particularly Roscher's *Grundlagen*, which had supplanted Rau in the third quarter of the 19th century as the 'new' standard German textbook (it reached 26 editions!), written by a man to whom Menger had dedicated his own *Principles* four years ago. Some passages in the Notebooks can be traced to Hermann, Riedel, Schäffle and Stein, all well-known professors. As all of them wrote textbooks, their treatments overlap to a considerable degree; but sometimes the source used by Menger can be reconstructed with near certainty because of some unusual word faithfully reproduced by the imperial pupil or because of the exact sequence of arguments presented. At least one important idea can be traced only to Peter Mischler, Menger's own teacher, a source I was the first to discover – Menger himself never mentioning him.[4] Menger depends on Mischler rather more than he ever admitted.

Now a loaf baked with so few ingredients would not seem to be exciting food. Can Menger, copy-cat of a very few standard textbooks and of one world classic, be of any interest to the history of thought? Most definitely. After all, Menger presented to Rudolf 10 per cent of Adam Smith's *Wealth of Nations* at the most (and in a very abbreviated form) and not much more than 1 per cent of the four volumes of Rau's work: it is the selection which is fascinating. The Rudolf Notebooks remind me of the first seminar paper a Chinese student once presented to me: it consisted of nothing but quotations, but these were arranged, mosaic-like, in such a way that they presented an original picture, rendered not by the authors quoted, but by the young Chinese scholar himself.

Menger uses exactly the same technique of hiding behind his authorities, a fact, which, as I said, points to his uneasy awareness of the dangers of his position.

4 Streissler (1990a), pp. 36 f., 60.

In particular he is an artist in omission, not only of whole topics but here and there even of certain arguments. I shall go into the details of this aspect of the Notebooks later in this introduction.

By using the 'ancients' in his arguments Menger could present his own world view and his own views on economic policy, but not his new theoretical framework, because that, being new, simply cannot be found in the works of the 'ancients'. But this gives us a fascinating insight into Menger's own priorities: evidently, what was of paramount importance to him was a classical liberal policy stance coupled to methodological individualism, which he could fully communicate to the Crown Prince by selective references taken from Adam Smith, Rau, and others. Incidentally, this suggests a further reason why he used old treatises and old textbooks: they were much more liberal than many of the contemporary books on economics. Menger evidently preferred the 'ancients' on ideological grounds as well. On the other hand, Menger, the creator of subjective value theory, seems not to have minded that in many instances he taught the Crown Prince the exact opposite of what he had forcefully argued was the only possible correct theoretical position (see below). And this may imply that subjective value notions were not as important to Menger himself as they became to his followers: his pupils and his pupils' pupils.

MENGER'S DIDACTICS

In order to illustrate Menger's technique of selectivity we have, however, first to turn to Menger's didactics. For the Notebooks can also serve as a model for teaching economics, and their analysis is, among other things, a study in pedagogy. Menger was, as has been generally attested, a great teacher.

Crown Prince Rudolf Franz Karl Joseph of Austria was born on 21 August 1858. At the time when most of the lectures were held (January–March 1876) he was a young man of seventeen and a half years of age, unusually intelligent, very well educated and interested, but also very nervous and highly strung. The lectures were to be a crash-course in economics, the Crown Prince's first and last such course in Menger's scientific field. How could one catch the attention of such a young man? Menger used a method which appears to be quite modern, but which is, in fact, quite old: he mainly taught using case studies connected by a thin line of general argument. For these case studies he frequently had to rely on other sources than Adam Smith.

In Notebook II the importance of private property, seen in particular as an incentive to thrift and initiative, is brought out by using 'communist' arguments against private property as case study no. 1. These arguments are fully rejected, of course. For this Menger could rely on Roscher's masterly marshalling of arguments against socialism in his textbook. Case study no. 2 follows immediately: modern production relies on all manner of machinery, much of it only recently developed. The treatment is wholly optimistic, much more so than in Ricardo's (1821) famous chapter XXXI 'On Machinery'. Menger achieves this by referring to a suitably optimistic author, the Prussian Riedel, and to elaborations on Riedel's theme by his own teacher, Mischler. While Notebook III is pure theory and consequently follows Adam Smith nearly exclusively, Notebook IV develops case study no. 3, which, at first sight, seems to be a *non sequitur*. The Notebook treats the theory of value (following Smith), and the case study is on the viability of small-scale handicraft industry. The link is that tastes shift away from the demand for handicraft products and that therefore nothing can (or should) be done politically against the inevitable decline and demise of handicraft production. The case study is taken from Rau and uses some arguments of Smith's. Here, one idea is Menger's own: the importance of product differentiation; but curiously enough it is used as an argument against, and not in favour of, the survival of handicraft manufacturers, who are – more by implication – too hidebound and tradition-minded to seize the opportunities of product differentiation. Notebook V on the origin of money is straight Adam Smith. Having discussed 'industrial policy' – or rather the fact that in the sense of protecting existing industries it is quite useless – and having said something about money (mainly that it is an institution developing according to human needs and one with which the sovereign should not tamper) Menger turns to the general principles which ought to guide government action: they are recorded in the two Notebooks entitled *On the Benefits and Limits of Government Intervention in the Economy*. The topics dealt with all conform to Adam Smith's duties two and three of the sovereign:

> secondly, the duty of protecting, as far as possible, every member of the society from the injustice and oppression of every other member of it ... and thirdly, the duty of erecting and maintaining certain publick works and certain publick institutions, which it can never be for the interest of any individual, or small number of individuals, to erect and maintain' (*Wealth of Nations* IV.ix.51).

The actual treatment, apart from Smith, strongly relies on Rau, who had made the external effect argument, implicit in Smith's third duty, much more explicit. Interspersed are two case studies, case study no. 4 on labour regulation (hours and conditions of work) and child labour and case study no. 5 on forest management to guard against deforestation. Both are taken from Rau, this time from the latter's book on economic policy. The next two Notebooks may *in toto* be considered a case study of the abuse of governmental power through the misuses of a paper currency in Austria. Notebook X returns to topics of the *Wealth of Nations* and presents the theory of wages. This is, in fact, treated in another case study, no. 6, which examines the question of the appropriate payment of civil servants. The arguments are nearly all taken from Smith, in spite of the fact that Smith had not examined the pay of civil servants, as this human subspecies was mostly absent from the England of his day. Menger deals with civil service pay purely on opportunity cost lines: as recompense for the cost of the necessary higher education and the costs of exercising official duties. Of course, civil servant remuneration is a most fitting case study for the Crown Prince: it is wage theory from the perspective of government. The same is true of case study no. 7: interest theory is presented by way of an investigation of the factors determining interest on government loans, a topic which gives Menger another opportunity to stress the need for thrift and financial rectitude in government affairs. (Here he has to rely much more on Rau than on Smith, but is also able to quote just about the only classical liberal argument in the public finance text of his senior colleague, Lorenz von Stein, viz. the need for scrupulously correct dealing in debt management.) Notebook XII is another case study, no. 8, this time in the theory of rent: here the only question examined is why rents are constantly rising in real terms, thereby enriching the aristocracy. Once more, Menger relies on Adam Smith, while at the same time demonstrating perhaps the most common ability of all economists, the ability to forecast wrongly (within a very few years Austrian rents were to go into a precipitate decline, due to the importation of corn from the United States and other 'newly developed' countries, a decline that ruined the Austrian landed aristocracy). Most of Notebook XIII amounts to yet another case study, no. 9: instead of presenting a systematic commodity price theory, Menger examines the problem of famines. Is there a need for the government to interfere in the pricing process of the corn market? No, for this would be both unnecessary and, if attempted, useless. Menger relies on Rau, who elaborates on a couple of paragraphs by Adam Smith. The last two Notebooks, on taxation, fall within Menger's own academic province, public finance. They deal with taxation along the lines of Smith elaborated by Rau, this time in the latter's two volumes on public finance. These final lectures make for somewhat dry reading and must have been rather tough going for Rudolf, considering that they were given during his summer holidays (and judging from Menger's numerous alterations in the pupil's manuscripts). These two Notebooks are dated from Ischl, the imperial summer resort, the final date given being 11 August 1876, shortly before Rudolf's 18th birthday (the other Notebooks are dated January to April).

As to the technique of presentation, Menger generally begins by giving a brief preview of the topic to be analysed, then elaborates on the subject and finally repeats some of the key issues. The Crown Prince has not been trained and is not being trained in proper exposition. He is not enjoined to rearrange the arguments on his own in their logical (in contrast to their didactic) order. Therefore, in places his presentation is decidedly repetitious. This, together with the many case studies interspersed in the more general line of argument, makes the Notebooks somewhat unsystematic and muddled. One has to reconstitute their logical order if one wishes to see their unity and cohesion. Basically, we are presented with the raw materials of didactic endeavours which have not yet been moulded into a pleasing whole.

In imperial education memory training was very important to the Habsburg family. After all, a future Emperor had to remember countless legal provisions and regulations, any number of people by name, and several languages at that. (Rudolf was proficient in German, Latin, French, English, Hungarian, Czech and Polish.) Therefore, the Crown Prince was enjoined to follow Menger's lectures attentively without taking notes or with only a minimum of notes. (At least, in contrast to some of the other lecture courses, there are no 'rough books' on Political Economy in the Archives.) Rudolf had to reproduce them from memory by writing them down in notebooks. As far as we know, he was not given any textbooks to read or to refer to when writing his essays. (Otherwise, sentences or half-sentences in the originals which Menger left out, evidently for ideological reasons, would inevitably have cropped up in the Notebooks.) The notebooks were then handed in to Menger for correction. Rarely did Menger delete repetitions, and only in a few places did he change the order of argument. Apart from the notebooks on the paper currency of Austria, where Menger had stuck out his neck in dealing with a subject without shielding himself behind a textbook, and in which he corrected so much that they had to be rewritten, and the notebooks on taxes which are rather heavily 'edited', Menger usually corrected only certain words or phrases. Much of the text is therefore by Rudolf, unaided. And it is quite astonishing to see the calibre of Menger's pupil, a pupil in the prime age for memorative learning: the Crown Prince shows near-perfect recall. In quite a few instances, the German textbook used by Menger can be deduced merely from an unusual word or two which Rudolf renders faithfully. The various detailed arguments are written down almost exactly in the sequences presented in the books – which the Crown Prince did not have before him. Usually the major part of the arguments in a fairly long line of reasoning is reproduced; and sometimes Menger himself may have abbreviated such a line of reasoning (in fact, one can sometimes find him deleting arguments he did not like). The reader can easily verify these statements from the footnotes to the text, which have been compiled to a large extent in order to show not only that Menger hardly ever lectured without a text, but also how faithfully the Crown Prince reproduced both the lines of argument and also the exact words in which they were stated. The Notebooks are certainly proof of Menger's didactic success.

IDEOLOGICAL AND POLITICAL CONTENT OF THE RUDOLF LECTURES

Apart from occasional naive remarks and a certain effusiveness, we can thus be sure that on the whole the Notebooks reproduce faithfully what Menger said.

What light then do the Rudolf Lectures throw on Menger's ideological stance, the degree to which he was a pure classical liberal, and also on the policy recommendations he endorsed?

The question of what Menger really thought on matters of economic policy would be of relatively little interest were it not for the fact that the Neo-Austrian School now thriving in the United States and in Great Britain has a notable and commonly recognized policy bias, and that the last generation of the Austrian School proper, especially F.A. von Hayek, G. von Haberler, and F. Machlup, are (or were) classical economic liberals of the strictest kind and are (or were) very much concerned with the fundamental principles of economic policy. Is this due only to Ludwig von Mises, who, as he did not become a full-time academic, could uninhibitedly (and, of course, magisterially) discourse on matters of economic policy?

Upon reading Menger's sole pronouncement on the fundamental principles of economic policy, his article in the main Austrian newspaper on the occasion of the centenary of the death of Adam Smith (1891),[5] one might be tempted to conclude that Menger in his time stood far to the 'left' of Mises, that Menger was, in fact, a socially minded 'liberal' or a liberal socialist. Evidently the subject of the economic policy of the classical school touched Menger deeply: it was to be the topic on which he made Richard Schüller write the last *Habilitation* thesis completed under his supervision.[6] His newspaper article is in a sense one on economic theory, being merely an inquisition into the history of economic thought, but of course with a political impact. It points out what the classicists and Adam Smith had actually said on questions of social policy and how much they were wronged in contemporary (late 19th century) German and Austrian political discourse. In this essay in persuasion Menger may give the impression that he himself was fully in sympathy with all types of legislative measures in favour of the 'working man', including massive intervention in free enterprise and numerous redistributive measures. This is what one might gather in hindsight, reading his text after another century of social (and socialist) policies.[7] However, in this article Menger does not even mention the Austrian social security system (a health care and old-age pension scheme with heavy redistributional subsidization by the state), which had been introduced a few years earlier. What he says is simply that Adam Smith did not consider justice always to be on the side of the employers in all their conflicts with and all their demands against

5 See Menger (1891) 1970.

6 See Schüller (1895).

7 Menger uses florid terminology, e.g. when he says: 'A. Smith stellt sich in allen Fällen des Interessen-Conflictes zwischen den Armen und Reichen, zwischen den Starken und den Schwachen *ausnahmslos* auf die Seite der Letzteren' (1970, p. 223). Or: 'Die staatliche Einmischung *zu Gunsten* der Armen und Schwachen weist er (i.e. Smith) so wenig zurück, dass er sie vielmehr in allen Fällen billigt, in welchen er von der Einmischung des Staates eine *Begünstigung* ... der besitzlosen Volksclassen erwartet' (p. 224). See also Streissler (1990b).

their workers (obviously true); and that Smith was not against all types of state actions in all cases (again obviously true). In fact, in similar endeavours Jacob Viner, Lionel Robbins, and George Stigler (to take them in historical order) distilled a far more copious agenda for economic policy out of Adam Smith [8] than Menger dwells upon – though admittedly they were writing on economic policy of the classicists in general, and not only on social policy.

In contrast, the Rudolf Notebooks show Menger to have been a classical liberal of the purest water with a much smaller agenda for the state in mind than even Adam Smith. (And when carefully rereading Menger's 1891 article on Smith and the classicists one can see that he had not changed his mind – in spite of the eloquence which might be misconstrued.) No mention whatsoever is made of Smith's antimonopolist strictures or his condemnation of actions in restraint of trade. (One recalls that the Austrian School as a whole was never much in favour of active antimonopoly legislation.) Even more astonishing is the fact that no mention is made that national security might ever be a legitimate reason for regulative or protective action – regardless of the fact that Rudolf was trained as a member and prospective commander-in-chief of the Austrian armed forces! To Smith, on the other hand, the first 'duty of the sovereign' was the 'duty of protecting the society from the violence and invasion of other independent societies' (*Wealth of Nations* IV.ix.51); he thought economic interventionism 'wise' if it furthered national security, 'as defence ... is of much more importance than opulence' (ibid. IV.ii.30). On this 'duty' Menger is silent. Obviously he thought that unsuccessful wars in 1859 and 1866 and excessive attention towards the armed forces had already sufficiently ruined Austrian finances and that speaking of them might open a Pandora's box of unsound fiscal measures. Many other economic activities of the Austrian state are not mentioned either. Austria had, for example, a well developed and reliable postal service; even Smith had thought mail services 'perhaps the only mercantile project which has been successfully managed by, I believe, every sort of government' (*Wealth of Nations* V.ii.a.5). But even this sole exception of Smith's to the rule that the state should refrain from running economic operations directly does not appear in the Notebooks. Rudolf says: 'The building of schools, too, is a suitable field for government to prove its concern with the success of its citizens' economic efforts'. One must take care not to misconstrue this sentence by an extensive interpretation: for it is quite intentional that Rudolf speaks only of building schools, and not of running them – notwithstanding the fact that free (and compulsory) public education had long been one of the major concerns of the Austrian state and teachers constituted a large part of the civil service establishment. Menger evidently follows Smith, who points out expressly that the 'publick' should on the whole limit itself to 'establishing'

8 See Viner (1927); Robbins (1952); Stigler (1972).

schools, 'the master being partly, but not wholly paid by the publick; because if he was wholly, or even principally paid by it, he would soon learn to neglect his business' (*Wealth of Nations* V.i.f.55). It is part of Menger's technique to speak only of what the state should do, and not what it should not. Therefore, his omissions are most significant.

These omissions of advisable state activities are extensive indeed. They are, perhaps, best explained in the terminology of R. Musgrave: there certainly was to be no distributive division to state activity. Not that such an activity was unthought of at the time; we should remember that in 1872 the Verein fuer Socialpolitik had been founded, the society of those German economists who made the propagation of income redistribution their main concern. And only a little later Bismarck established the first social security system with redistributive intent, the state, the employers and the employees each paying one third. Furthermore, there certainly was to be no stabilization division to economic policy. Again, such activity was then not at all unheard of. Roscher (the foremost living German economist to whom Menger had dedicated his own *Principles*) in his magisterial long essay on market crises had examined practically all Keynesian and also all monetarist measures for coping with economic recessions (Roscher 1861); and the Emperor, Rudolf's father, had shown himself not at all averse to countenancing quasi-Keynesian employment-creating state activities during the Great Depression starting in 1873, at the very trough of which Menger was lecturing. In fact, among the most significant omissions in the whole course of the lectures are unemployment, the possible negative effects of financial speculation, and the possibility that the government might have to take over the running of railways that had gone bankrupt while privately run; nor is bankruptcy itself ever mentioned – regardless of the fact that all these questions were burning issues of the day. Not once does Menger suggest that the free enterprise system as such is not running smoothly. What Menger admitted was only an allocative division to government activity, and that only on a narrow basis.

As to the allocative division Menger once more misses out on an important line of Austrian policy. In a curious mixture of private business and state activity large industrial banks had been established in Austria, the first and largest being the Creditanstalt[9] (founded in 1855). The express intent of this banking policy was to stimulate industrial development. Adam Smith had pleaded for bank regulation (*Wealth of Nations* II.ii.94) and linked it with building regulations. But Menger does not even mention banks, so important in the Austria of his day; and he carefully refrains from speaking of the need for regulation of any commercial or industrial enterprise as such or even of the need of regulating

9 See März (1968); Good (1984).

private building activities. Allocative state intervention is only to be due to palpable and direct positive or negative external effects.

The Crown Prince lists 12 examples of government intervention in Notebooks VI and VII, in all of which the external effect is clearly explained. Six of them concern the prevention of negative external effects by measures to prevent the spread of cattle plague (case 1), of phylloxera (case 2), of the bark beetle (case 3) and measures to control deforestation (case 4). In other words, all these are cases of agricultural regulation. In this connection it is perhaps relevant to remember that Rau thought agriculture much more prone to cause negative external effects than industry! Cases 5 and 6 have to do with the limitation of hours of work (very modestly to 15 hours a day in case of hard labour!) and the limitation of child labour. The other six cases concern positive external effects: the building of roads (7), railways (8), canals (9), schools (10), the provision of prime breeding animals for poor farmers (11), and finally the negotiation of commercial treaties (12). One may be tempted to consider these examples only as a demonstrative enumeration, as mere examples which could be explained easily to the young Crown Prince, examples readily to be enlarged upon. But this would run counter to the explicit conclusion drawn by Rudolf: 'The state may interfere with the citizens' economic activities only in the manner described in the above examples'! The 12 examples show that Menger's state is indeed minimal in its economic activity.

Two of these examples deserve to be enlarged upon. Menger suggests the negotiation of commercial treaties as a proper field for government activity. Here, the state provides a pure public good. But note: Menger introduces commercial treaties merely as measures to make exports possible, i.e. as measures furthering free trade, and not as measures to limit imports. That it may ever be sensible to limit imports is not even touched upon anywhere in the lectures, though even Adam Smith had thought some import duties not totally amiss (*Wealth of Nations* V.ii.k.31,32). With regard to labour regulation the limitation of hours of work and the limitation of child labour are suggested. All this is couched in somewhat highflown language. The actual measures envisaged are, in contrast, extremely meagre, e.g. limitation of hours of work to no more than 15 a day in the case of hard labour. No mention is made of safety regulations at the workplace, by then in effect in many countries. Nor are factory inspectors mentioned, who make sure that labour regulation laws are complied with. The possibility that the payment of workers in kind could be forbidden, a prohibition which Adam Smith had thought justified (ibid. I.x.c.61), goes unmentioned. And, of course, no mention whatsoever is made of a state-run scheme of unemployment relief. In all these omissions, the Rudolf Lectures parallel another document commonly thought to be an important milestone on the road towards a social policy with regard to industrial labour, viz. the papal encyclical *Rerum Novarum* of 1891, 15 years later than the lectures. Both Menger and Pope Leo

XIII actually suggest very little of substance and rely mainly on private self-help organizations and the exhortation to workers to be thrifty, Menger dwelling on co-operatives as self-help organizations in his chapter on handicraft business. Neither Menger nor Leo XIII mentions unemployment and unemployment relief. This seems quite incredible to today's readers, including the present pope, John Paul II, who strongly suggests in his centenary encyclical *Centesimus Annus* (1991) that Leo XIII had addressed the problem of unemployment, while, if one checks the actual text of *Rerum Novarum*, this is not the case. Both thc Rudolf Lectures and *Rerum Novarum* thus reflect the classical liberals' concern with the so-called 'social question', but concern without consequent action apart from a few limitations and the appeal to self-help.

A similar do-nothing 'concern' is shown by Menger in the case of the decline of handicraft industry and in the case of famines. The intended moral to be drawn by the Crown Prince is to leave well alone. In order to alleviate famines government may purchase grain abroad; but nothing is said about what should be done with it. What is recommended explicitly is that the court and the nobility should set a good example in frugality. Measures to safeguard a sound currency and to pay interest on the public debt punctually, on the other hand, are typical concerns of a policy of *laissez-faire*, as defined by Immanuel Kant,[10] for example.

Menger's Rudolf Lectures are, in fact, probably one of the most extreme statements of the principles of *laissez-faire* ever put to paper in the academic literature of economics. There is just cause for economic action only in 'abnormal' circumstances. Only when 'disaster' is impending, only where 'government support becomes indispensable' should the state step in. Otherwise 'government interference' is 'always ... harmful'. Rudolf says in Notebook VI:

> There are instances in the life of a state when the economic performance of individuals or of groups of citizens runs up against obstacles that require the government's powers to remove them, since individual resources would not possibly be enough.
>
> We deal with abnormal situations here, since only these justify government interference; in everyday economic life we shall always have to denounce such action as harmful.
>
> For the most part, these are such powerful phenomena that they either require special laws, which, of course, only the state can pass, or involve such high costs – because of the size of the obstacle – that government support becomes indispensable.

Many of Menger's classically liberal examples are taken from German authors, at least as to their actual wording. In his history of German economics Roscher had pointed out that German economists of the late 18th and of the

10 Kant (quoted in Habermas, 1962, p. 325, n.79) relates the story of how a wise old merchant replied to the request of a French Minister (Colbert?) for policy advice: "Schafft gute Wege, schlagt gut Geld, gebt ein promptes Wechselrecht und dgl., übrigens aber 'laβt uns machen'!"

19th century tended to water down the classically liberal precepts of English and French authors in favour of more government intervention;[11] and among historians of thought this is the prevailing conception of the typical line of argument even before the rise of the Younger Historical School. It comes as quite a surprise to see to what extent German economists – skilfully edited by Menger – prove to be classical liberals.

There is, however, one important aspect in which Menger differed from English classical liberals. To him government is an agency with a moral duty. The state is conceived of as a *moralische Anstalt* (the term is Friedrich Schiller's), a moral agency, institution, edifice or endeavour (all this could be signified by the word *Anstalt*). This notion is in contrast to the state as it is commonly used in England, where – from the Restoration onwards – moral exhortation had been the province of the Anglican church.[12] Menger had in this case probably been influenced by his teacher Mischler, though he transformed Mischler's ideas so as to make them agree better with methodological individualism. Both Mischler and Menger think it important duties of the state to inform its citizens on the one hand, and, on the other, to belabour them with exhortation and moral persuasion and to set them a good example by its own economic behaviour. But for Menger the subject matter of such admonition is different from what Mischler would have thought appropriate: it has to serve in stimulating the liberal virtues of initiative, self-help and thrift. If and when government takes such a moral initiative there is then all the more reason for a policy of *laissez-faire*.

The topic of insufficient information is central to Menger's thinking, of course, as is well known among historians of thought. It is this concern which Menger bequeathed to his school. Throughout the Notebooks there runs, however, also another, secondary, concern. The typical English liberal position is well expressed by Bagehot's dictum: 'The human heart is strong and the human reason weak'.[13] In the *Wealth of Nations* Adam Smith never doubted that private people would have economic incentives. To Smith 'statesmen' are 'the greatest spendthrifts in society', whereas 'private people' not only know much better what is useful to them but are also characterised by 'application and industry'. To Menger, on the other hand, private man is faint-hearted, lack-lustre and full of sloth. It is therefore important that government strengthen incentives and foster the economic initiatives of its citizens besides providing them with information on which to act.

11 Wilhelm Roscher, *Geschichte der National-Oekonomik*, Munich 1874, p. 1014 f. says it is 'eine nationale Eigenthümlichkeit der Deutschen, ... die aus England und Frankreich eingeführte Regel der *Verkehrsfreiheit* durch zahlreiche Ausnahmen der Staatseinmischung zu unterbrechen'.

12 As to the paramount importance of Anglican theorizing on the purpose of government and of the extremely close symbiosis of church and state in England see Clark (1985).

13 Walter Bagehot, *The English Constitution* (1867), intr. R.H.S. Crossman, London, Glasgow 1968, p. 86.

And here Menger invents two among the very few new arguments in the long history of classical economic liberalism. Firstly, even justified state action always has a deleterious side effect as well. In consequence, it is advisable only if the grounds for justification are very strong. As Rudolf puts it in Notebook VI: '... the state can greatly harm the citizens' interests by interfering too much ... Being responsible and caring for the well-being of one's self and family is a powerful incentive for work and industry... If the state seizes some of these responsibilities, the individual will feel imposed upon and not free, even in such matters as pertain to his most personal interests'. Secondly, Menger uses to great effect a key idea of Austrian subjectivism, the notion that different individuals have different preference functions – an idea at variance with, for example, the predilection of the Cambridge tradition of arguing in terms of 'representative' individuals. This fundamental diversity of individuals can never be served well by state provision, which of necessity has to be of a standardized and stereotyped kind. Rudolf writes, again in Notebook VI: 'Government cannot possibly know the interests of all citizens ... However carefully designed and well-meant institutions may be, they will never suit everybody ...: the variety ... would be altogether lost with comprehensive bureaucratic controls. Even the most devoted civil servant is but a blind tool within a big machine who treats all problems in a stereotyped manner according to regulations and instructions and can cope neither with the requirements of contemporary progress nor with the diversity of practical life'.

What could be worse in the eyes of a liberal than drab uniformity! At the same time we realize how much Mises and Hayek had already benefited from Menger when they formulated their arguments in the course of the debate on the impossibility of rational planning in socialism.

HOW MARGINALIST WAS MENGER?

Was Menger a marginalist? The unanimous answer of all the treatises on the history of economic thought is: of course he was, at least if we do not construe marginalism too narrowly and include all of subjective value theory; and he was even more, he was one of the three founding fathers of the Marginalist Revolution. Yet it is one of the most fascinating aspects of the Rudolf Lectures that from them alone we would never have been able to guess as much. Quite the contrary: in spite of the fact that Menger lectured five years after the publication of his *Principles*, which contain all his subjective value theories as fully as he ever developed them, he did not teach the Crown Prince a single one of the important contributions to the body of economic theory with which he is commonly credited. If one judges by the Notebooks Menger must have considered his innovations only unimportant frills on the great edifice of classical economics created by Adam Smith. What he did teach were, in fact, quite a few notions which he himself had proved to be faulty, if not downright wrong-headed.

Not only in matters of economic policy, but also in matters of theory, in matters of the foundations of economics, the Crown Prince was taught – let us stress once more, in the centenary year of the first publication of the *Wealth of Nations* – nearly undiluted Adam Smith (in the German version of Rau and Hermann from the 1820s and 1830s). True, in what I have called the German protoneoclassical vein of the latter two, Rudolf was at the very outset introduced to 'the importance of satisfying needs for man' and to the division of goods into economic and non-economic goods (Hermann's classification) – goods, of course, including (since Hermann's work of 1832) also 'labour services' and 'relationships'. But that was standard German economics, by then more than 40 years old. The 'basic principles according to which men economize' were taken from Rau and Hermann; since the publication of their work it had become common practice to stress how important it was 'to satisfy the more important needs before the less important ones'. 'The ability to rank needs and disregard less important, though often pleasurable, things characterizes the economizing person, while uneconomic man typically satisfies less important needs at the expense of the more important ones; this is true of the individual as well as the state' (Notebook I).

But from these brief first passages onwards Adam Smith rules supreme. With the 'second principle of economy' (we are not told what the first is) we come to Smith's division of labour, followed by the theory of incentives already remarked upon, a basically classical theory, as it is supply-oriented. We then proceed to the factors of production, the concepts of income, of wealth, and of capital. Here the Crown Prince was instructed, very much in Smithian vein, that 'for many people ... their labour potential constitutes their capital' (Notebook III) – surely reminiscent of Smith's pronouncement that 'the property which every man has in his own labour, as it is the original foundation of all other property, so it is the most sacred and inviolable' (*Wealth of Nations* I.x.c.12). Menger goes on to explain the importance of thrift and saving, no topic being more Smithian; then he comes to the theory of value, here treated (in contrast to Smith) in the German protoneoclassical vein, and concludes the theoretical survey by explaining the importance of money, a topic likewise treated by Adam Smith in this context.

That the theory of value is treated somewhat differently from Smith must not surprise us. The labour theory of value was rejected by the Germans from Rau and Hermann onwards and was characterized by Roscher as a mere English aberration.[14] In pre-Smithian manner (but well known to Smith and referred to

14 Roscher (1864), § 107, p. 200: 'Echt national ist die englische Ansicht, als wenn das Gleichgewicht der Preise darauf beruhete, dass alle Güter soviel Werth hätten, wie sie Arbeit gekostet'.

by him: *Wealth of Nations* I.iv.13), Menger distinguishes 'value in use' and 'value in exchange'. He suggests two definitions of value: 'Value is the importance that a good acquires for the individual because it can satisfy his needs'; and 'Value is the importance that a specific good acquires for us once we recognize that one of our needs could less fully be satisfied if we had no command over the good' (Notebook III). Again, however, these had been standard German textbook definitions long before Menger. As one of only two authors mentioned in the Notebooks (the other being Adam Smith), Menger here expressly gives the 18th century French writer Condillac as his source – Condillac being the source typically quoted by Roscher on this point, so typically that Karl Marx attacked Roscher for having taken his value theory from Condillac.[15] The only sentence where we may scent a whiff of Menger's own thought is the following: '(The) standard of measurement (of value) is quite relative and depends upon the most varied influences of taste, character, and customs of whole peoples and of individuals.' This sentence, though, is negated right away in a phrase which seems rather untypical for the originator of subjective value theory: 'But to render communication possible, items of trade must be assigned more or less definitive values that are fixed according to civilized peoples' longstanding experience and needs.'

Nowhere in the Notebooks can we find even a hint at marginal valuation, despite the fact that Hermann had already come very close to it in 1832.[16] Nowhere is the concept of marginal utility – or of utility itself – used, even in passing. Rudolf merely renders the very muddled statement: 'For some objects value is determined by their scarcity, for others by the importance of the need satisfied, and for still others by the quantity of the object available' (Notebook IV). Declining marginal utility of income is suggested in passing in a half-sentence. But this notion had been briefly suggested by John Stuart Mill and other classicists. Nowhere, above all, are factor prices introduced as derived utilities depending on their productive contribution to final satisfaction.

The Crown Prince was taught pure classical wage theory, in absolute contrast to Menger's *Principles*. He is explicitly taught the 'Iron Law of Wages,' as F. Lassalle had termed this theory memorably for German speakers. 'The simplest sort of labour,' Rudolf recorded, 'for which no training at all is required, will be paid just enough to provide the means of subsistence for working-class families. The more advanced ... highly skilled types of labour require previous training and will be paid more, in proportion to the cost of the necessary training' (Notebook X). This is the classical supply-side argument, running counter

[15] See Marx (1867) 1987, p. 157.

[16] See Hermann (1832), both in his long discussion about the productivity of various employments ('In the eyes of the consumer that service will appear as productive, which, when the product is exchanged, entails no higher subjective cost than would be necessary when an alternative method is used', p. 32) and on optimal consumption.

to demand-based marginal productivity theory. Wage theory in general is, however, only noticed in passing in this Notebook. Its main concern is the appropriate remuneration of civil servants. What principle should guide us here? 'It is (the state's) foremost duty to see to it that those who devote their services to the common good, to the state, are paid wages in proportion to their training and their sphere of activity.' Smith, as is well known, was the originator of the theory of human capital. This is nothing but a brief statement of his opportunity-cost-of-investment-in-education argument for the determination of wage differentials for the highly skilled (*Wealth of Nations* I.x.b.6). It is just this argument, particularly in its application to the learned professions, which the whole marginalist school, and Menger especially, had set out to refute.

The Rudolf Lectures provide us then with a most astounding case of self-effacement by a world-famous economic theoretician. Can one believe that Menger taught something he considered absolutely wrong? This appears unlikely even if it had been suggested to him that he should teach a course based on Adam Smith. For it would still have been easy to point out that Adam Smith had considered costs merely as given, while the 'moderns' went 'deeper' and showed that in the last instance costs, too, have to conform to the valuation of factor services in terms of their utility rendered to the final consumer. In fact, German economists had pioneered marginal productivity theory from Rau and Hermann onwards, and magisterially so in the case of Thünen, who was in this respect not at all an isolated maverick. Menger could just as well have taken the tack of showing that the supply-side considerations, on which Smith based his whole theoretical argument, were valid only in the long-run and, for short-run purposes, had to be balanced out by considerations of demand. Any number of courses of merely 'supplementing' Adam Smith's notions of value while still adhering to a Smithian framework otherwise would have been open to him. But he took none of them. This forces us to draw two conclusions: Menger evidently regarded the classical notions of value still as useful first approximations for an introductory course; and possibly he also thought the supply-side considerations he taught a better basis for those classically liberal ideas he wanted to convey,[17] above all on the questions of how the economy is run and how it should be run, including the topic of incentives and self-help.

In view of the moral imperatives that Menger associated with the subject of government duties and individual initiative, he may have preferred to take a supply-side approach rather than bring in any hedonistic overtones by speaking of desires and their satisfactions.

17 Mark Blaug, *Economic Theory in Retrospect*, 4th ed., Cambridge, Cambridge University Press, p. 302, in evaluating a possible ideological bias of the marginal utility theory points out: 'Actually, classical economics is a far better instrument for defending private property'. Did Menger realize this?

DO THE NOTEBOOKS REFLECT THE CONSIDERED OPINIONS OF CARL MENGER?

This introduction takes the lecture notes of Crown Prince Rudolf of Austria as an accurate mirror of Menger's own opinions on questions of economic policy, and even on the relative importance of various alternative paradigms of economic theory. Furthermore, it considers the Notebooks as reflections of the mature judgement of Carl Menger. Other interpretations are possible. They will be discussed in what follows as alternative interpretations. The reader will have to make up his own mind.

The first alternative interpretation is that Menger, who had only a few months for teaching the Crown Prince, though they were months of intensive studies, gave Rudolf merely the traditional and standard 'crash course' for undergraduates. To my mind this argument does not hold water; it is, I think, the weakest of all alternative interpretations. First of all, it was not Menger's own crash course: he did not teach economic policy. And secondly, a classically liberal course was not at all traditional or standard for the Austria of the 1870s. Adam Smith had been taken up early in Austria, in the 1780s and 1790s, but since the era of Metternich liberal thought had been anathema for a long while; and the Austrian state was traditionally highly paternalistic and interventionist. In fact, Menger was the rediscoverer of Adam Smith in Austria – and he communicated this rediscovery to the Crown Prince.

A second alternative interpretation is that those responsible for Rudolf's education – e.g. Count Latour-Thurmburg or even Empress Elisabeth, well-known to have been of liberal persuasion – set Menger the task of teaching the Crown Prince a classically liberal course, based on Adam Smith. Here again, nothing can be proved conclusively, as instructions to Menger have not survived. But from possible (vague) instructions we cannot build up an argument for Menger's rendering an even more classically liberal version of Adam Smith with fewer exceptions in favour of state action, instead of giving a more toned-down version. At least Smith must have fitted in exactly with Menger's own predilections. And when Menger supplements Adam Smith by extracts from then already old German texts, this to my mind again only argues that Menger thought the (classically liberal) ancients had much more of importance to say on questions of economic policy than the moderns. It is not at all typical of a teacher to try consciously to be old-fashioned and to teach a budding statesman outdated ideas.

A third alternative interpretation would single out the fact that Menger presents even fewer exceptions to classical liberal non-interventionism than Smith. This argument runs as follows: in giving a first undergraduate course to an 18-year-old student one simplifies; only the main argument is presented, without the exceptions. To this I reply that one leaves out the exceptions only if one does not think them vital; and this was not only the first, but also, as Menger knew, the last course to be taught to the Crown Prince. By leaving out even Smith's own caveats Menger, to my mind, shows that he fully endorsed Smith.

The same argument might be made with respect to Menger's own theoretical notions: that he did not have time to go into his own complex new arguments. But he could easily have slipped in some of his key ideas on marginal productivity pricing of factors of production or on the pricing of commodities, and still have used up only a few minutes. After all, he had developed a 'unified theory of price', as he proudly remarks in the Preface to his *Principles*; and a unified theory is easier and therefore quicker to teach than a theory for each particular case, which is what he actually presents in conformity with the classicists. And if he was short of time, why then did he mention explicitly such nonsense (in the eyes of the Marginalist Revolutionaries) as that commodities are highly valued if they are scarce in any absolute sense; or that wages are determined by the subsistence level according to the 'Iron Law of Wages'?

So, after having considered various alternatives we are, I think, forced to the conclusion: Both politically and theoretically Carl Menger was much more of a classical economist than is commonly realized. Even his clash with Gustav Schmoller in the so-called '*Methodenstreit*' of 1883–84 does not argue to the contrary: for on the surface it was a clash on the role of economic theory as such, and not on subjective value theory alone; and the classical economists had, of course, presented a great wealth of theory, and of theory unconditioned by any historical relativity. The hidden agenda was methodological individualism versus the holistic notions of the state espoused by the Younger Historical School. And here Menger as a follower of Adam Smith would have had to take the very line he did.

Politically his disclaimer of not being a 'Manchester liberal' and of not being opposed to all reforms in the matter of economic policy appears somewhat forced, or at least liable to be misconstrued.[18] Menger certainly was a minimalist as regards state action. Theoretically, as is well known, in his *Principles* he presented himself not as a scientific revolutionary but rather as a mere reformer – or should we even say as a reviver of a well-established train of thought? The Rudolf Lectures reinforce this impression. If there was one man whom it took extremely long to realize fully Carl Menger's revolutionary impact on economics, it was Carl Menger himself.

18 Menger (1884), p. 83. Menger denies as 'frivolous' the charge that he is a member of the *Manchesterpartei,* points out that it is impossible to deduce such a thing from his writings on economic theory, asserts that it would be altogether honourable to see in the free play of private self-interest the main source of the common economic good, and finally remarks that his caution, that in designing reforms one should take into account what has already been achieved, does not mean that he is always against reform. Again the oblique phraseology makes Menger appear far more interventionist than he actually was.

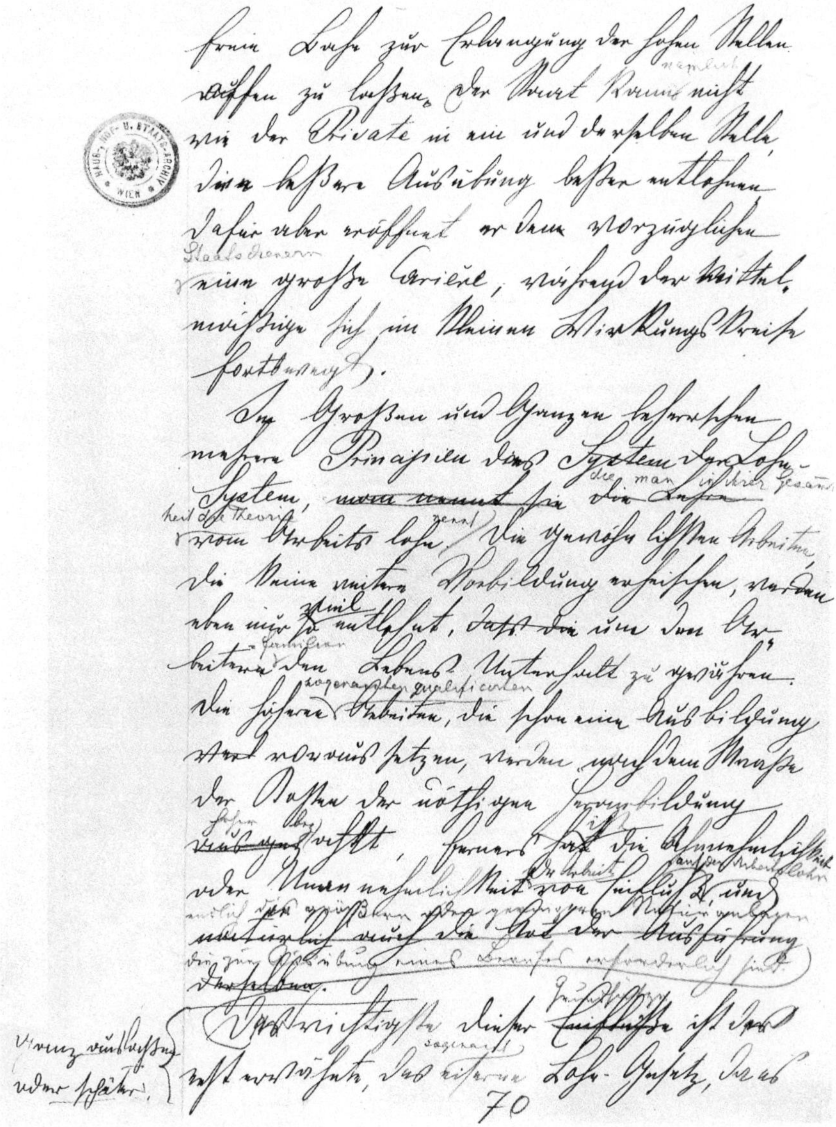

A page from Rudolf's Notebooks showing Menger's editing of the text

The Notebooks

Politische Ökonomie I. 1876 Jänner

[Auf der Innenseite des Umschlages:

Inhalt:
I. Heft: Einleitung. Wichtigkeit der Befriedigung der Bedürfnisse für den Menschen
Einteilung dieser Wissenschaft in

1. Volkswirtschaftspolitik
2. Finanzwissenschaft
3. Theoretische Volkswirtschaftslehre.

Die Lehre von den Gütern und von der Wirtschaft
Über die Hauptgrundsätze, nach welchen die Menschen wirtschaften
Zweiter Hauptgrundsatz der Wirtschaftlichkeit
Teilung der Arbeit
Aneiferung der Arbeit
Stücklohn
Das reine Tantiemen-System
Das Kommissionssystem
Über Institution und wirtschaftliche Bedeutung des Eigentums.]

1 r Die Wichtigkeit für den Menschen, die in der Befriedigung seiner Bedürfnisse liegt, und der enge Zusammenhang derselben mit dem ganzen geistigen und materiellen Leben, ist eine Tatsache.[1] Auch erfüllen die Sorgen über die Befriedigung der einfachsten Lebensbedürfnisse den ganzen Gedankenkreis der größten Mehrzahl der Menschen und werden zu den Hebeln, welche sie zu den unangenehmsten Arbeiten drängen.[2]

Der geringste Teil der Menschheit kann sich durch seine Stellung, befreit von diesen hemmenden Sorgen, idealen geistigen Bestrebungen widmen; dabei aber dürfen diese wenigen die ernsten Bestrebungen der Vielheit nicht außer

[1] Rau (1855), betont S. 11 ff. den engen Zusammenhang zwischen der materiellen und der immateriellen Kultur.

[2] Auffällige Ähnlichkeit mit den ersten eineinviertel Seiten von Schäffle (1867). Siehe weiters Menger (1871), S. 32, in Anlehnung an seinen eigenen Lehrer Peter Mischler (1857), S. 13–18 (§§ 8 und 9). §9 beginnt: 'Der Hebel der wirthschaftlichen Thätigkeiten, wie er in der Sorge für das eigene Wohl wirkt...'.

Political economy I. 1876 January

[On the inside of the front cover:

Contents:
Notebook I: Introduction. Importance of satisfying needs for man
Classification of political economy into

1. economic policy
2. public finance
3. economic theory

The theory of goods and of economy
On the basic principles according to which men economize
Second principle of economy
Division of labour
Incentives to work
Piece-rate
The simple system of shares
The system of commissions
On the institutions and economic significance of property.]

The importance of satisfying needs for man and its close connection to the whole of intellectual and material life is a fact.[1] Worrying about how to satisfy the most basic needs entirely occupies the minds of the large majority of men and acts as a lever pushing them to perform the most unpleasant kinds of work.[2] 1 r

Only the smallest part of mankind is free of these hampering worries and in a position where it can devote time to intellectual endeavours; but those few must not be oblivious to the serious endeavours of the multitude and must recognize these as matters of life and death for the overwhelming majority of citizens.

1 Rau (1855), speaks of the close connection between material and immaterial culture on p. 11 ff.
2 Obvious similarity to the introductory page of Schäffle (1867). See also Menger (1976), p. 77, closely following his own teacher Peter Mischler (1857), pp. 13–16. Mischler uses the simile of the lever.

Acht lassen und müssen in denselben die Existenzfragen für den größten Teil der Staatsbürger erkennen.

Darum müssen diejenigen, die an der Spitze der Staaten stehen, besonders ihr Augenmerk auf diese Verhältnisse richten und durch erfolgreiche Förderung der wirtschaftlichen Bestrebungen der Bürger, durch Wohlfahrt und Zufriedenheit die Macht des Staates herbeiführen. Doch auch diese Eingriffe des Staates müssen ihre Grenzen haben, denn es ist zum allgemeinen Wohle der Gesellschaft besser, wenn der einzelne selbst seine und seiner Familie Existenz zu verantworten und zu besorgen hat; denn in dieser Sorge liegt der unaufhörliche Impuls zu
1 v steter Tätigkeit, welche das Wohl der gesamten Menschheit herbeiführt. Doch soll der einzelne Bürger, ohne bevormundet zu werden, den Schutz des Staates und die Unterstützung desselben bereit wissen, für solche Fälle wo sein einzelner Wille zu schwach ist, Hindernisse wegzuschaffen, welche den gesamten wirtschaftlichen Bestrebungen im Wege stehen, oder Maßregeln anzuwenden, welche dieselben fördern würden.[3]

Zu diesem Zwecke streben die Regierungen mit großer Sorgfalt die Hebung des Volkswohlstandes an und richten sich dabei nach bestimmten Regeln, welche die Wissenschaft von der Volkswirtschaftspflege oder die Volkswirtschaftspolitik[4] genannt wird; sie besteht aus den Erfahrungen, welche im Laufe der Zeiten gesammelt wurden, und bildet einen wichtigen Teil der Regierungskunst.

Wie der einzelne zur Erhaltung und Verbesserung seiner Existenz der Mittel bedarf, so auch der Staat; damit er allen seinen vielen Zwecken nachkommen kann. Zur Befriedigung seiner notwendigen Bedürfnisse braucht er aber ein geregeltes Einkommen.[5] Wie dieses Einkommen am zweckmäßigsten verschafft

[3] Dieser Absatz (und seine Weiterführung in den folgenden Heften) ist Mengers originellster, ja fast einziger eigener Beitrag zu den Rudolf-Vorlesungen. Während Smith (1776) in der auf Eigeninteresse beruhenden Initiative der einzelnen die sichere Grundlage einer Privatwirtschaftsordnung sieht, die eine Staatstätigkeit weitgehend unnötig macht, sieht Menger es als Staatsaufgabe an, die einzelnen zu dieser Eigeninitiative zu erziehen und dieselbe zu schützen.

Im übrigen baut dieser Absatz die entsprechende Passage bei Rau (1855), S.15, aus. Rau sagt: 'Es liegt weder in den Kräften noch in den Pflichten der Regierung, die Wirthschaft jedes Staatsbürgers unter ihre Aufsicht und Leitung zu nehmen, aber die Volkswirthschaft im Ganzen und in ihren Zweigen bedarf einer Einwirkung von Seiten der Staatsgewalt, damit sie in solchen Fällen von Hindernissen befreit und befördert werde, wo die Bemühungen der Einzelnen keinen befriedigenden Erfolg haben'. Rau setzt diesen Gedanken mit folgendem Halbsatz fort, den Menger charakteristischerweise unterschlägt: '..., und damit sie ferner auf die wirthschaftliche Wohlfahrt Aller im Staat hingelenkt und mit den Zwecken desselben in Übereinstimmung gebracht werde'. Das Erste erscheint Menger, Smith folgend, wohl nicht notwendig, während von den individuellen Zwecken verschiedene Staatszwecke seinem methodischen Individualismus widersprächen.

[4] Terminologie (insbesondere 'Volkswirtschaftspflege') von Rau (1855), S.16.

[5] Hier folgt Menger Rau (1855), S.15, wo es heißt: 'Die Aufgabe der Regierung ... ist eine doppelte: 1) Die Beförderung der wirthschaftlichen Zwecke des Volkes ... 2) Befriedigung der eigenen Bedürfnisse der Regierung', wobei die Untersuchung der zweitgenannten Bemühung bei Rau (§ 17) erstmals 'Finanzwissenschaft' heißt. (Davor hieß die Disziplin 'Kameralwissenschaften' o.ä.) Die erstgenannte Aktivität nennt Menger 'Hebung des Volkswohlstandes'.

Therefore heads of states must pay particular attention to these circumstances and through welfare and contentment make their country powerful by successfully promoting the citizens' economic endeavours. But there has to be a limit to such interference on the part of the state, as it is better for the general welfare of society if the individual has the responsibility of caring for his own and his family's livelihood; for such responsibility constantly drives him to an unceasing activity that fosters the well-being of all mankind. Without being imposed upon, the individual citizen should understand, however, that the state is prepared to 1 v
protect and support him when and where his own willpower is insufficient to overcome obstacles in the way of all economic endeavours or to take measures to promote these.[3]

To this end, governments strive carefully to improve the general prosperity and in so doing pay attention to certain rules which are called the theory of improving the economy or economic policy;[4] it consists of the experiences gathered over time and is an important part of the art of government.

Just as the individual requires means to maintain and improve his existence, so does the state in order to achieve its many objectives. To satisfy its essential needs, however, it has to have a regular income.[5] How to acquire and then use this most expediently is the subject of a special discipline, public finance or the

3 This paragraph (and enlargements on it in subsequent notebooks) is/are Menger's most original, if not to say his only original, contribution to the Rudolf Lectures. While for Smith (1776) individual initiative as propelled by self-interest is a reliable foundation of a private enterprise economy, which has hardly any need for government activity, Menger considers it the task of the state to develop and foster such individual initiative in its members.

Apart from that, this paragraph elaborates on the respective passage in Rau (1855), p. 15, where the author justifies government intervention in the economy whenever and wherever handicaps or barriers to be removed are so substantial as to defy individual effort. Rau follows this up with a half-sentence that Menger typically leaves out: '... in order that (the national economy) will furthermore be directed towards the economic welfare of all members of the state and be matched to their purposes'. To Menger, who follows Smith, the first reason given seems redundant, while the second idea – of the national economy having purposes of its own, only to be brought in line with the individuals' purposes – would run counter to his methodological individualism.

4 In his terminology, Menger follows the older standard German textbook of his time, viz. Rau (1855), p. 16.

5 Menger very closely follows Rau (1855), p. 15. Rau sees two spheres of economic activity for the government: 1) advancing the economic aims of the people, and 2) satisfying its own needs by gathering revenue. For the study of the latter activity Menger uses the German term for 'public finance' (Finanzwissenschaft), which Rau had created. Menger makes only one, though very significant innovation: while Rau speaks of gathering revenue to satisfy the government's own needs, Menger limits this activity to essential needs.

und dann verwendet wird, ist der Gegenstand einer besonderen Wissenschaft,
2 r der Finanzwissenschaft, oder der Lehre vom Staatshaushalte. Die Wissenschaft von der Regierungskunst teilt sich mithin in volkswirtschaftlichen Dingen in zwei Hauptzweige:

1. in die Volkswirtschaftspolitik, welche sich mit den Mitteln der Förderung der Wirtschaft eines Volkes beschäftigt;
2. in die Finanzwissenschaft, welche sich mit der Art der zweckmäßigsten Einrichtung des Staatshaushaltes beschäftigt.

Diesen Wissenschaften, welche schon fördernd in das Staatsleben eingreifen, muß eine andere Wissenschaft als Vorkenntnis vorausgehen, nämlich die theoretische Volkswirtschaftslehre.

2. Die Lehre von den Gütern und von der Wirtschaft

Unter einem Gut versteht man ein Ding, welches zur Befriedigung menschlicher Bedürfnisse dienlich ist, in seiner Tauglichkeit vom Menschen erkannt und ihm verfügbar ist.[6]

Die Güter werden eingeteilt:[7]

1. in Arbeitsleistungen;
2. in Sachgüter;
3. in Verhältnisse.

2 v Die Güter lassen sich ferner einteilen:[8]

1. in wirtschaftliche Güter, d.i. jene Güter, welche uns in einer geringeren Menge zur Verfügung stehen, als unser voller Bedarf beträgt, und mit denen wir deshalb wirtschaften.
2. in nichtwirtschaftliche Güter, d.i. jene Güter, bei welchen das umgekehrte Verhältnis eintritt, mit denen wir deshalb zu wirtschaften nicht genötigt sind.

[6] Bis auf die Verfügbarkeit, die Menger seit den Grundsätzen (siehe S. 3) hinzufügt, folgt die Definition in ihrer ersten Formulierung Hufeland (1807) (siehe Grundsätze, S. 2), in ihrer zweiten Roscher (siehe ebenda): 'Alles dasjenige, was zur Befriedigung eines wahren menschlichen Bedürfnisses anerkannt brauchbar ist'.

[7] Folgt in etwa der bekannten Einteilung von Hermann (1832), S. 1 f., in der Formulierung von Schäffle (1867), S. 47 f.

[8] Der Text von hier an bis zum vorletzten Satz vor der nächsten Überschrift folgt – ausnahmsweise – Mengers eigener Arbeit, die hier kaum Anklänge in deutschen Lehrbüchern findet. Die erste Passage entspricht den Grundsätzen, S. 51 und S. 57 ff. Menger selbst folgt in seiner Unterscheidung wirtschaftlicher und freier Güter Hermann (1832), S. 3.

theory of the budget. Concerning economic matters then, the theory of the art of government has two main branches: 2 r

1. economic policy, which deals with the means of improving a country's economy;
2. public finance, which deals with the optimal management of the budget.

These disciplines, which already positively affect political life, presuppose acquaintance with another discipline, viz. economic theory.

2. Theory of Goods and of Economy

A good is a thing which can serve to satisfy human needs, which has been recognized as such, and of which man has command.[6]

Goods are classified into[7]

1. labour services;
2. material goods;
3. relationships.

Furthermore, goods may be classified into[8] 2 v

1. economic goods, i.e. those goods of which we have a smaller amount than would satisfy all our needs and which we therefore economize;
2. non-economic goods, i.e. those goods where the relationship is the other way around, therefore we do not have to economize them.

6 Apart from the condition of availability, which Menger added since the Principles, the first formulation of the definition follows Hufeland (1807), the second formulation Roscher's definition: 'All that is recognized as being applicable to the satisfaction of a true human need' (see Menger (1976), p. 288, note 9).

7 This looks much like the well-known classification by Hermann (1832), p. 1 f., in the wording of Schäffle (1867), p. 47 f.

8 It is quite exceptional in these lectures for Menger to present his own ideas and formulations, as he does here for once (down to the last but one sentence before the next heading). The first passage follows the Principles (1976), p. 94 f. and p. 98. In the distinction between economic goods and 'free' goods Menger himself follows the generally noted and quoted author of this distinction, viz. Hermann (1832), p. 3.

Wenn nun wahrgenommen wird, daß ein Gut in geringerer Menge vorhanden ist, als der Bedarf von demselben beträgt, so suchen die Menschen ihr Bedürfnis nach diesem Gute so gut es geht zu befriedigen, und daraus entsteht in ihnen das Bestreben,[9]

1. Jede Teilquantität der betreffenden Güter gegen den Verlust derselben zu verwahren.
2. Jede Teilquantität in ihren nützlichen Eigenschaften zu erhalten.
3. Eine Wahl zu treffen zwischen den wichtigeren und minder wichtigen Bedürfnissen, die sie zu befriedigen haben.
4. Die ihnen verfügbare Quantität dieser Güter so zu verwenden, daß bestimmte Bedürfnisse mit der geringsten Menge derselben, und damit wieder
3 r möglichst viele Bedürfnisse erfüllt werden.

Unter einem Vermögen versteht man die Gesamtheit der ökonomischen Güter eines Menschen; nichtökonomische Güter sind keine Vermögensteile.[10]

Unter Reichtum versteht man den Besitz eines für die Lebensverhältnisse einer Person großen Vermögens.[11]

Über die Hauptgrundsätze, nach welchen die Menschen wirtschaften[12]

Die Menschen, zur Erkenntnis gelangt, daß ein großer Teil der Güter ihnen nur in geringer Quantität zur Verfügung steht, suchen daher mit denselben zu wirtschaften; diese Art der Güter werden die wirtschaftlichen oder ökonomischen genannt.

Indem die Menschen wirtschaften, suchen sie:

1. Diese Güter vollständig in ihrem Besitz zu erhalten.

[9] Diese Aufzählung entspricht genau Menger (1871), S. 52 f.

[10] Menger (1871), S. 70. Menger folgt in seiner Vermögensdefinition sehr eng Roscher (1864), § 7, S. 11.

[11] Roscher 1864, § 9, S. 13 (Menger selbst definiert Reichtum nicht).

[12] Hier treffen wir zum ersten Mal auf Mengers Vortragstechnik, die sich in den Rudolf-Vorlesungen immer wieder findet. Nach einer kurzen Darstellung der zu erläuternden Hauptideen ('Thema') schreitet er zur Ausführung derselben und schließlich zu einer Zusammenfassung. Der Kronprinz, der, wie man gerade bei der meist wortgetreuen Wiedergabe der deutschen Quellen erkennt, ein sehr präzises Gedächtnis hat, unterscheidet nicht zwischen Thema und Ausführung und bringt diese hintereinander, so daß sich manchmal eine bis zu viermalige Wiederholung wichtiger Gedanken ergibt (man erkennt freilich gleichzeitig, was Menger so wichtig war, daß er es wiederholte). Hier ist die 'Ausführung' kaum länger als das 'Thema', so daß diese Seite mit der vorangehenden fast identisch ist.

Der Kronprinz gibt Menger oft unsystematisch wieder. Wir erfahren auf der folgenden Seite ausdrücklich, was der zweite Hauptsatz der Wirtschaftlichkeit ist, jedoch nur implizit, was der erste ist.

When people realize that there is less of a good available than is needed, they will satisfy their need for this good as well as they can, and thus they endeavour[9]

1. to guard each particular quantity of such goods against loss;
2. to preserve the useful properties of them;
3. to choose between the more important and the less important needs they have to satisfy;
4. to employ the quantity of these goods available so as to satisfy needs with the smallest possible amount, thereby satisfying the greatest possible number of needs. 3 r

Wealth is understood to be the sum total of a person's economic goods; non-economic goods are not part of such wealth.[10]

Riches denote the command over wealth which is large as compared to a person's way of life.[11]

On the Basic Principles According to which Men Economize[12]

When men realize that many goods are available only in small quantities, they strive to economize; such goods are called economic goods.

In economizing, men strive:

1. to retain full command of these goods;

[9] This passage and the four 'endeavours' enumerated correspond nearly verbatim to Menger (1976), p. 95 f.

[10] The definition is taken from Menger (1976) p. 109. His definition, however, comes very close to Roscher (1864), § 7, p. 11.

[11] Roscher (1864), § 9, p. 13. (Menger himself does not define riches.)

[12] This is our first sample of Menger's method of teaching, which we will encounter time and again in the Rudolf Lectures: after a short exposition of the main ideas ('theme') Menger proceeds to develop them and then summarize them. Rudolf does not distinguish between the theme and its development. His memory is photographic, as it were, and he reproduces theme and development in such a way that important ideas are repeated up to four times (at the same time this shows, of course, what Menger considered important enough to repeat it). Here, the development is hardly longer than the 'theme', so that the following passage is almost identical with the last one.

Rudolf, however, often reproduces Menger's exposition somewhat unsystematically: from the next page we learn explicitly what the second principle of economy is while gathering the first principle only by implication.

2. sie in ihren nützlichen Eigenschaften zu konservieren.[13]
3. die wichtigeren Bedürfnisse an denselben vor den minder wichtigen zu befriedigen.
4. dieselben so zu verwenden, daß die Bedürfnisse mit einer geringen Menge derselben befriedigt werden.

Daraus können wir das Bestreben der Menschen erkennen, diese wirtschaftlichen Güter gegen Verluste und vor Verderben zu beschützen; weiters läßt sich das
3 v Trachten der Menschen beobachten, zwischen den wichtigeren und minder wichtigen Bedürfnissen eine Wahl zu treffen, und letztere unbefriedigt zu lassen.

Die Größe der Wichtigkeit bestimmter Güter steht im umgekehrten Verhältnisse zu dem Vermögen der einzelnen Personen;[14] der Arme wird oft die notwendigsten Bedürfnisse nicht befriedigen können, während der Reiche sich nur die Lust nach unnützen Luxusgegenständen versagen muß.

In der richtigen Wahl der Bedürfnisse und in der Hintansetzung minder wichtiger, oft angenehmer Dinge erkennt man den tüchtig wirtschaftenden Menschen, während der unwirtschaftliche Mensch sich dadurch charakterisiert, daß er die minder wichtigen Bedürfnisse auf Kosten der wichtigeren befriedigt; es gilt dies, so wie für das Leben des Individuums, so auch für das Leben der Staaten.[15]

Die richtige Beurteilung des Grades der Bedürfnisse ist im Staatsleben wegen der komplizierten Verhältnisse viel schwieriger als im Privatleben; auch kann im Staatsleben ein Konflikt zwischen den Interessen der Leiter der Staatswirtschaft und den wirtschaftlichen Interessen des Staates selbst entstehen; im letzteren Falle müssen die Staatsinteressen den Privatinteressen vorangehen.

[13] Rudolf verwendet häufig einfacheres und moderneres Deutsch als Menger in seinen Schriften, der sich dort nicht selten lateinischer Lehnworte bedient; in der Erstfassung auf der Vorseite sagt Rudolf 'erhalten', nunmehr spricht er von 'konservieren', wie Menger (1871), S. 52 (genau: 'conserviren'). Im Unterschied zur ersten Wiedergabe fehlen diesmal jedoch die 'Teilquantitäten', die im Original bei Menger stehen und wohl von ihm erwähnt wurden.

[14] Hier klingt zum einzigen Mal die Idee des bei zunehmendem Vermögen abnehmenden (Grenz-) Nutzens an. Sie wird in Mengers Schriften nie so einfach ausgedrückt, entspricht aber ungefähr den Grundsätzen, S. 92 ff. Der mit zunehmendem Vorrat abnehmende Grenznutzen war der deutschen Nationalökonomie vor Menger keineswegs unbekannt, wird von Hildebrand (1848) klar herausgearbeitet und von Roscher (1864), § 6, S. 10, gerade vor der Darstellung der Vermögensbegriffe (§ 7) erwähnt ('daß bei gleichbleibendem Bedürfnisse jede Vorrathsminderung eine specifische Werthserhöhung bewirkt'). Mit der Formulierung vom 'umgekehrten Verhältnis' gibt Menger eher Hildebrand als seine eigenen Formulierungen wieder. Siehe zu all dem Streissler (1990a).

[15] Dieser und der nächste Absatz beruhen offenbar auf der zweiten Auflage von Hermann (1870). Menger hatte in seinen Grundsätzen ausführlich die erste Auflage (1832) verwendet, die zweite aber noch nicht gekannt. Diese behandelt eingehend die Bedürfnisse, und zwar nach ihrer Stärke, wobei absolute oder unabweisliche und relative unterschieden werden. Daß private Wirtschaftstreibende Fehler in der Abwägung der Bedürfnisse gegeneinander machen können, wird von Hermann nicht ausdrücklich betont, aber unterstellt. Umso expliziter ist Hermann bezüglich entsprechender staatlicher Fehler, was Menger sichtlich interessiert und was er dem

2. to preserve their useful properties;[13]
3. to satisfy their more important needs of them before the less important ones;
4. to satisfy the needs using a small amount of the goods.

From this, we can deduce that man strives to guard economic goods against loss and ruin; furthermore, it can be observed that people strive to choose between more important and less important needs, leaving the latter unsatisfied. 3 v

The importance of certain goods is inversely proportional to a person's wealth;[14] a poor man very often is not able to satisfy his most pressing needs while a wealthy man has to refrain only from consuming useless luxuries.

The ability to rank needs and disregard less important, though often pleasurable, things characterizes the economizing person, while uneconomic man typically satisfies less important needs at the expense of the more important ones; this is true of the individual as well as the state.[15]

Due to the complexity of the situation it is much more difficult for the state than for an individual to judge correctly the relative importance of needs; furthermore, in political life there may arise a conflict between the interests of those responsible for the public sector and the interests of the national economy as a whole; in this case, public interest must take precedence over private interest.

13 Often, Rudolf uses simpler and more modern language than Menger, whose writings abound with somewhat stilted loan-words from Latin.
In the first version (preceding page) Rudolf used the word 'erhalten', now he speaks of 'konservieren' (to be exact: 'conserviren') as does Menger (1871), p. 52. (Differing from the first version, though, the 'particular quantities' from Menger's original are omitted.)

14 This is the only time that the idea of (marginal) utility decreasing with increasing wealth crops up. In Menger's writings it is never expressed so simply, but the passage roughly corresponds to Principles, (1976), p. 126 ff. The idea of marginal utility decreasing with increasing stock was not at all unknown to German economists before Menger: it was developed plainly by Hildebrand (1848), while Roscher (1864), § 6, p. 10, just preceding his exposition of the concepts of wealth/riches (§ 7), mentioned 'that with needs unchanging any decrease of stocks causes an increase in respective value'. The 'inverse proportionality' is Hildebrand's rather than Menger's wording, cf. Streissler (1990a).

15 This paragraph and the following one obviously refer to the second edition of Hermann (1832), published in Munich in 1870. In his Principles Menger had made extensive use of the first edition, but had not seen the second one in time. This deals at length with needs – which are distinguished by their intensity into absolute (or irrepressible) and relative needs. That private economic agents may make mistakes when weighing their needs against each other, is not expressly stated but implied by Hermann, who is quite explicit, however, with regard to government mistakes of such sort. This clearly interests Menger and he wants to call Rudolf's attention to the problem. The pertinent passage in Hermann (1870) is found on p. 83.

4 r Zweiter Hauptgrundsatz der Wirtschaftlichkeit

Es genügt aber nicht bei unseren wirtschaftlichen Bestrebungen, daß wir unsere wichtigeren Bedürfnisse mit Hintansetzung unserer minder wichtigen befriedigen, sondern es ist ebenso wichtig, daß wir jedes zur Befriedigung gelangende Bedürfnis so ökonomisch als möglich befriedigen. Dieser Grundsatz gilt ebenso sehr bei der Konsumtion als bei der Produktion.[16]

Ein wichtiges Mittel, um billig und ökonomisch zu produzieren, ist die Arbeitsteilung; man versteht darunter jene Organisation der Arbeit, bei welcher ein jeder Gegenstand, oder selbst nur ein Teil desselben von einem besonderen Arbeiter ausgeführt wird.

Der Beginn dieser Organisation war die Teilung in einzelne Gewerbe; mit fortschreitender Kultur teilen sich dieselben wieder in vielfache Berufe.[17] Die großen Vorteile dieses Systemes sind:

4 v A. Die Erlangung großer Virtuosität der einzelnen Arbeiter.[18] Denn durch die stets gleiche Arbeit wird der höchste Grad von Geschicklichkeit in dieser Verrichtung erzielt, und dadurch wieder vorzügliche Arbeiten geliefert.

B. Ersparnisse von Zeit und Mühe. Je geringer die Operation des einzelnen Arbeiters, desto schneller erlernt er sie, desto kürzer ist er Lehrling und desto rascher wird er Meister und Virtuos in seiner täglichen Beschäftigung.

Dadurch wird Zeit gewonnen, denn die an viele Arbeitskräfte verteilte Arbeit wird rascher vollendet, als wenn eine Person die ganze Tätigkeit

Kronprinzen vermitteln will. Hermann (1870), S. 83, sagt: ‘Von besonderer Wichtigkeit ist der Unterschied zwischen dem absolut und relativ Nothwendigen bei den Staatsbedürfnissen ... Müßte der Privatbedarf eines Theils der Mitglieder fühlbar beschränkt werden, um ... Beiträge für relative öffentliche Bedürfnisse zu leisten, so wäre deren Befriedigung eine ökonomische Verfehlung. Sonderbar, daß gerade unter der Zustimmung von Landesvertretern für blos relative Bedürfnisse oft genug leichthin große Summen verwendet werden. Ich verweise blos auf den Bau so mancher unnöthiger Eisenbahn...’.

16 Schäffle (1867), S. 3. Der Schwabe Schäffle war an der Wirtschaftlichkeitsforderung besonders interessiert und zieht von dort aus seine Überlegungen auf.

17 Rau (1855), S. 133; Roscher (1864), § 48 f., S. 88 ff. Von hier an folgt Menger Adam Smith (1776), zumindest als letzte Quelle. Auch dieser zählt drei Vorteile auf (I.i.5): die größere Fertigkeit jedes einzelnen Arbeiters, die Zeitersparnis und schließlich die Erfindung einer großen Zahl arbeitserleichternder Maschinen.

Menger läßt Smiths dritten Umstand, die Erfindung von Maschinen, weg und nennt statt dessen die Vorteile der internationalen Arbeitsteilung. Das läßt darauf schließen, daß er als unmittelbare Quelle Roscher (1864) benützte; hier § 50, S. 91 f. Roscher führt genau diese drei Argumente an, die er mit A, B und C bezeichnet, verwendet den im Deutschen ungewöhnlichen Ausdruck ‘Virtuosität’ für Fertigkeit (im Unterschied zu Rau, der von ‘Geschicklichkeit’ spricht und damit näher bei Smiths ‘dexterity’ bleibt) und führt unter B das Argument des Lernens an, das er als eine Art langfristige Zeitersparnis sieht, gerade so wie Rudólf. Wir haben hier wieder ein Beispiel für dessen wortgetreues Gedächtnis.

18 Rudolf reproduziert hier wortgetreu den Vortrag nach Roscher (1864), § 50, S. 91 f. Roscher bringt genau die Einteilung in A, B und C wie Rudolf. Es heißt dort, die Arbeitsteilung, ‘besteht in Folgendem: A. Größerer Virtuosität der Arbeiter ... B. Einer Menge von Ersparnissen an Zeit und Mühe ... C. ... insbesondere die internationale Arbeitstheilung’.

Second Principle of Economy 4 r

In our economic striving, it is not enough to satisfy our more important needs while disregarding our less important ones, but it is just as important that we satisfy those needs in the most economical manner possible. This principle applies to consumption as well as to production.[16]

The division of labour is an important preliminary condition for inexpensive and economical production; the term denotes the organization of work in such a way that each product or part of a product is executed by a different worker.

This organization goes back to the development of different trades; these were subdivided into many different vocations with the progress of civilization. The great advantages of this system are:[17]

A. The resulting virtuosity of the individual worker.[18] For performing the same work all the time permits him to reach the highest degree of skill in that operation and, in turn, to produce excellent results. 4 v

B. Saving of time and effort. The narrower the task of the individual worker, the faster he becomes familiar with it, the shorter his apprenticeship and the quicker his mastery of and virtuosity in his daily routine.

   This saves time, as work divided up among many workers is performed more quickly than if a single worker were in charge of the whole process; in addition, the effort of slowly learning how to perform many separate operations is saved.

16 Schäffle 1867, p. 3. Schäffle, a Swabian, was particularly interested in the principle of economizing and uses this as the starting point of his reasoning.

17 From here, Menger follows Smith (1776), at least as the ultimate source. Smith (1776), I.i.5, also gives three advantages: 'This great increase of the quantity of work, which, in consequence of the division of labour, the same number of people are capable of performing, is owing to three different circumstances; first to the increase of dexterity in every particular workman; secondly, to the saving of the time which is commonly lost in passing from one species of work to another; and lastly to the invention of a great number of machines which facilitate and abridge labour, and enable one man to do the work of many'.

Menger leaves out Smith's third circumstance, the invention of machinery, and substitutes the advantages of the international division of labour for it. This shows that his immediate source is Roscher (1864), § 50, pp. 91 f. Roscher gives exactly these three arguments, numbering them A), B), and C), he uses the unusual German term 'Virtuosität' for proficiency (in contrast to Rau, who uses 'Geschicklichkeit', closer to Smith's 'dexterity'), and he advances the argument of learning – a kind of long-term time saving – under B), just as Rudolf does. This is another example of Rudolf's precise memory.

18 This seems to be a verbatim reproduction of Menger's lecture, after Roscher (1864), § 50, p. 91 f., where the division of labour is said to consist in A) increased proficiency ('virtuosity') of the workers, B) certain savings of time and effort, C) especially the international division of labour.

verrichten müßte; und auch die Mühe des langsamen Erlernens vieler Verrichtungen wird durch die Teilung erspart.

C. Die internationale Arbeitsteilung, durch welche die Produkte fremder Länder ins Inland gelangen können und jedes Land seine spezifischen Arbeiten verrichtet und sie dann den anderen Ländern verhandelt.

Die Teilung der Arbeit findet bei diesen Tätigkeiten ihre Grenze:

5 r I. wo die Natur in gewissen Zeiten eine bestimmte Arbeit unmöglich macht. Dies ist namentlich beim Landbau der Fall.[19]

II. Wo die Ausdehnung des Marktes eine so geringe ist, daß der Produzent durch Betrieb eines einzelnen Gewerbes sich nicht erhalten könnte, da der Absatz ein zu geringer ist.[20] *Wollte man die Arbeitsteilung steigern, so muß man deshalb vor allem auf die Verbesserung der Kommunikationsmittel*[21] *und namentlich die Verbindung der Produktionsgebiete mit den Märkten hinwirken.*

Wegen der Geringfügigkeit des Marktes pflegen in kleineren Ortschaften viele oder doch mehrere Geschäfte von einer Person getrieben zu werden, die in größeren Ortschaften unter mehreren Personen geteilt sind.[22]

5 v ***Aneiferung der Arbeit***

Nächst der Arbeitsteilung trägt der Eifer, mit welchem gearbeitet wird, wesentlich zur Vermehrung der Quantität und somit zur Billigkeit der Produkte bei. Daher kann man jede Anspornung der Arbeiter zur größeren Tätigkeit als einen Gewinn der Volkswirtschaft betrachten.[23]

[19] Smith, (1776) I.i.4. Ähnlich Roscher (1864), § 51, S. 93 f.

[20] Smith, (1776) I.iii; Roscher (1864), § 52.

[21] Genau die Wortfolge bei Roscher (1864), § 53, S. 95 f.: 'Wer darum die Arbeitstheilung im Volke steigern will, der muß vor Allem den Markt desselben vergrößern; und das geschieht besonders wirksam durch Verbesserung der Communicationsmittel' (meine Hervorhebung gleicher Wörter).

[22] Roscher (1864), § 52 (erstes Unterargument), S. 94 f.

[23] Das ist ein allgemeiner klassischer und sogar vorklassischer Gedanke. Es ist ganz erstaunlich, daß Menger ihn ohne jeden Vorbehalt äußert; denn er beruht entschieden auf irgendeiner Art von Arbeitswertlehre und ist mit Mengers eigener Theorie eines subjektiven Wertes unvereinbar. Denn wenn der durch den Anreiz gewonnene Zusatznutzen genau dem zusätzlichen Grenzleid der Arbeit entspricht, was unter 'schönen neoklassischen Bedingungen' jedenfalls marginal zutreffen müßte, so kommt es netto zu keinem Nutzenzuwachs und somit auch nicht zu einem 'Gewinn für die Volkswirtschaft'. Man kann also mit Recht fragen, ob Menger – im Unterschied zu W.St. Jevons – das Arbeitsleid überhaupt berücksichtigt. Smith, (1776) I.viii.40, spricht lediglich von den Anreizeffekten hoher Löhne.

Rau (1855) behandelt den Fleiß der Arbeiter in § 112 in engem Zusammenhang mit der Arbeitsteilung (§ 114 ff.). In diesem Absatz gibt Rau eine kurze Zusammenfassung der Anreize – in gewissem Sinn in Vorwegnahme von Mengers eigener Darstellung. Der Gedanke der

C. International division of labour through which a country imports the products of foreign countries; each country pursues its specific activities, and then trades with the other countries.

The division of labour has its limits:

I. where nature makes some kinds of work impossible at certain times. This is especially true for agriculture;[19] 5 r

II. where the market is so small that if the producer restricted himself to only one trade, the respective sales would be insufficient for him to subsist.[20] Increasing the division of labour requires above all improving the means of communication,[21] in particular transportation from the areas of production to the markets.

Because of the thin markets in small communities one person may run many or at least several types of business, which in larger places are divided among different persons.[22]

Incentives to Work 5 v

In addition to the division of labour the intensity of work contributes substantially to increasing the quantity and thereby the cheapness of products. Thus, any incentive which makes the workers work harder may be regarded as a gain to the economy.[23]

19 Smith (1776), I.i.4: 'The nature of agriculture, indeed, does not admit of so many subdivisions of labour'. Similarly Roscher (1864), § 51.

20 This is the main idea of Smith (1776), I.iii., entitled: 'That the Division of Labour is Limited by the Extent of the Market'. Smith then goes on to consider extensively the importance of the means of transport for the division of labour. See also Roscher (1864), § 52.

21 The exact wording of Roscher (1864), § 53, p. 95.

22 Roscher (1864), § 52, p. 94 f., first subargument.

23 This is a general classical and even preclassical idea. It is quite astonishing that Menger renders it without any qualifications, as it squarely rests on some kind of labour theory of value and is, in fact, inconsistent with his own subjective value theory. For if the additional utility derived from the incentive just equals the additional disutility of labour, as it certainly should, at least at the margin, with 'smoothly neoclassical' conditions, there is no net increase in utility and thus no 'gain to the economy'. One can thus legitimately question whether Menger – in contrast to W.S. Jevons – ever considered the disutility of labour at all.

Smith (1776), I.viii.40, only speaks of the incentive effects of high wages: 'The liberal reward of labour ... increases the industry of the common people'.

Rau (1855), treats of industriousness of workers in § 112 in close connection with the division of labour (§ 114 ff.). In this paragraph Rau gives a brief synopsis of incentives, foreshadowing Menger's own treatment. To deal with incentives in connection with the division of labour is

Der größte Sporn zur Tätigkeit der Arbeiter ist, wenn sie erkennen, daß es von ihrem eigenen Fleiße abhängt, in welchem Maße ihnen der Lohn der Arbeit zuteil wird.[24] *Am wenigsten Fleiß wird der Sklave bezeugen, weil er sich bewußt ist, daß er keinen Lohn für die Arbeit erhält und seine Mehranstrengung nur dem Herrn zu Gute kommt.*[25]

6 r *In ähnlicher, wenn auch weniger einschneidender Weise wirkt die Leibeigenschaft, beziehungsweise das Frohndenwesen lähmend auf die Energie der Arbeiter und dadurch schädlich auf die Volkswirtschaft.*[26] *Die Aufhebung der Leibeigenschaft, bzw. der Fronarbeiten brachte Fleiß und Tätigkeit mit sich, und durch dieselben wuchs in gleichem Maße die Bodenkultur.*

Eine weitere Art der Aneiferung der Arbeitsenergie ist die Einrichtung des Stücklohnes, welche darin besteht, daß der Arbeiter keinen Taglohn bezieht, sondern der Lohn im Verhältnisse zur Anzahl der gelieferten Stücke besteht.[27]
6 v *In diesem Bezahlungsmodus des Arbeiters liegt gegenüber dem Taglohne*[28] *das Zugeständnis einer größeren Freiheit des Arbeiters, indem beim Stücklohne die Tätigkeit des Arbeiters weder erzwungen noch auch kontrolliert wird, sondern dem eigenen Willen des Arbeiters überlassen bleibt.*

Neben den großen Vorteilen dieses Systems kann als Nachteil desselben bezeichnet werden, daß der Arbeiter in seinem Bestreben, sich durch Lieferung möglichst vieler Stücke viel zu erwerben, schleuderisch arbeitet und die Volkswirtschaft hiedurch, was sie an Quantität der Produkte gewinnt, an Qualität derselben verliert.[29] *Das System des Stücklohnes ist deshalb in allen*
7 r *jenen Fällen nicht wohl anwendbar, wo der Wert der Produkte hauptsächlich in der Sorgfalt der Ausarbeitung beruht.*

Behandlung von Anreizen im Zusammenhang mit der Arbeitsteilung stammt also von Rau, während die Art der Darstellung Roscher (1864) folgt, der auch die unmittelbare Quelle für das Thema der Arbeitsteilung war.

24 Von hier an folgt der ganze Absatz Roscher (1864), § 39, S. 67 f.

25 Negativ über Sklavenarbeit äußert sich Smith (1776) u.a. in I.viii.41 und III.ii.12. Die hier gewählten Formulierungen halten sich eng an Roscher (1864), § 39, S. 67.

26 Roscher (1864), § 39, S. 67 f.

27 Smith erwähnt auch die Akkordarbeit als möglichen Anreiz. Interessanterweise sieht Menger nur die positive, produktionssteigernde Seite der Stückarbeit bzw. bedauert er nur die dadurch wahrscheinlich eintretende Qualitätsminderung des Produkts, während Smith insgesamt skeptisch ist und von gut bezahlter Akkordarbeit hauptsächlich Überarbeitung und Gesundheitsschädigung der Arbeiter befürchtet. Rudolf hörte hier also weniger von sozialen Erwägungen, als Smith sie anstellt – der in diesem Punkt stärker der subjektiven Wertlehre zuneigt als Menger!

Bei Roscher (1864), § 39, S. 67, findet sich die Akkordarbeit unmittelbar im Anschluß an die Sklaverei (und Tagelöhnerei) behandelt, ebenso wie hier bei Menger. Dieser gibt im gegebenen Zusammenhang Roschers Gedankenfolge exakt wieder. Roscher ist der Meinung, daß das 'Vorherrschen der Akkordarbeit' England seine wirtschaftliche Führungsposition verschafft hätte (er zitiert hierzu Howlett aus 1788).

28 Von Roscher (1864), § 39, S. 67, erwähnt.

29 Dies kritisiert Roscher (1864), § 39, S. 67 f.

The most effective inducement for the workers lies in their recognizing that their reward depends on their own diligence.[24] The slave will be least diligent, since he knows that he receives no reward for his labour and that any extra effort on his part benefits only his owner.[25]

In a similar, though less pronounced manner, serfdom or forced labour 6 r
paralyses the energies of workers and thus has a detrimental effect on the economy.[26] The abolition of serfdom (or forced labour) caused diligence and activity to develop, and in step with them agriculture improved.

Another type of incentive to work is the piece-rate system, where the worker receives his wage not for the days worked but rather in proportion to the number of pieces produced. As compared to the day-wage,[28] this method of payment
entails greater freedom for the worker; under the piece-rate system his activity 6 v
is not forced or even controlled, but is left to his own judgement.

Although it has substantial advantages, this system has the disadvantage that the worker works carelessly – in the attempt to produce as many pieces as possible. The national product will increase in quantity but suffer a corresponding loss in quality.[29] Using the piece-rate system is therefore not advisable in all those instances where the value of the products depends above all on meticulous
workmanship. 7 r

thus suggested by Rau, while the actual treatment follows Roscher, who had also been the immediate source for the division of labour.

24 From here, the whole passage follows Roscher (1864), § 39, p. 67 f.

25 Smith (1776), I.viii.41: 'It appears … from the experience of all ages and nations, I believe, that the work done by freemen comes cheaper in the end than that performed by slaves'. Smith (1776), III.ii.12: 'A slave … who can acquire nothing but his maintenance, consults his own ease by making the land produce as little as possible'. Smith goes on to make these principles responsible for the decline of villeinage. The formulations used in the Rudolf Lectures follow Roscher (1864), § 39, p. 67.

26 Roscher (1864), § 39, p. 67 f.

27 Smith (1776), I.viii.44, also mentions piecework as an incentive scheme. It is interesting that Menger sees only the positive, production enhancing side of piecework or rather deplores only the likely reduction in quality of the product, while Smith is in the main sceptical: 'Workmen … when they are liberally paid by the piece, are very apt to over-work themselves, and to ruin their health and constitution in a few years'. Thus, the Crown Prince was taught less social concern than that evinced by Smith, and in this respect Smith can be said to be more of a subjective value theorist than Menger.

Roscher (1864), § 39, p. 67, continues with the discussion of piecework immediately after serfdom (and day-work), just as Menger does here. So Menger, in this passage, follows Roscher's ideas one by one. Roscher, by the way, thinks that the 'prevalence of piecework' had made England economically paramount (he quotes Howlett, who wrote in 1788).

28 Mentioned by Roscher (1864) in the same passage.

29 This criticism is made by Roscher (1864), § 39, p. 67 f.

Das reine Tantiemen-System besteht in der Entlohnung des Arbeiters ausschließlich durch einen Anteil am Geschäftsgewinne (Tantieme).[30] *Der Vorteil dieses Systems ist, daß der Arbeiter mit den Schicksalen der Unternehmung auf das innigste verknüpft ist, und deshalb sein Eifer für das Aufblühen des Unternehmens nahezu identisch ist mit jenem für sein eigenes Wohl.*

Dagegen sprechen aber folgende Gründe: Wenn die Unternehmung stockt oder gar Verlust bringt, der Arbeiter weder das Stocken des Zuflusses seiner
7 v *Einkünfte, noch viel weniger aber einen Verlust ertragen kann.*[31]

Das Kommissionssystem ist eine Verbindung des Lohnsystems mit dem Tantiemen-System. In diesem Falle erhält der Arbeiter einen Arbeitslohn, überdies aber im Falle des Gewinnes eine Tantieme.

Auch muß als ein Hebel für die Arbeit die Achtung vor derselben betrachtet werden.[32] Nur in rohen oder unkultivierten Ländern ist die Arbeit verachtet und als sklavisch betrachtet; durch dieselbe wird die Blüte eines Staates und die Kultur der Völker herbeigeführt. Die Arbeit jeder Art ist ehrenvoll, und nur der Müßiggang ist verächtlich.[33]

Doch die Arbeitsamkeit muß von den Lenkern des Staates gepflegt und geachtet sein, damit sie in allen Schichten der Bevölkerung blühe.[34]

8 r Über die Institution und die wirtschaftliche Bedeutung des Privateigentums

Kein Vermögen, und wäre es das größte, gestattet dem Besitzer, alle seine Wünsche und Bedürfnisse zu befriedigen; er entwickelt deshalb eine Tätigkeit, die wir die Wirtschaft nennen; ein Teil derselben ist das Bestreben, das Eigentum vor Verderben aller Art und besonders vor fremden Eingriffen zu schützen.[35]

Doch diesen Schutz kann sich der einzelne aus eigenen Mitteln nicht verschaffen; und so wäre er den Angriffen jedes Stärkeren preisgegeben, und das ganze Streben nach Ansammlung von Vermögen durch Arbeit wäre untergraben. Daher wird nur dann die Volkswirtschaft wirklich blühen, wenn der Staat das Eigentum seiner Bürger schützt, und durch diesen Schutz dieselben zu Wirtschaft, Mäßigung und Fleiß anspornt.

30 Als nächstes erwähnt Roscher die Gewinnbeteiligung: ebenda, S. 68.

31 Roscher, ebenda.

32 Roscher, ebenda.

33 Smith, (1776) I.ix.20, bemerkt, daß in Holland Untätigkeit unmodern und verachtet sei, weil durch den großen Reichtum des Landes der Zinssatz so niedrig sei, daß außer den Allerreichsten kaum jemand von seinem Kapitaleinkommen leben könne. Das führt Roscher (1864), § 41, S. 73, aus.

34 Das ist, in etwas anderen Worten, der letzte Gedanke von Roscher (1864), § 39, S. 68. Zwei Seiten von Mengers Niederschrift entsprechen fast genau zwei Seiten von Roscher.

35 Menger folgt wiederum ziemlich genau Smith und dessen "zweiter Pflicht des Souveräns". Siehe Smith, (1776) IV.ix.51, und insbesondere die Ausführungen in V.i.b, zumal i.b.2. Interessanterweise wird die Bedeutung des Privat- oder Sondereigentums von Menger stärker hervorgekehrt als von Smith.

In the simple share system the worker's payment consists exclusively of a share in the profits.[30] This has the advantage of intimately involving the worker with the fate of the firm so that his interest in the firm's performance is nearly identical with his interest in his own well-being.

There is, however, the following objection: If the firm stagnates or even incurs a loss, the worker cannot bear the interruption in his flow of income, much less a loss of income.[31] 7 v

Payment by commission is a combination of wages and profit shares. In this case, the worker is paid a wage and, if a profit accrues to the firm, a share of that, too.

The high esteem of such work must be regarded as still another incentive.[32] Only in primitive and uncivilized countries is work looked down upon and considered the business of slaves; it causes nations and civilizations to flourish. Work of whatever kind is honourable, and only idleness is to be despised.[33]

But in order to thrive in all strata of the population diligence must be fostered and respected by the rulers.[34]

On the Institution and Economic Importance of Private Property 8 r

No amount of assets, be there ever so many, is sufficient to satisfy all the desires and needs of its owner; therefore he develops an activity that we call economy; a part of it is striving to guard property against perils of all sorts, especially against trespasses by third persons.[35]

But the individual cannot provide such protection out of his own means and would therefore be exposed to assaults by anyone stronger than himself; and in that case all efforts to accumulate wealth by work would be in vain. Therefore the national economy will truly prosper only if and when the state protects the citizens' property and thereby spurs them to thrift, moderation, and industry.

30 Roscher (1864) next mentions profit sharing: see § 39, p. 68.
31 Roscher ibid.
32 Roscher ibid.
33 Smith (1776), I.ix.20, remarks that idleness is unfashionable and despised in Holland because the country is so rich that the rate of interest becomes so low that hardly anybody 'but the very wealthiest people' can live passively on interest income. This is elaborated on by Roscher (1864), §41, p. 73.
34 In slightly different words this is the last idea of Roscher (1864), § 39, p. 68. Two pages in the notebook correspond nearly exactly to two pages in Roscher.
35 Once more, Menger closely follows Smith in what the latter calls the 'second duty of the sovereign'. See Smith (1776), IV.ix.51, and especially the elaboration in V.i.b (in particular V.i.b.2). Note that the importance of private property is stressed more by Menger than by Smith.

8 v Darum ist dieser Schutz eine der wichtigsten wirtschaftlichen Aufgaben jeder Regierung.

Die Institution des Eigentums hat aber auch ihre unleugbaren Schattenseiten;[36] eines der größten Übel derselben ist der im Laufe der Entwicklung entstandene krasse Unterschied zwischen arm und reich,[37] der uns furchtbar entgegentritt bei den so häufigen Gegensätzen eines genußreichen Lebens ohne Tätigkeit und Arbeit, gegen ein Leben voll Elend und Mangel oft an der Befriedigung der notwendigsten Bedürfnisse.

[36] In der Behandlung zunächst der sozialen Vorteile des Privateigentums, dann des Sozialismus und Kommunismus als Versuche, dasselbe zu beschränken oder abzuschaffen, folgt Menger der kurzen Erörterung in den späteren Ausgaben von Rau (1855), § 45a, und der ausführlichen Darstellung in Roscher (1864), §§ 78–85.

[37] Roscher (1864), § 78, Bedingung A, S. 140 f.

For this reason, such protection is one of the most important economic duties of any government. 8 v

The institution of property has, however, its undeniable drawbacks;[36] one of its worst effects emerging in the course of development is the crass difference between rich and poor,[37] dreadfully obtrusive when one contrasts, as happens so often, a pleasurable life without activities or work with a life of misery and deprivation without even the most basic satisfactions.

36 In discussing first the social advantages of private property, then socialism and communism as the attempts to limit or abolish the same, Menger follows the short discussion in the later editions of Rau (1855), § 45a, and the extensive discussion in Roscher (1864), §§ 78–85.

37 Roscher (1864), § 78, p. 140 f. (condition A).

Politische Ökonomie II. 1876 Jänner

9 r *Durch diese Übelstände sind einzelne Personen auf die Idee gekommen, die Institution des Eigentums als die Ursache des bestehenden Elends zu bezeichnen und auf die Abschaffung derselben zu dringen.*

Auf diesen Ideen beruhen die Ansichten der Kommunisten. Dieselben verlangen

1. *daß alles Vermögen vom Staate eingezogen werden soll (damit entfällt auch jedes Erbrecht);*[1]
2. *daß jeder seine Arbeitskraft dem Staate zur Verfügung stellen solle;*[2]
3. *daß dagegen der Staat für die Bedürfnisse aller sorgen solle;*[3]
4. *daß der Staat insbesonders für das Aufziehen der Kinder sorgen solle.*

9 v *Nicht so weit als die Kommunisten gehen die sogenannten Sozialisten. Sie verlangen weder die völlige Abschaffung des Eigentums noch jene des Erbrechtes, sondern lediglich eine Beschränkung der obigen Institutionen, namentlich des Grundeigentums.*

Die obigen Vorschläge sind vielleicht überhaupt, jedenfalls aber unter den gegenwärtigen Verhältnissen nicht durchführbar. Sie setzen einen großen Gemeinsinn, eine allgemeine Bildung, wenigen Egoismus der Beherrschten und große Mäßigung, Weisheit und Uneigennützigkeit der Herrschenden voraus.[4]

Selbst diese Eigenschaften vorausgesetzt, würden immer noch große Übelstände zu Tage treten:

10 r

1. *es würde die Selbstverantwortung für das persönliche Wohl, die Verantwortung für das Los der Kinder und damit die hohe Arbeitsenergie, wie wir sie gegenwärtig beobachten können, sehr geschwächt werden, indem dieselbe durch kein persönliches (individuelles) Motiv getrieben würde;*[5]

1 Rau (1855), S. 55.
2 Roscher (1864), § 82, S. 151.
3 Ebenda: 'Eine Centralleitung aller Production und Consumtion durch die … Staatsgewalt'.
4 Roscher (1864), § 81, S. 147 f. Die Betonung eines praktisch unwahrscheinlichen Maßes von Gemeinsinn und des Nichtvorhandenseins von Egoismus als Voraussetzungen eines sozialistischen Systems rückt diesen Absatz in die Nähe von F.A. von Hayek, insbesondere seinen Überlegungen in Hayek (1988).
5 Roscher (1864), § 82, S. 151.

Political economy II. 1876 January

These drawbacks led some people to consider the institution of private property as the cause of existing misery and to urge its abolition. 9 r

These ideas are at the core of the Communists' view. They demand

1. that all property be confiscated by the state (thus rendering unnecessary any sort of inheritance law);[1]
2. that everybody put his labour at the disposal of the state;[2]
3. that in return the state provide for the needs of everybody;[3]
4. that the state provide especially for the rearing of children.

The so-called Socialists do not go as far as the Communists. They do not demand that private property and inheritance laws be abolished, but rather that the institutions named above, in particular landed property, be limited. 9 v

The proposals listed may not be realizable at all, but definitely not under present conditions. They presuppose a well-developed community spirit, a high level of education, little egoism among subjects, and great moderation, wisdom, and unselfishness among rulers.[4]

Even if these prerequisites were given, there would still be considerable drawbacks:

1. individual responsibility for one's personal welfare, responsibility for the fate of one's children, and with it the large supply of individual energy that we find at present, would seriously diminish as they would lack all personal (individual) motivation.[5] 10 r

1 Rau (1855), p. 55.
2 Roscher (1864), § 82, p. 151.
3 Ibid.: 'central direction of all production and consumption by … government authorities'.
4 This passage with its emphasis on an unlikely degree of community spirit and the absence of egoism as a prerequisite of socialism comes close to foreshadowing F.A. von Hayek, in particular Hayek (1988). It is taken from Roscher (1864), § 81, p. 147 f.
5 Roscher (1864), § 82, p. 151. With Roscher, this argument follows the next one, so that Menger altered the sequence here.

2. *es würde sich unter der Herrschaft des Kommunismus und selbst des Sozialismus eine Despotie*[6] *herausbilden, welche jede Selbstbestimmung unterdrücken würde. Niemand würde seinen Beruf selbst wählen können, sondern sich in allem den Anordnungen des Staates fügen müssen.*

10 v *Eine Institution, gegen welche die Angriffe des Kommunismus und Sozialismus sich vornehmlich richten, ist das Erbrecht,*[7] *weil dadurch Personen ohne Arbeit in den Besitz von Vermögen gelangen. Für das Erbrecht sprechen dagegen sehr gewichtige Gründe:*

1. *das historische* [?Hrsg.] *Recht eines jeden, über sein Vermögen frei zu verfügen, somit auch zu testieren;*[8]
2. *ist die Institution des Erbrechtes einer der wichtigsten Hebel für die Arbeitsamkeit, für die Selbstbeherrschung und Sparsamkeit der Menschen, da der einzelne seine Familie zu sichern strebt und das natürliche Verlangen hat, eine wohlsituierte Familie zu begründen.*[9]

Eine weitere Institution, gegen welche sich insbesondere die Angriffe der
11 r *Sozialisten richten, ist das Grundeigentum. Der Grund hiervon liegt darin, daß die Sozialisten behaupten, das Grundeigentum sei – nicht wie das übrige Vermögen – ursprünglich nicht durch Arbeit erworben, sondern durch Okkupation oder durch Gewalt.*[10]

Dagegen ist aber einzuwenden, daß die Okkupation von Grund und Boden, fern davon, ein Gewaltakt zu sein, einen Kulturfortschritt bedeutet und allfällige Eroberungen durch den verjährten Besitz längst gerechtfertigt sind; auch befinden sich die Grundstücke längst nicht mehr in den Händen der Nachkommen der ersten Okkupanten.

Der moderne Staat soll demnach die Interessen der besitzenden Klassen (Grundbesitzer, Häuserbesitzer, Fabrikanten, Handelsleute, Kapitalisten etc.)
11 v *gegen die undurchführbaren Projekte der Sozialisten und Kommunisten schützen; auf der anderen Seite aber darf sich die Regierung nicht gegen das wirklich vorhandene Elend eines Teiles der besitzlosen Klassen verschließen und soll dahinstreben, alles aufzuwenden, um die arbeitenden Klassen zu heben und das Elend derselben, wo es zu Tage tritt, zu lindern.*

6 Ebenda, den Ausdruck 'Despotie' verwendend. Menger dreht jedoch die Reihenfolge dieser Argumente um. Man beachte, wie genau Menger – genauer: Roscher – F.A. von Hayeks Weg zur Knechtschaft (1944) vorwegnimmt.

7 Roscher (1864), § 86, S. 158 f.

8 Roscher, ebenda, stellt das Familienerbrecht der 'Testamentsfreiheit' gegenüber. Der Text stellt das offensichtlich falsch dar: die Testierfreiheit spricht nicht für das Erbrecht.

9 Roscher (1864), § 86, nunmehr richtig wiedergegeben.

10 Roscher (1864) diskutiert in den §§ 87 und 88 das Grundeigentum, ohne freilich diese Argumente zu bringen.

2. under Communism and even under Socialism a despotic[6] system would develop that would suppress any kind of self-determination. Nobody could choose his vocation or profession for himself, but would have to comply with government regulations in all matters.

Among the institutions that Communists and Socialists attack particularly 10 v
are the inheritance laws[7] through which individuals acquire property without having worked for it. There are, however, important arguments in favour of inheritance laws:

1. everybody's historical [?ed.] right to dispose of his property as he sees fit, i.e. by last will and testament;[8]
2. the institution of inheritance laws provides one of the most important levers to human industry, self-restraint and thrift, as the individual seeks to provide for his family and has a natural desire to found a well-situated family.[9]

Another institution that Socialists attack especially is landed property. For
the Socialists argue that landed property, in contrast to other kinds of property, 11 r
originally was not acquired through labour, but rather by occupation or by force.[10]

Far from being an act of force, it may be countered, the occupation of land brings progress to civilization, and those conquests that occurred have long been justified by many years of occupation; furthermore, for a long time now the parcels of land concerned have not been in the hands of the original occupants' heirs.

Accordingly, the modern state ought to guard the interests of the propertied classes (real estate owners, owners of houses and factories, merchants, capitalists,
etc.) against the unworkable projects of Socialists and Communists; on the other 11 v
hand, however, the state must not ignore the palpable misery of a part of the unpropertied classes and should strive to do everything in its power to improve the situation of the working classes by relieving their misery where it becomes apparent.

6 Ibid. Menger, following Roscher, here foreshadows F.A. von Hayek (1944).

7 Roscher (1864), § 86, p. 158 f.

8 The respective sentence in Roscher, ibid., contrasts family-bound inheritance and freedom of testamentation. The latter is not an argument for inheritance laws.
Roscher mentions that freedom of testamentation often did not exist with respect to landed property. What Menger, following Roscher, may have wanted to convey was that freedom of testamentation as well as inheritance laws were likely to increase the incentive effects of private property.

9 Roscher (1864), § 86, now correctly reproduced.

10 Roscher discusses landed property in §§ 87 and 88 immediately after inheritance, though without the arguments presented here.

12 r **Werkzeuge und Maschinen**[11]

Unter einem Werkzeug verstehen wir eine Vorrichtung, welche den Zweck hat, die Wirkung der physischen Kraft des Menschen zu verstärken (z.B. Hammer, Schere, Säbel, Zange, Nadel, etc.).

Unter einer Maschine versteht man dagegen eine Vorrichtung, welche gewisse Wirkungen in einer mehr selbständigen Weise, wenn auch unter Leitung des Menschen, hervorbringt.

Die Maschinen teilt man:

l. in Motoren;
2. in Arbeitsmaschinen.

Unter Motoren versteht man jene Maschinen, welche eine Kraft hervorbringen,
12 v *die dann zu Produktionszwecken verwendet werden kann (z.B. Wasserräder, die Flügel der Windmühle, die Dampfmaschine). In gewissem Sinne kann man auch die Tiere als Maschinen in dem obigen Sinne betrachten.*

Der älteste Motor war die physische Kraft des Menschen. Die zweite Stufe bildet die Kraft der Tiere.[12] *Die letztere hat vor der ersteren den Vorzug der Billigkeit, die größere Fügsamkeit , und in den meisten Fällen den Vorzug der größeren Intensität.*

Abgesehen von den obigen Vorteilen ist auch das Moment zu berücksichtigen, daß durch den Übergang von der Benützung des Menschen als Motor zum Tier als Motor auch ein sittlicher Gewinn[13] *hervortritt .*

13 r *Die dritte Stufe ist dann der Übergang von den lebenden Motoren zu den leblosen Motorkräften und zwar zunächst zu der Kraft des Wassers und des Windes.*[14]

Es bedeutet dieser Übergang einen nicht unwesentlichen Fortschritt gegen die frühere Stufe. Der Hauptgrund liegt darin,

1. daß die leblosen Maschinenkräfte eine größere und zumeist auch andauerndere[15] *Tätigkeit äußern als die Tiere;*

11 Im folgenden mischt Menger die Darstellung von Rau (1855) und Roscher (1864). Der Satz über das Werkzeug folgt Rau, der es 'einfache Mittel zur Unterstützung der menschlichen Kraftäußerung' nennt (1855), S. 146 (Riedel folgend). Roscher (1864), § 42, S. 75, sagt, daß bei einer Maschine 'die bewegende Kraft nicht unmittelbar vom menschlichen Körper ausgeht (nur die leitende)'.

12 Menger folgt ungefähr, jedoch eher frei, den ausführlichen Überlegungen zu diesem Thema bei Riedel (1838), S. 315–30. Riedel unterscheidet 'Menschen- oder Handmaschinen … Thiermaschinen, Wassermaschinen, Luft- und Dampfmaschinen' (S. 320). Diese vier Arten werden bei Menger zu vier Stufen. Man beachte, daß hier ausgerechnet Menger eine historische Stufentheorie entwickelt. Mengers eigener Lehrer Mischler (1857, II, S. 101 ff.) folgt Riedel.

13 Mischler (1857), II, S. 102.

14 Ebenda, S. 103 f.

15 Ebenda, S. 104, beschreibt eingehend Vorkehrungen, um die 'Regelmäßigkeit' der Wasserkraft zu gewährleisten.

Tools and Machinery[11] 12 r

A tool is an instrument for increasing the effects of the physical power of man (e.g. hammer, scissors, sabre, prongs, needle, etc.).

A machine, by contrast, is an instrument which produces certain effects rather more autonomously, though under man's direction.

Machinery is classified into:

1. engines;
2. machines proper.

Engines are machines that produce energy employed for productive purposes (e.g. water wheels, the sails of a windmill, the steam engine). In a certain sense, 12 v
animals may be regarded as machines, as here described.

The first engine was the physical power of man. The second phase is the energy of animals.[12] The latter is preferable to the former because of cheapness, greater pliancy, and in most cases greater intensity.

Apart from these advantages the substitution of human energy by animal energy in engines constitutes a moral advance.[13]

The subsequent third stage is the substitution of animal power by inanimate 13 r
power, first of all by water and wind.[14]
This is a noticeable step forward as compared with the previous stage. The main reasons are

1. that inanimate power produces greater and in most cases steadier[15] activity than animals;

[11] Here, Menger follows Rau (1855), p. 146, and Roscher (1864), § 42, p. 75, the first passage on tools following the words used by Rau, the second on machines those used by Roscher – both authors in their turn following Riedel (1838).

[12] Menger recognizably appropriates the extensive discussion of the topic in Riedel (1838), pp. 315–30. In § 391, Riedel distinguishes 'human or hand-engines ... animal engines, water engines, air and steam engines'. With Menger, these four types of engines become four stages of development. Note that of all people Menger here avails himself of a theory of historical stages. Menger's own teacher Mischler (1857), Part II, p. 101 ff., followed Riedel.

[13] Mischler (1857), Part II, p. 102.

[14] Ibid., p. 103 f.

[15] Mischler (1857), p. 104, provides a detailed description of gadgets for ensuring the 'steadiness' of water power.

2. *daß dieselben um vieles weniger kostspielig sind als die lebenden Motoren, weil sie weder ernährt werden müssen, noch auch sich nach und nach abnützen.*

Als die 4. Stufe müssen wir betrachten die Benützung des Dampfes als Motor.
13 v *Die Vorzüge des Dampfes als Motor bestehen:*[16]

1. *in der sehr großen Intensität seiner Wirkung;*
2. *in der großen Stabilität und Andauer seiner Wirkung;*
3. *in dem Umstande, daß der Dampf unabhängig von der Lokalität überall dort angewandt werden kann, wo sich genügendes Brennmaterial vorfindet.*

Die Nachteile des Dampfes als Motor sind die große Kostspieligkeit der Errichtung und Speisung der Dampfmaschinen.

14 r **2. Arbeitsmaschinen**

Unter einer Arbeitsmaschine versteht man eine solche Vorrichtung, welche die Kraft eines Motors in einer gewissen selbständigen Weise, wenn auch unter Leitung eines Menschen, zur Verrichtung gewisser Arbeiten verwendet. Z.B. Mähmaschinen, Dreschmaschinen, Nähmaschinen etc.

Jede Arbeitsmaschine setzt einen Motor voraus.

Vorteile der Maschinen für die Volkswirtschaft

Als Hauptvorzug der Maschinen kann man bezeichnen, daß durch dieselben die nämliche Arbeit, welche sonst durch eine größere Anzahl von Arbeitern ausgeführt wurde, nunmehr von einer viel geringeren Anzahl von Arbeitern ausgeführt werden kann.[17]

14 v *Es kommen deshalb viele Arbeiter in Ersparnis, was ein sehr bedeutender Vorteil für die Volkswirtschaft ist.*

Als weiterer Vorteil der Maschinenarbeit muß die Präzision und Genauigkeit hervorgehoben werden, mit welcher Maschinen der Regel nach arbeiten.[18]

Unter solchen Umständen kann der Nutzen der Maschinen mit jenem der Arbeitsteilung für die Volkswirtschaft in eine Parallele gestellt werden.[19] *Die*

[16] Der Dampf ist 'eine Kraftquelle, die nie versiegt, jede Ausdehnung des Betriebes zuläßt und dabei die unbeschränkte Freiheit in der Wahl des Standortes der Gewerbsanlagen gestattet'; so Mischler (1857), II, S. 105, das Ganze gesperrt gedruckt.

[17] Smith (1776) I.i.8.

[18] Riedel (1838), S. 322, betont, daß Maschinen 'Quantität und Qualität des Products' erhöhen. 'Ohne Maschinen gewisse Erzeugnisse in der Güte darzustellen, worin sie dem Maschinenwesen verdankt werden, erscheint als baare Unmöglichkeit und oft ist dabei zugleich die Menge, worin sie für denselben Kostenaufwand gewonnen werden, um mehr als das Hundertfache vergrössert'.

[19] Hier geht Menger über Smith und Riedel hinaus.

2. that it is far <u>less costly</u> than animal power since it neither has to be fed nor wears out in the course of time.

The fourth stage is using <u>steam</u> in engines.
The advantages of steam as motive power are:[16] 13 v

1. the great <u>intensity</u> of its effect;
2. the great stability and long <u>duration</u> of its effect;
3. that, independent of locality, steam can be used wherever there is sufficient fuel.

The <u>disadvantages</u> of steam as motive power are the high costs of setting up and fueling steam engines.

2. Machines 14 r

A <u>machine</u> is an instrument that uses the power of an engine for performing certain operations in a quasi autonomous manner even though it is under man's direction. E.g. mowing machines, threshing machines, sewing machines etc.

Every machine requires an engine.

Advantages of Machinery for the Economy

The main advantage of machinery is that the same amount of work previously performed by a larger number of workers can now be performed by a much smaller number.[17]

This saves the input of many workers, which is a substantial advantage to the national economy. 14 v

Another advantage of machinery to be pointed out is the <u>precision</u> and <u>accuracy</u> with which machines operate, as a rule.[18]

Under such circumstances the <u>benefits of machinery</u> to the economy correspond to those of the <u>division of labour</u>.[19] Just like machinery, the division of labour

16 Steam is 'a source of energy that never runs out, that allows each and every enlargement of plant, without at all restricting the freedom of choosing the location of plant' (Mischler, ibid., p. 105, all in spaced letters).

17 Smith (1776), I.i.8: 'Everybody must be sensible how much labour is facilitated and abridged by the application of proper machinery'.

18 Riedel (1838), p. 322, stresses the improvement not only in quantity, but also in quality.

19 While, according to Notebook I, Menger had skipped the remarks on the development of machinery as a consequence of the division of labour, as expounded by Smith (1776), I.i.8,9, he now considers machinery as, in effect, corresponding to the division of labour. This is not to be found in Riedel (1838), otherwise a proximate source of much of the matter treated here. As

15 r *Arbeitsteilung erspart gerade so wie die Maschine Arbeitskräfte und somit Kosten, zum Teile auch Zeit. Zugleich wird sowohl durch die Arbeitsteilung, als auch durch die Maschinen die Qualität des Produktes wesentlich vervollkommnet. Es werden demnach durch die beiden obigen Einrichtungen sowohl Quantität als Qualität der Produkte um vieles verbessert.*

Als ein Nachteil, sowohl der Arbeitsteilung als auch der Einführung der Maschinen, wurde vielfach der Umstand genannt, daß durch die obigen Einrichtungen eine große Anzahl von Arbeitern brotlos werde. Zunächst ist es allerdings wahr, daß durch die obigen Momente viele Arbeiter überflüssig und dadurch brotlos werden. Dagegen läßt sich aber bemerken,[20]

1. *daß die Arbeiter zu neuen Tätigkeiten zu greifen in der Lage sind;*

15 v

2. *daß durch die obigen billigeren Produktionsmethoden die Produkte billiger und in Folge dessen mehr gekauft werden. Wird aber mehr gekauft, so muß auch mehr produziert werden und wird mehr produziert, so müssen wieder neue Arbeiter in die Fabriken aufgenommen werden, so zwar, daß die brotlos gewordenen Arbeiter allmählich wieder in die Lage kommen, Arbeit zu finden.*

Das Endresultat der Einführung der Arbeitsteilung und der Maschinen ist demnach,

1. *daß die wirtschaftliche Kultur des Landes zunimmt;*
2. *daß die Arbeiter hierdurch entweder überhaupt nicht, oder doch nur vorübergehend einen Nachteil erfahren.*

16 r [CM am Rand: *Unter Einkommen (überhaupt) versteht man alle jene wirtschaftlichen Güter, welche in gewissen Zeitperioden neu in das Vermögen einer Person treten.*[21] *Ertrag ist die Summe der Vermögensobjekte, welche aus einer bestimmten Einkommensquelle neu in das Vermögen einer Person zufließen.*[22]]

Unter Vermögensstamm[23] versteht man das Haupteigentum des einzelnen, welches demselben die Basis bildet, die ihm jene Mittel einträgt, mit denen er seine Bedürfnisse befriedigt, ohne aber diesen Grundstock, der sein eigentliches Vermögen bildet, angreifen zu dürfen.[24] Der Vermögensstamm kann in beweglichem oder unbeweglichem Gute bestehen, er ist stets die Grundlage,

20 Die Überlegungen folgen wieder Riedel (1838), S. 327 ff. Riedel ist optimistischer als Ricardo (1821), 'On Machinery'.

21 Das entspricht ungefähr Smith (1776) I.v.l, erster Satz; jedoch geht Smith sofort zur verfügbaren Arbeitsmenge als der wahren Ursache des Reichtums einer Person über. Die unmittelbare Quelle ist Rau (1855), S. 161.

22 Diese Definition folgt Smith (1776) I.vi.18, ohne erkennbare deutsche Quelle.

23 Der merkwürdige deutsche Ausdruck stammt aus Rau (1855), S. 161.

24 Ausnahmsweise ist Menger hier viel 'subjektiver' als Smith, indem er Kapital als 'Mittel zur Bedürfnisbefriedigung' ansieht, während Smith, (1776) II.i.2, Kapital definiert als 'den Teil

saves labour-input and thereby costs and, to a certain extent, time. In addition, 15 r
product quality is greatly improved by the division of labour and by the use of machinery. Thus, both phenomena greatly increase the quantity and quality of products.

It was often judged a disadvantage of the division of labour and of machinery that they caused a large number of workers to lose their jobs. It is indeed true that, for the reasons mentioned, many workers at first become redundant and thus unemployed. Against this, it may be argued, however,[20]

1. that workers are capable of turning to new activities;
2. that, through cheaper production methods, products become cheaper and 15 v
   will therefore be in higher demand. If more is bought, more will have to be produced. If more is produced, additional workers will have to be employed in the factories, so that unemployed workers will eventually find jobs again.

Eventually, introducing the division of labour and machinery results in:

1. improvements in a country's economy;
2. no disadvantage at all or, at most, a temporary disadvantage to the workers.

[CM in the margin: Income (in general) denotes all those economic goods 16 r
accruing to a person's property in specified periods of time.[21] Returns are the sum of assets newly accruing to a person's property from a particular source of income.[22]]

A person's capital[23] is the stock of assets that provides him with the means to satisfy his needs without encroaching upon the actual stock of assets that constitutes this capital.[24] Capital may be mobile or immobile; in either case, it is the foundation for the means of subsistence earned by economic activity.

to Smith, he had not suggested anywhere that either the division of labour or machinery improve the quality of the product.

20 The argument again follows Riedel (1838), p. 327 ff. Riedel is more optimistic than Ricardo (1821 edition, ch. XXXI, 'On Machinery').

21 This looks somewhat like Smith (1776), I.v.l, first sentence, but Smith quickly switches to the quantity of labour a man can 'command' as the real essence of his 'riches'. The proximate source is Rau (1855), p. 161.

22 This definition follows Smith (1776), I.vi.18, without any apparent German source.

23 The curious German expression used derives from Rau (1855), p. 161.

24 Here Menger is, for once, much more subjective than Smith, considering capital 'the means

von der aus das Leben durch jene Summen, die durch die wirtschaftliche Tätigkeit einkommen, erhalten wird.

Unter Einkommen *aus Vermögen* versteht man jene *wirtschaftlichen Güter*, welche durch die Verwertung und Bewirtschaftung des Vermögensstammes aus demselben zur Benützung dem Besitzer zufallen.

Es gibt nicht nur Einkommen aus einem Vermögensstamm, sondern auch aus anderen Erwerbsquellen.

Dieses Einkommen also hat als Hauptzweck die Befriedigung der Bedürfnisse des Eigentümers;[25] er kann es, ohne dem Hauptstamm zu schaden, in einer bestimmten Zeit verausgaben; fließt der Hauptstamm des Vermögens aus unbeweglichen Gütern, welche aber Einflüssen jeder Art unterworfen sind, die, um in gleichem Werte zu bleiben, manchmal verbessert werden müssen, dann ist es gut, wenn die Mittel, die dazu nötig sind, aus dem Einkommen genommen
16 v werden und dasselbe also nicht vollständig verzehrt wird, sondern ein Teil desselben stets zurückgelegt wird.

Auch ohne jeden bestimmten Zweck wird man es als vorsichtiger und klüger gehandelt bezeichnen müssen, wenn einem ein Teil des Einkommens zur Sicherung gegen eventuelle Fälle aufgespart wird und den Staatsbürgerpflichten ebenfalls aus dem Einkommen nachgekommen wird und man dann deshalb nicht den Hauptstamm antasten muß.[26]

Für die Volkswirtschaft ist es nützlicher, wenn der einzelne diese wirtschaftlichen Prinzipien verfolgt. Im ersten Augenblick sollte man meinen, daß es für das Gemeinwohl vorteilhafter wäre, wenn der einzelne sein Einkommen, statt es zu behalten, verbraucht, denn es kommt dadurch in den Umlauf und in die Benützung wieder.

Doch dies ist unrichtig;[27] durch das Sparen und Zurücklegen von Teilen des Einkommens entstehen wohlhabende, selbst reiche Leute, und viele derselben machen ein reiches Land aus.

Das Verbrauchen des ganzen Einkommens ist für die Gesellschaft verderblich, denn es ist das Hindernis zur Erreichung einer großen Blüte der Wohlhabenheit.

(des Vermögens einer Person), von dem sie einen Ertrag erwartet'. Die Betonung der Wichtigkeit der Erhaltung des Kapitals und der Notwendigkeit, bei der Berechnung des Einkommens (nach Smith Nettoeinkommen) solche Erhaltungsaufwendungen zu berücksichtigen, ist jedoch zur Gänze Smith (so in guten Teilen von II.ii).

25 Hermann (1832), S. 297, definiert Einkommen als hauptsächlich auf die Befriedigung von Bedürfnissen gerichtet.

26 Von hier an folgt Menger – offensichtlich nach dem Original und ohne Verwendung deutscher Lehrbücher – ziemlich genau Smith, und zwar lassen sich die Gedanken in den Schlüsselpassagen II.iii.14–20 absatzweise nachlesen. (Wie aber das nächste Heft zeigt, sollte das nur ein kurzes Vorspiel bleiben.)

27 Etwas verkürzt und vereinfacht ist dies das Argument des prototypischen Sayschen 'Gesetzes', wie es sich bei Smith, (1776) II.iii.18, findet. Der Kronprinz wurde also ein 'Gesetz' gelehrt, wobei Menger es zweifellos ausführlicher entwickelte.

Income from assets denotes all those economic goods that accrue to the owner from using and employing capital and may be used by him.

Income is not only derived from capital, but also from other sources.

The main purpose of income is to satisfy the owner's needs;[25] he can spend it in a certain period of time without encroaching upon his capital; if his capital consists of immobile assets which, however, are subject to various influences and therefore have to be repaired from time to time to maintain their value, the requisite means should be taken from income, i.e. income must not be completely consumed, but part of it invariably saved. 16 v

If a person saves part of his income, even without any definite purpose but with a view to possible emergencies, and if he meets civic duties out of his income instead of encroaching upon capital, he must be deemed more prudent and judicious.[26]

For the economy as a whole it is better if the individual pursues these economic principles. At first sight, it may seem in the interest of the common good if the individual were to spend his income instead of saving it, for then it would remain in circulation and could be employed anew.

This is incorrect, however;[27] by saving and accumulating parts of their incomes, people become prosperous, even wealthy, and many wealthy people make up a wealthy country.

Consuming the entire income is perilous to society, since that is the obstacle on the way to flourishing prosperity.

for the satisfaction of his needs', while Smith (1776), II.i.2, defined capital as 'that part (of a man's stock) which, he expects, is to afford him revenue'. The emphasis on the importance of the maintenance of capital and the need to deduct maintenance in the calculation of income (net revenue according to Smith) corresponds, however, to Smith in much of II.ii.

25 Hermann (1832), p. 297, defines income as mainly intended for the satisfaction of needs.

26 From here on, Menger follows – evidently from the original and mostly without using German textbooks – Smith (1776), II.iii.14–20, in one idea after the other in this key passage. (But, as Notebook III will show, this was only to be a short prelude.) In II.iii.14, for example, Smith expounds: 'Capitals are increased by parsimony, and diminished by prodigality and misconduct'; in 18: 'What is annually saved is as regularly consumed as what is annually spent ... but it is consumed by a different set of people'; in 19: 'By what a frugal man annually saves, he ... like the founder of a public workhouse, ... establishes ... a perpetual fund for the maintenance of a ... number in all times to come'.

27 This is – in a somewhat foreshortened and simplified way – the argument which forms the prototype of Say's so-called 'law', as given by Smith (1776) in II.iii.18 – a 'law' which Rudolf is thus taught. Without doubt, Menger presented it more fully.

Politische Ökonomie III. 1876 Jänner

17 r Der Begriff 'Vermögen' kann von zwei Gesichtspunkten aus betrachtet, definiert werden, nämlich im wissenschaftlichen Sinne und im populären.

Wissenschaftlich genommen verstehen wir unter einem Vermögen alle wirtschaftlichen Güter einer Person; diese können nun in Geld, Häusern, Landgütern, Gegenständen aller Art, Aktien, Haustieren etc. etc. bestehen. Es ist also der Inbegriff aller Habe im weitesten Sinne.

Populär betrachtet, werden nur jene wirtschaftlichen Güter Vermögen genannt, die ein Einkommen tragen, z.B. Geldsummen, Häuser, Landgüter, Unternehmungen, Papiere etc. etc. Dies ist also ein engerer Begriff wie der vorige, denn er ist nicht der Inbegriff aller Habe des einzelnen, sondern nur jener Teile derselben, die ein Einkommen tragen.[1]

Unter Einkommen verstehen wir jene wirtschaftlichen Güter, welche in gewissen Zeitperioden neu in das Vermögen einer Person treten.[2]

Das Einkommen kann aus verschiedenen Quellen entspringen, es kann z.B.
17 v der Lohn für Arbeit oder das Erträgnis des Vermögens im engeren Sinne genommen sein. Man kann das Einkommen in zwei Hauptabteilungen teilen, nämlich: in das reine Einkommen und in das Bruttoeinkommen.

Unter ersterem versteht man das Einkommen einer Person *in jener Ausdehnung*, wie es von derselben verwertet werden kann, also nach Abschlag aller Kosten, die damit gleich bestritten werden müssen, z.B. Steuern oder Mietgeld etc. etc. Das reine Einkommen ist immer ein sehr verschiedenes, um vieles kleineres, als das Bruttoeinkommen, denn meistens muß ein großer *Teil davon*, in jedem Falle aber die Steuern, gleich abgerechnet werden.[3]

Was Bruttoeinkommen ist, wird durch das Vorhergehende leicht verstanden, es ist das gesamte Einkommen einer Person in seiner ersten oder rohen Form, bevor noch irgend etwas davon abgezogen ist. Es ist also sehr irrig, jemanden
18 r in bezug auf seine Wohlhabenheit nach seinem Bruttoeinkommen zu beurteilen, das wohl die Frucht seines übrigen Besitzes, aber für ihn nicht verwendbar ist.[4]

1 Menger weicht hier von Smith (1776) ab, der Mengers 'wissenschaftlichen' Begriff in II.i.2 'stock' und eben den 'populären' Begriff 'capital' nennt. Man beachte jedoch die etwas andere Wiederholung dieser Unterscheidung im folgenden, so daß der Kronprinz hier vielleicht eine leicht veränderte Fassung der Vorlesung wiedergibt.

2 Wiederholung der oben wiedergegebenen Definition von Rau (1855).

3 Smith, (1776) II.ii.3–5, unterscheidet ähnlich zwischen Brutto- und Nettoeinkommen, insbesondere Brutto- und Nettoeinnahmen eines landwirtschaftlich genutzten Grundstücks. Als unmittelbare Quelle diente Menger wahrscheinlich Roscher (1864), § 145, S. 293.

Political economy III. 1876 January

The concept of 'assets' may be defined from two angles, the scientific and the popular. 17 r

From a scientific point of view, assets are all of a person's economic goods; these may consist of money, houses, farms, objects of all kinds, stocks, domestic animals, etc. It is the sum total of belongings in the widest sense.

In a popular sense, only those economic goods are assets that yield an income, e.g. sums of money, houses, farms, firms, securities, etc. This concept is narrower than the former for it is not the sum total of all of an individual's belongings, but only those parts from which an income is drawn.[1]

Income denotes all those economic goods which newly accrue to a person's assets within specified periods of time.[2]

Income may be derived from various sources, e.g. it may be the wage for work performed or the returns from assets in the narrower sense. Income may 17 v be divided into two major classes: net income and gross income.

The net income of a person is that amount of income that may be disposed of after deducting all costs that have to be met, e.g. taxes, rent payments, etc. Net income is invariably very different from, and much smaller than, gross income, since usually a large part, and in any case taxes, has to be deducted from it.[3]

Gross income is easily visualized from the aforesaid; it is the entire income of a person in its original or crude form, before anything has been deducted from it. It is a big mistake, therefore, to judge a person's wealth by his gross income, which – though it is the returns from all his assets – he cannot use as such.[4] 18 r

1 Here, Menger deviates from Smith. To Smith (here II.i.2), Menger's 'scientific' concept would be 'stock', while Menger's 'popular' concept would be 'capital'. But see the somewhat different reiteration of this distinction below. Rudolf may be rendering a slightly garbled version of the lecture.

2 Repetition of the definition from Rau (1855), given above.

3 Smith (1776), II.ii.3–5, similarly distinguishes gross and neat revenue and especially gross and neat rent of an agricultural estate. Menger's proximate source was probably Roscher (1864), § 145, p. 293.

4 Smith (1776), II.ii.4: 'Neat rent (is)...what, without hurting his estate, he can afford to place in his stock reserved for immediate consumption, or to spend upon his table, equipage, the

Vom Einkommen in vielem verschieden ist der Begriff des Ertrages.

Man versteht darunter die Summe von Vermögensobjekten, die aus einer bestimmten Einkommensquelle in das Vermögen neu zufließt.

Der Ertrag folgt immer aus der Verwertung einer bestimmten Sache, nicht aus allen wirtschaftlichen Gütern, sondern nur aus Teilen.[5]

Das Einkommen ist die Frucht des gesamten Vermögens im populären Sinne, während der Ertrag nur aus Teilen desselben entspringt.[6]

Darum spricht man vom Einkommen einer Person und dem Ertrag eines bestimmten Vermögensteiles.

Der Ertrag wird auch in den Rein- und Bruttoertrag eingeteilt. Ersterer besteht aus dem übriggebliebenen Teile nach Abschlag aller Kosten, letzterer aus dem Gesamtertrag, ohne Abrechnung der Kosten. Gegenstand eines Ertrages kann
18 v z.B. ein Feld, Geldsummen, oder ein Nutztier, wie die Milch einer Kuh sein etc. etc.

Unter Vermögensstamm versteht man die dauernde Grundlage eines jeden Einkommens;[7] in diesem Falle wird auch die Arbeitskraft eines Menschen als Vermögensstamm zu betrachten sein;[8] im populären Sinne dagegen versteht man unter Vermögensstamm nur jene übertragbaren Vermögensobjekte, welche ein von der Arbeit des Besitzers unabhängiges dauerndes Einkommen liefern.

Es gibt aber verschiedene Arten von Vermögensstämmen, man könnte sie in drei Hauptgruppen gliedern:[9]

1. In Grundbesitz und Häuser,
2. in Geldsummen und
3. in Unternehmungen.

Diese Einteilung der Vermögensstämme könnte man als populär bezeichnen, denn es ist der Begriff nur im engeren Sinne gegeben. Wissenschaftlich müßte man den Begriff erweitern und auch die Arbeitskraft hineinnehmen.[10]

Unter jedem Falle muß man sagen, daß es noch viele andere Einkommensquellen gibt, die nicht aus dem Vermögensstamme im populären Sinne entspringen.

4 Vgl. Smith, (1776) II.ii.4, über 'rohe' und 'reine' Einnahmen und ihr Verhältnis zum Vermögen einer Person.

5 Smith (1776) V.vi.18.

6 Smith (1776) II.i.2.

7 Daß jegliche 'Verbesserung' der Kapitalakkumulation bedarf, erwähnt Smith (1776) bereits in II. Einleitung 4; daß Kapital ein 'dauernder Fonds' sei, in II.iii.19.

8 Vgl. Smith (1776) I.x.c.12.

9 Die Unterteilung weicht etwas von Smith, (1776) I.i.13–17, ab. Menger betrachtet besonders Unternehmen, unabhängig von dem in ihnen gebundenen Realkapital, als Vermögen; das heißt, er bewertet den 'Good-Will' oder, wie er sagt, 'Kunden-Kreise, Publicum, Monopole etc.' getrennt; siehe Menger (1871) S. 6 f.

10 Genau wie in Smith (1776) II.i.17, vierter Punkt.

The concept of returns differs in many ways from that of income.

It denotes the sum of additional assets accruing to a person's capital from a particular source of income.

The returns derive from using particular goods – not from any and all economic goods, but only from some of them.[5]

Income is the yield from the sum total of assets in the popular sense, while returns derive only from parts of these assets.[6]

Therefore we speak of a person's income and of the return on a particular asset.

Returns are also classified as net and gross. The former are what remains after deducting all costs, the latter are the total returns before deducting costs. Returns may accrue from objects like a field, sums of money or a domestic animal, e.g. the milk of a cow, etc. etc. 18 v

A stock of capital is the continuing foundation of any income;[7] seen in this way, a person's labour potential is to be regarded as capital;[8] in the popular sense, though, capital denotes only those transferable assets that yield a continuing income independent of their owner's labour.

There are, however, different types of capital; they could be classified in three categories as :[9]

1. real estate and housing;
2. sums of money; and
3. firms.

This classification of capital could be called popular, since it pertains to the narrower concept of capital only. From the scientific point of view, the concept would have to be extended to include labour potential.[10]

For each one of these cases there are many more sources of income which have nothing to do with capital in the popular sense.

ornaments of his house and furniture, his private enjoyments and amusements'.

5 Smith (1776), V.vi.18.

6 Smith (1776), II.i.2: 'That part (of his stock) which, he expects, is to afford him…revenue, is called his capital'.

7 That the 'accumulation of stock' is necessary for all 'improvement' is announced by Smith (1776) already in II. introduction. 4; that it is a 'perpetual fund' in II.iii.19.

8 Smith (1776), I.x.c.12: 'The property which every man has in his own labour, as it is the original foundation of all other property, so it is the most sacred and inviolable. The patrimony of a poor man lies in the strength and dexterity of his hands.' Also Smith's valuation theory of human capital in I.x.b. 5–7, e.g.: 'A man educated at the expense of much labour and time to any of those employments which require extraordinary dexterity and skill, may be compared to one of those expensive machines'.

9 The division differs somewhat from that given by Smith (1776), I.i.13–17. In particular, Menger typically includes firms in contrast to their assets, as he considers goodwill a part of

19 r Viele Menschen haben als Einkommen den Lohn für ihre Arbeit, denselben bildet dann ihre Arbeitskraft ihren Vermögensstamm. In diese Gruppe gehört jeder Arbeitslohn, ob er jetzt der Gehalt für geistige Arbeit oder der Sold des Soldaten oder der Lohn für jede Händearbeit ist; auch Almosen, Lebensrenten etc. etc. muß man hierher rechnen.

Der Begriff des Kapitals kann von zwei Standpunkten aus betrachtet definiert werden:[11]

1. Im wissenschaftlichen Sinne versteht man unter einem Kapital jeden Vermögensstamm;
2. im populären Sinne wird jede Geldsumme, die ein Einkommen oder einen Ertrag liefert, Kapital genannt.[12] Erstere Definition ist viel weiter, denn sie schließt in sich jedes dauernde Einkommen. Letztere ist enger, denn es werden nur Geldsummen Kapital genannt. Besitzer derselben werden Kapitalisten[13] genannt und sind meistens bestrebt, dieses Kapital durch Sparen aus dem Einkommen zu vergrößern, dadurch sind sie für den Staat von Vorteil.[14]

19 v Für den Staat ist es ein Glück und ein Segen, wenn seine Bewohner wirtschaftlich und sparsam sind und den Stamm ihres Vermögens gar nicht antasten, das Einkommen aber so verwenden, daß ihnen ein Teil desselben übrig bleibt, den sie dann zurücklegen.[15]

11 Menger verwendet nun Rau (1855), S. 66 ff., als Quelle. Der Kronprinz gibt das Argument anscheinend nicht ganz genau wieder: Rau unterscheidet zwischen der Summe nützlicher Güter, die in der weiteren Produktion eingesetzt werden und die vom volkswirtschaftlichen Standpunkt Kapital vorstellen, einerseits, und Geldkapital – vom Standpunkt des einzelnen aus Kapital – dessen Aggregation zu Doppelzählungen führen müßte.

Die erste Definition ist also die 'fundamentalere', die zweite genau die 'weitere'. Vielleicht aber führte Menger als zusätzliche Überlegung einen Gedanken von Mischler (1857), I, S. 269) ein, daß der Begriff des nationalen Kapitals weiter ist als die Summe der individuellen privaten Kapitalien, weil er das Kapital in öffentlichem Eigentum einschließt; dann hätte der Kronprinz zwei verschiedene Argumente zusammengeworfen.

12 Im Unterschied zu den Ausführungen am Anfang dieses Heftes scheint der übliche Trugschluß nunmehr viel eher darin zu bestehen, daß eine 'Geldsumme' als Kapital betrachtet wird. Das würde genau Smith (1776) entsprechen, für den Geld sicherlich nicht Teil der 'revenue' ist (ein Ausdruck, dem im Deutschen nichts genau entspricht). Vgl. Smith (1776) II.ii.14. Unmittelbar bezieht sich Menger hier auf Rau (1855), § 54, S. 67.

13 Der Ausdruck 'Capitalisten' wird bereits von Rau (1855), S. 68, ursprünglich 1826, verwendet und beweist, daß sich Menger hier auf Rau stützt, da der Ausdruck sonst noch eher unüblich war. Rau verwendet ihn genau wie hier einschränkend auf die Eigentümer von Geldsummen bezogen: 'Unter Capitalisten pflegt man nur jene Zinsgläubiger zu verstehen'. Ein weiteres 'Leitfossil' für die Verwendung von Rau (1855) ist der Ausdruck 'Vermögensstamm' (z.B. S. 161), manchmal 'Erwerbsstamm' (z.B. S. 65).

14 Roscher (1864), § 201, S. 414: '...productionsfördernde Concentrirung der Capitalien...' (man beachte, daß dies vor Marx (1867), l. Band, geschrieben ist); ähnlich § 45, S. 83.

15 Eine Wiederholung dieses zentralen Anliegens von Smith, möglicherweise auch Roscher (1864), § 222, S. 455.

For many people income consists of the wages for their labour; for these people their labour potential constitutes their capital. Every sort of wage belongs in this category – be it the remuneration for intellectual work or the soldier's pay or the wage for any sort of manual labour; also alms, annuities, etc. etc. 19 r

The concept of capital may be defined from two angles:[11]

1. in a scientific sense, capital denotes any stock of assets;
2. in the popular sense any sum of money that yields an income or a return is called capital.[12] The first definition is much wider, since it includes any continuing income. The latter definition is narrower, since it includes only sums of money. The owners of these are called capitalists[13] and for the most part are eager to increase this capital by saving part of their income, thus they are useful to the state.[14]

A country is fortunate and blessed if its inhabitants are economical and thrifty and do not touch their stock of capital at all, but dispose of their income in such a way that part of it is left over and saved.[15] 19 v

capital, cf. Menger (1976), p. 55.

10 Exactly as in Smith (1776), II.i.17, where 'fourthly...the acquired and useful abilities of all the inhabitants or members of society' are enumerated as part of fixed capital.

11 Menger now uses Rau as his source; cf. Rau (1855), p. 66 ff. The Crown Prince apparently does not reproduce the argument quite accurately: Rau distinguishes between the sum of useful commodities used for further production on the one hand, which constitute capital from the point of view of the economy; and monetary capital, capital from the point of view of the individual, which would entail double counting if aggregated. The first definition is more fundamental, while it is exactly the second that is 'wider'. Possibly, however, Menger introduced – as a further consideration – an argument from Mischler (1857), I, p. 269, that the concept of national capital is wider than the sum of individual private capitals because it includes publicly owned capital. In that case the Crown Prince condensed two different arguments into one.

12 In contrast to the beginning of this notebook, the popular fallacy now seems much rather to consider a 'sum of money' as capital. That would be in close conformity to Smith, for whom money is certainly not part of 'revenue' (a term with no exact German equivalent). Cf. II.ii.14: 'money, by means of which the whole revenue of the society is regularly distributed...makes itself no part of that revenue'. Menger's proximate source is Rau (1855), p. 66 ff.

13 Rau (originally 1826) (1855), p. 68, already uses the term 'capitalist'. In 1876 the term was still rather unusual. Its appearance seems to prove that Menger relied on Rau here. Rau uses it, in exactly the restrictive sense employed here, viz. for the owners of sums of money. Another 'clue' indicating that Menger had recourse to Rau's book is the term 'Vermögensstamm', occasionally 'Erwerbsstamm' (ibid., p. 65).

14 Roscher (1864), § 201, p. 414, speaks of the 'production-enhancing concentration of capital'; see also § 45, p. 83. Note that this was written before the publication of Marx's Capital.

15 Repetition of this central concern of Smith, possibly also Roscher (1864), § 222, p. 455.

Aus diesem Verfahren, wenn es nämlich allgemein angewendet wird, entsteht ein wohlhabendes, gut kultiviertes Land, welches dadurch ein geordnetes, ruhiges Leben im Inneren und eine sichere Haltung gegen die Gefahren von außen einnehmen kann.[16] Oft hört man aber dagegen einwenden, daß die Handwerker und Kaufleute viel mehr beschäftigt seien und weniger Arbeiter brotlos wären, wenn die einzelnen besonders die Reichen, ihr ganzes Einkommen und vielleicht auch Teile des Vermögensstammes für ihre persönlichen Bedürfnisse verbrauchen würden.

Diese Einwendung kann in vielem richtig sein, doch in der Hauptsache ist diese Tendenz zu mißbilligen. Einzelne Gewerbe, besonders jene, die sich mit dem Handel von Putz-Luxus und ähnlichen unwichtigen, nur für den
20 r augenblicklichen Genuß bestimmten Waren beschäftigen, würden durch die Sparsamkeit leiden,[17] und indem die Mehrzahl der Menschen in den Städten solche Kaufläden vor Augen hat und das Klagen dieser Gewerbsleute stets zu hören bekommt, könnte sich leicht die Ansicht verbreiten, daß das ganze Gewerbe durch die Wirtschaft und den Mangel an Verschwendung zugrunde ginge.

Es ist richtig, daß vielleicht einige Arten von Geschäften ihre Tätigkeit beschränken und Arbeiter entlassen müßten, doch im großen und ganzen würde durch Sparsamkeit der Reichtum des Landes und mithin auch die Arbeit zunehmen, denn der einzelne, der sein Kapital erspart und es zu vergrößern strebt, läßt sein Geld eben deshalb nicht tot liegen.[18]

Er wird es entweder durch Geldgeschäfte zu vermehren suchen und es anlegen; oder er wird seinen Vermögensstamm, der vielleicht in Landgütern besteht, durch Bauten, bei welchen viele Arbeiter beschäftigt sind, oder durch gute Maschinen, bei deren Ankauf die Kaufleute, die damit handeln, profitieren, zu vergrößern trachten.

20 v Durch sein durch Wirtschaft und Sparsamkeit vergrößertes Kapital, das er, indem er es noch zu vergrößern strebt, bei Unternehmungen verwendet, werden viel mehr Leute profitieren,[19] als hätte er stets sein Einkommen und vielleicht auch über dasselbe hinaus ausgegeben. Auch wird der wirtschaftliche Mensch mehr solchen Menschen durch die Anwendung seines Geldes Profit verschaffen, die es besser brauchen, da sie für den Staat nützlichere Geschäfte betreiben,[20]

16 Die Bedeutung des Sparens für den internationalen Wettbewerb zu betonen, entspricht nicht Smith, war aber ein zentrales Anliegen der Österreicher.

17 Wiederum eine – leicht veränderte – Wiederholung, die nunmehr Smith, (1776) II.iii.18, anklingen läßt. Man vergleiche auch II.iii.28 über den 'augenblicklichen Genuß', sowie die Beschreibung unnötiger Luxusgüter in II.iii.38.

18 Smith (1776) II.iii.18.

19 Wiederholung mit Variation; entspricht genau Smith (1776) II.iii.19, 20.

20 Menger gibt hier Smiths Lehre vom Unterschied zwischen 'produktiver und unproduktiver Arbeit' wieder (1776, II.iii, erster Teil), die völlig im Widerspruch zu seiner eigenen Lehre vom subjektiven Wert steht; denn unter den Voraussetzungen methodologischen Individualismus ist jede Arbeit 'produktiv', die vom einzelnen als subjektiv wertvoll angesehen wird; sie ist umso wertvoller, je höher sie vom Grenzkonsumenten geschätzt wird. Menger kann es auch nicht unterlassen, objektive Urteile über Bedürfnisse zu fällen.Vgl. Menger (1871), S. 4.

If and when this sort of behaviour is generally adopted, there will develop a prosperous, well-cultivated country which can be orderly and quiet inside and can show self-assurance in the face of dangers from abroad.[16] Often it is objected, however, that craftsmen and traders would have much more to do and that fewer labourers would be out of work if people, particularly the rich, were to spend all of their income and perhaps even part of their capital in satisfying their personal needs.

There may be some truth in this, but on the whole, such an attitude should be frowned upon. Certain trades, especially those that are concerned with mongering millinery, luxuries, and similar trifles intended only for instant pleasure would suffer by general thriftiness,[17] and since the majority of 20 r
townspeople would see such shops and keep hearing the complaints of the tradespeople, it could easily become general opinion that all trade is doomed to failure because of thrift and the lack of extravagance.

It is true that some kinds of shops may have to cut down on their activities and dismiss some employees, but on the whole the wealth of the country and the amount of labour employed would increase by thrift because an individual who saves his capital and is intent on making it grow, will not simply let it lie.[18]

He will either attempt to make his money grow by putting it to work and investing it; or he will try to increase his capital, e.g. in the case of farming property, by constructing more buildings (which employs many workers) or by purchasing good machinery (which renders a profit to the respective merchants).

Many more people will profit from his capital – which he has increased by 20 v
economy and thrift and which he strives to increase still further, by making it work – than if he had always spent his entire income and perhaps more than that.[19] Furthermore, by investing his money, economic man will generate a profit for other people who will employ the money better because they perform services that are of greater use to the general public,[20] e.g. labourers in various

[16] The emphasis on the importance of (domestic) saving for international competitiveness is not to be found in Smith (1776); it was a major concern of the Austrians.

[17] Again a repetition, with slight variation, now echoing Smith (1776), II.iii.18, with its strictures on 'idle guests and menial servants, who leave nothing behind them in return'. See also II.iii.28 on the 'passion for present enjoyment' and II.iii.38 on 'unnecessary luxuries'.

[18] Smith (1776), II.iii.18: 'Saving a part... that part is for the sake of the profit immediately employed as capital'.

[19] Repetition with variation, corresponding to Smith (1776), II.iii.19, 20, where 'the prodigal...diminishes the quantity...of labour' and 'the real wealth and revenue'.

[20] Menger echoes Smith's doctrine of the distinction between 'productive and unproductive labour' (1776, first part of II.iii), which is completely at variance with his own subjective value theory; for on the basis of methodological individualism any labour is 'productive' which is considered

z.B. Arbeiter bei den verschiedenartigen Bauten, oder Gewerbsleute und Fabrikanten von für die Volkswirtschaft wichtigen Gegenständen.

Man kann auch den Vorteil der Sparsamkeit auf folgende Weise deutlich beweisen: jener, der sein Vermögen in Kleinigkeiten vergeudet, gibt zwar dem damit Handelnden den Geldpreis, doch dieser gibt ihm dafür eine Sache, die vielleicht im ersten Gebrauche aufgeht, oder wenigstens bald verbraucht ist, ohne durch ihren Gebrauch den Besitz des Eigentümers zu vergrößern oder auf irgend eine Art nützlich zu sein.

21 r Der Sparsame hingegen verwendet sein Geld bei Ankäufen von Gegenständen, die im Gebrauche etwas nutzen, und ihm sein Vermögen vergrößern; dadurch wird der Gewerbsmann, der es ihm verkaufte, unterstützt, und das Geld, das er demselben gegeben und noch mehr auch durch die Verwertung des gekauften Gegenstandes wieder hereingebracht.[21]

Dadurch hat also der allgemeine Reichtum nur zugenommen, der bei dem früher geschilderten Falle, trotz der irrigen allgemeinen Ansicht, abgenommen hat.

Auch wird der wirtschaftende Mensch sein Vermögen für öffentliche Unternehmungen, wie Eisenbahnen, Kanäle, Dampfschiffahrts-gesellschaften verwerten.[22] Durch dieses Verfahren wächst sein eigenes Einkommen, sowie der Reichtum und die Kultur des ganzen Landes, die durch solche Unternehmung natürlich gehoben wird. Durch Gründung von Fabriken werden viele Arbeiter beschäftigt, und durch das Wachstum des Verkaufes der Produkte wächst der allgemeine Reichtum.[23]

21 v So geht es auch bei Dammbauten oder Kanalisierungen auf den eigenen Landgütern, welche, nebst dem, daß sie viele Menschen beschäftigen, den ganzen Wert und Reichtum eines Landstriches oft begründen, sicher aber erhöhen.

Zu allen diesen Unternehmungen und Tätigkeiten, welche dahin gerichtet sind, den eigenen Reichtum zu erhöhen, und da dieselbe unzertrennlich ist von der allgemeinen Sache, auch dem allgemeinen Wohlstande zugute kommen, braucht man Geld, und dasselbe erlangt man nur durch Wirtschaft und Sparsamkeit in genügendem Maße.[24]

21 Wir stoßen hier wieder auf die "produktiven Hände" und den 'dauernden Fonds' aus Smith (1776) II.iii.19. Man beachte, wie der Text darauf immer wieder zurückkommt. Offensichtlich konnte Menger diesen Punkt gar nicht genug betonen.

22 Eine interessante etatistische Abwandlung des Smithschen Themas durch Menger.

23 Die vierte Wiederholung von Smith (1776) II.iii.19, nunmehr in Verbindung mit II.Einleitung.3, daß Kapitalakkumulation notwendig ist, um der Vorteile der Ausweitung des Marktes teilhaftig zu werden.

24 In diesen zwei Absätzen erwähnt Menger positive externe Effekte (d.s. externe Effekte regionaler Entwicklung) als weiteren Vorteil von Akkumulation, ein Gedanke, der Hermann (1832) wichtig war, von Smith aber in seiner Tragweite noch nicht erkannt wurde.

types of construction work, tradesmen, and manufacturers of objects important to the national economy.

The advantages of thrift may also clearly be proved in the following way: anybody who squanders his money on trifles surrenders the money-price asked to the tradesman but in turn receives an object used up at once or quite soon without either increasing its owner's assets or being useful in any way.

The thrifty person, on the other hand, spends his money by purchasing objects 21 r
that can be usefully employed and can increase their owner's wealth; in this way the tradesman who sold him the object is supported, and through the utility of the object purchased the buyer gets back his money's worth and more than that.[21]

Thus, general wealth will have increased while in the first case described it will have decreased, contrary to erroneous general opinion.

Furthermore, economizing man will invest his capital in public enterprises like railways, canals, and steamship companies.[22] This increases his own income and the wealth of his country whose level of civilization is thereby naturally improved. With the foundation of factories, many labourers are employed and with expanding sales general wealth increases.[23]

The same is true for the construction of dams and drainage on landed estates. 21 v
In addition to creating employment for many people, such construction certainly increases the value and wealth of a stretch of land and often is the entire basis of such value.

Money is needed for all undertakings and activities aimed at increasing individual wealth and – as this is inseparable from the common good – positively affecting the general welfare. It is acquired only by a sufficient measure of economy and thrift.[24]

subjectively valuable by an individual, and the more so the more it is esteemed by the marginal consumer. Menger cannot refrain from objective judgements on needs either; cf. Menger (1976), p. 53.

21 Once again the 'productive hands' and the 'perpetual fund' created by saving in Smith (1776), II.iii.19. Note how the text comes back again and again to this point, which Menger evidently thought could not be emphasized enough.

22 An interesting statist variation on the Smithian theme by Menger.

23 The fourth repetition of Smith (1776), II.iii.19, now coupled with II. introduction. 3, that accumulation of capital is necessary in order to achieve the advantages of an extension of the market.

24 In these two paragraphs Menger adduces positive external effects, i.e. external effects of regional development, as a further benefit of accumulation, an idea close to Hermann, but not yet appreciated by Smith.

Die allgemeine Erkenntnis dieser Wahrheiten zeigt einen hohen Grad von Kultur und wird zum Segen für die Völker, die sie zu schätzen wissen.

Beim einzelnen ist Verschwendung eine Versündigung an dem Wohle des Staates, und ein Frevel, wenn man dagegen die aufreibende Arbeit der größten Mehrzahl der Menschen betrachtet.[25]

Beim Staate, wenn seine Regierung mit den Staatsgeldern leichtsinnig verfährt
22 r und sie für unnütze Dinge verwendet, ist es ein unverantwortliches Vergehen an allen Mitgliedern des Staates und eine Versündigung an der Menschheit und ihrem Fortschritte.[26]

Unter einer Unternehmung verstehen wir ein Geschäft, das auf eigene Gefahr unternommen wurde und auf die *nutzbringende* Anlage eines Kapitals gerichtet ist.[27]

Eine Unternehmung kann von einem einzelnen so gut wie von einer Anzahl von Menschen, von einer Gesellschaft, unternommen werden; stets ist derselbe Zweck vor Augen, nämlich der größtmögliche Profit, zur Befriedigung aller Bedürfnisse, das treibende Moment aller Menschen.

Die Gefahr des Verlustes und des Mißglückens ist eine charakteristische Eigenschaft der Unternehmung.[28] Zum Beginn oder zur Beteiligung daran muß schon ein durch Sparsamkeit *erworbenes Kapital* vorhanden sein. *Das Kapital wird in zwei Arten geteilt*:

Die meisten Unternehmungen bestehen in der Produktion, oder im Handel
22 v mit rohen Produkten, oder mit schon verarbeiteten Gegenständen [CM am Rand: *Manufakten auch Fabrikat*], dazu sind aber nebst denselben auch andere Sachen notwendig, die der Unternehmer unbedingt und stets zu seinem Geschäfte braucht, um dasselbe führen zu können [am Rand: Adam Smith]; diese bilden sein fixes Kapital. Der Begriff desselben ist: 'Jenes Kapital, welches dem Unternehmer dadurch Gewinn bringt, daß er es nicht aus seiner Hand gibt, *sondern lediglich für seine Produktion nutzt*'.[29]

25 Nachdem wir uns nun lange genug mit Smiths (1776) Argumenten in II.iii.14–19 befaßt haben, schreiten wir zu einer genauen Wiedergabe von II.iii.20 fort; interessanterweise jedoch wird das Fehlverhalten, nämlich die Fehlinvestition (II.iii.26) nicht erwähnt: Anleger erscheinen also in einem viel günstigeren Licht als bei Smith (1776); unkluge Projekte gibt es offenbar nicht!

26 Wir wenden uns nun Smith (1776) II.iii.30 zu, wo es um öffentliche Verschwendung und Fehlverhalten geht, sowie dem herben Urteil über 'Könige und Minister' in II.iii.36. Die im allgemeinen ja sehr kurz gefaßten Hefte geben also das, was Smith auf etwa 15 Seiten behandelt hatte, am ausführlichsten von allen von Smith übernommenen Gedanken wieder: 7 Heftseiten befassen sich überwiegend mit der Bedeutung des Sparens und den Gedanken, die dem Sayschen Gesetz zugrundeliegen.

27 Menger folgt hier Rau in der Lehrsatzfassung von Roscher. Rau (1855), S. 158 f.: 'Zu einer Unternehmung gehört Folgendes: 1) Das Zusammenbringen der erforderlichen Güterquellen', insbesondere des 'Capitals'... 2) Die Leitung des Geschäftes ... 3) In den meisten Fällen auch die Übernahme der Gefahr'. Roscher (1864), § 195, S. 400: 'Das Wesentliche einer Unternehmung im nationalökonomischen Sinne des Worthes besteht darin, daß für den Verkehr auf eigene Gefahr producirt wird'.

Recognizing these truths implies a high level of civilization and will benefit the peoples who can appreciate them.

Individual squandering is an offence against the common good and an outrage considering the exhausting labour of the large majority of men.[25]

Public squandering, i.e. when a government is careless with its revenue and spends it irresponsibly, is an inexcusable crime against all members of society 22 r
and an offence against mankind and its progress.[26]

An enterprise is an operation undertaken at a person's own risk and aimed at the productive investment of capital.[27]

An enterprise can be undertaken by individuals alone or as a group, i.e. a corporation; the end is always the same, namely the greatest possible profit for satisfying all needs, the driving force of all humankind.

The risk of loss and failure is a characteristic feature of an enterprise.[28] Starting or taking part in one, requires capital accumulated by thrift. Such capital is of two kinds:

Most enterprises are involved with producing or trading raw products or finished
products [CM in the margin: manufactures or articles], apart from these, 22 v
however, the entrepreneur absolutely and invariably needs other items for his business; these constitute his fixed capital [in the margin: Adam Smith]. This is defined as 'that part of capital from which the entrepreneur draws a profit by not letting it go, but by employing it solely in his production processes'.[29]

25 After having circled long enough around Smith's (1776) arguments in II.iii.14–19, we now proceed to a close rendering of 20; interestingly, however, the 'misconduct', i.e. the malinvestment of 26, is not mentioned. Investors thus appear in a much more favourable light than with Smith; there are no 'injudicious projects', apparently.

26 We now switch to Smith (1776), III.iii.30, treating of 'public prodigality and misconduct' and the harsh condemnation of governments in 36. The notebooks, which are altogether quite brief, thus render what Smith had dealt with in about 15 pages most extensively of all the ideas taken over from Smith: nearly seven pages are filled with the importance of saving and the ideas behind Say's Law.

27 Menger follows Roscher who condenses what Rau had analysed. Cf. Rau (1855), p. 158 f.; Roscher (1864), § 195, p. 400.

28 In (1776) I.vi.5, Smith had remarked that 'something must be given for the profits of the undertaker of the work who hazards his stock in this adventure', but then hardly considers risk (in contrast to Cantillon (1755), I.xiii). Menger probably follows Rau, Hermann, or Roscher (see note 27). Roscher (1864, especially § 195) deals at length with the vicissitudes of enterprises and the risk of the entrepreneur.

29 The division into fixed and circulating capital was originally introduced by Smith (1776), II.i.4,5.

[Am Rand: Fixes Kapital ist jenes Kapital, welches bei der Produktion gebraucht, aber hiebei nicht bei einmaliger Benutzung verbraucht wird, im Handel benützt, aber nicht veräußert wird. Umlaufendes Kapital ist jenes Kapital, welches in der Produktion bei einmaliger Anwendung verbraucht und im Handel veräußert wird.]

Umlaufendes Kapital ist jenes Kapital, das dem Unternehmer dadurch Gewinn bringt, daß derselbe es *entweder unmittelbar oder mittelbar (seinem Werte nach) im Produkte* veräußert.

Beispiele für fixes Kapital wären: 'Die Maschinen in der Fabrik, der Kaufladen des Kaufmannes, die Fabrik selbst, die Lokomotive für die Eisenbahngesellschaft etc. etc.'[30]

Für umlaufendes Kapital wären Beispiele: 'Die in der Fabrik erzeugten Tuchstoffe, das Getreide des Getreidehändlers, die Verkaufsgegenstände des Kaufmannes, die Kohle für den Kohlenhändler, die Häuser für eine Baugesellschaft
23 r etc. etc.' Die Maschinen, die wir für den Fabriksbesitzer, der mit denselben produziert, als fixes Kapital bezeichnet haben, sind für den Maschinenfabrikanten umlaufendes Kapital, ebenso ist es bei der Lokomotive, die für die Eisenbahngesellschaft fixes, für die Lokomotiv- und Wagonsfabrik umlaufendes Kapital ist.[31]

Wert[32] ist ein Begriff, der fortwährend mit allen Unternehmungen und den meisten Lebensverhältnissen der Menschen in Zusammenhange steht, und so häufig er auch vorkommt und gebraucht wird, so schwer ist es dennoch, eine fixe Definition dieses Begriffes zu geben.

Die gewöhnlichsten Definitionen sind folgende: Wert ist die Bedeutung, welche ein Gut für den einzelnen dadurch gewinnt, daß dasselbe zur Befriedigung seiner Bedürfnisse tauglich ist. *Z.B. Wasser nur Nützlichkeit, noch nicht Wert.* [CM am Rand: *Condillac*][33]

28 Abgesehen von der Feststellung (Smith (1776) I. vi. 5,), daß derjenige, der eine Unternehmung finanziert, für sein Risiko entlohnt werden müsse, behandelt Smith im Unterschied zu Cantillon (vgl. Essai I.xiii) das Risiko so gut wie gar nicht. Menger folgt vermutlich Rau, Hermann oder Roscher (siehe Anm. 27). Roscher befaßt sich ausführlich mit den Gefahren für Unternehmen und dem Unternehmerrisiko.

29 Die Teilung in Fix- und Umlaufskapital stammt von Smith (1776) II.i.4,5 – was Menger seinem Schüler ausdrücklich mitteilte: neben dem Text findet sich in Rudolfs Schrift unterstrichen der Name Adam Smith. Allerdings sind die durch Anführungszeichen hervorgehobenen Sätze nicht mit dem Wortlaut von Smith identisch; sie entsprechen ihm sinngemäß.

30 Die Aufzählung entspricht Smith dem Sinn, wenn auch nicht dem Wortlaut nach; dieser gibt viel ausführlichere Beispiele.

31 Ähnlich Smith (1776) II.i.10.

32 Menger behandelt hier den Wert erst lange nach der Diskussion der Güter, ebenso wie in seinen Grundsätzen, wo diesem erst das 3. Kapitel gewidmet ist.

33 Ausnahmsweise gibt Menger hier eine voll subjektive Definition, aber eine, die durch lange deutsche Tradition sanktioniert ist: Rau, Hermann, Schäffle und Roscher. Die Definition kommt Roscher am nächsten, der selbst Schäffle, Mengers Vorgänger und k.k. Minister, ausdrücklich folgt. Roscher (1864), §4, S. 6, sagt: 'Wirthschaftlicher Werth eines Gutes ist die Bedeutung, welche dasselbe für das Zweckbewußtsein des wirthschaftenden Menschen hat'.

[In the margin: Fixed capital is that part of capital which is employed in production but not used up in one single process or which is employed in trade, but not sold. Circulating capital is that part of capital which is used up in one single process of production or sold in trade.]

Circulating capital is that part of capital embodied in his product which yields a profit to the entrepreneur when he sells it either directly or indirectly (i.e. in proportion to its value).

Examples of fixed capital would be: 'machinery in the factory, the tradesman's shop, the factory itself, the locomotive for the railway company, etc. etc.'[30]

Examples of circulating capital would be: 'the cloth produced in a factory, the grain of a grain merchant, the items for sale by a retailer, coal for the coal merchant, houses for a building company, etc. etc.' The machinery that is fixed capital for the factory owner who employs it in production is circulating capital 23 r
for the producer of machinery, the same is true for the locomotive that is part of fixed capital for the railway company, but is circulating capital for the locomotive and carriage factory.[31]

Value[32] is a concept that is forever connected with all enterprises and with most conditions of man, but despite its frequent occurrence and use, it is very difficult to define once and for all.

The most common definitions are the following: value is the importance that a good acquires for the individual because it can satisfy his needs. E.g.: Water only utility, not yet value. [CM in the margin: Condillac.][33]

Menger obviously made a point of that, if one may judge from Rudolf's inscription in the margin, where he wrote (in ink and underlined) the name 'Adam Smith' next to the definition. The lecture comes fairly close to II.i.5 ('things as yield a revenue or profit without changing masters'). The actual words, however, are not taken from Smith.

30 The enumeration is in the spirit of Smith who gives much more elaborate examples, however.

31 Again only in the spirit of Smith. That machinery can be fixed or circulating capital according to the type of enterprise is a modernization and adaptation of Smith (1776), II.i.10, where the same idea is discussed with reference to cattle and its importance for the cattle raiser, on the one hand, and for the dairy farmer, on the other.

32 Curiously, Menger discusses value here – long after the topic of goods, which had been discussed at the beginning of Notebook I, and after the division of labour and saving (the typical classical concerns). This corresponds to the sequence in his Principles. There, value is treated only in Chapter III.

33 For once, Menger gives a fully subjective definition; but in this he only follows Rau and especially Roscher. Roscher (1864), § 4, p. 6 says: 'The economic value of a good is its importance with respect to the purposes associated with it by economizing man'. Roscher in his turn explicitly followed Schäffle (Menger's predecessor and a recent imperial minister). Menger also finds it necessary to quote one more 18th century authority, the Abbé de Condillac. Etienne Bonnot de Mably de Condillac is Roscher's King's evidence for a subjective concept of utility and exchange. See Roscher (1864), § 60, p. 108, and § 107, p. 201. Roscher's reference to Condillac

Oder: Wert ist die Bedeutung, welche ein konkretes Gut für uns dadurch gewinnt,
23 v daß wir uns bewußt sind, daß wir irgendeines unserer Bedürfnisse nicht, oder nur minder vollständig befriedigen könnten, wenn wir dieses Gut nicht in unserer Gewalt hätten.

Oder: Wert ist die Bedeutung, die konkrete Güter dadurch gewinnen, daß bestimmte Bedürfnisse ohne ihren Besitz unvollständig*er* befriedigt würden.[34]

Mithin wäre der eigentliche Begriff des Wertes definiert, im allgemeinen Sinne, doch dieser Begriff kann ein sehr verschiedener sein; der Maßstab, nach welchem derselbe gemessen wird, ist ein sehr relativer, der von den mannigfaltigsten Einflüssen des Geschmacks, Charakters und der Sitten ganzer Völker, sowie der einzelnen beherrscht wird.[35]

In kleineren Details werden stets Verschiedenheit und geteilte Ansichten herrschen, denn, wie gesagt, der Maßstab und die Anforderungen der einzelnen sind zu großen Einflüssen unterworfen; darum kann man sagen, daß sich jeder Mensch seinen Wertmesser selbst schafft, der von seinen persönlichsten
24 r Interessen geleitet ist; doch um den Verkehr zu ermöglichen, müssen Gegenstände, mit denen Handel getrieben wird, mehr oder weniger bestimmte Werte erlangen, die fixiert sind nach den langjährigen Erfahrungen und den Bedürfnissen der kultivierten Völker.

Alle Interessen und Bestrebungen der Menschen sind nach einem Ziele gerichtet, nämlich nach der Befriedigung der Bedürfnisse auf die beste Art.[36] Aus diesem Grunde werden alle Güter, die zu diesem Zwecke dienlich sind, für den Menschen von Nutzen, doch nicht alle werden demselben von Werte sein; alles was gebraucht werden kann und daher nützlich ist, wird noch nicht wertvoll sein, denn Wert ist die Bedeutung, welche ein nützlicher Gegenstand erst durch die drohende Gefahr der Entbehrung erhält.

Es gibt einzelne konkrete Güter, die in fast allen denkbaren Fällen auch für
24 v alle Menschen von Wert sind, da sie in erster Linie zur Befriedigung der

Am Rand findet sich neben der angeführten Definition in Mengers Schrift mit Bleistift der Name 'Condillac' angeführt. Etienne Bonnot de Mably de Condillac ist für Roscher der Kronzeuge für eine subjektive Sicht von Nutzen und Tausch; siehe Roscher (1864), § 60, S. 108, und § 107, S. 201. Daß Condillac für die subjektive Wertlehre zentral ist, erkannte der Erzverteidiger einer objektiven Arbeitswertlehre, Karl Marx, der Roscher deswegen vehement angreift: 'Weil Condillac noch nicht die geringste Ahnung von der Natur des Tauschwerts besitzt, ist er der passende Gewährsmann des Herrn Prof. Wilhelm Roscher für seine eigenen Kinderbegriffe' (Das Kapital, Bd. I, Hamburg 1867, S. 174).

Das Wasser-Beispiel findet sich bei Menger (1871), S. 82 f.

34 Menger 1871, S. 77 f.: 'Bei allen Gütern... ist demnach von der Verfügung über jede concrete, practisch noch beachtenswerthe Quantität derselben die Befriedigung irgendeines menschlichen Bedürfnisses abhängig. Werden sich nun die wirthschaftenden Menschen dieses Umstandes bewusst, erkennen sie nämlich, dass von der Verfügung über jede Theilquantität der in Rede stehenden Güter ... die Befriedigung eines ihrer Bedürfnisse, oder doch die grössere oder geringere Vollständigkeit derselben abhängig ist, so gewinnen diese Güter für sie jene Bedeutung, die wir den Werth nennen, und es ist somit der Werth die Bedeutung, welche concrete Güter oder Güterquantitäten für uns dadurch erlangen, dass wir in der Befriedigung unserer Bedürfnisse von der Verfügung über dieselben abhängig zu sein uns bewusst sind'.

Or: value is the importance that a specific good acquires for us once we recognize that one of our needs could not be or could less fully be satisfied if we had no 23 v
command over the good.

Or: value is the importance that specific goods acquire if, without them, certain needs would be less fully satisfied.[34]

Thus, the actual concept of value has been defined, in a general sense, but it may have very different meanings; its standard of measurement is quite relative and depends upon the most varied influences of taste, character and customs of whole peoples and of individuals.[35]

Opinions will always differ on minor details for, as just remarked, individual standards and requirements are subject to strong influences; therefore one can say that everyone sets his own standard of value based on his most personal preferences; but to render communication possible, items of trade must be assigned more or less definite values that are fixed according to civilized 24 r
peoples' longstanding experience and needs.

All interests and endeavours of man are directed towards one end, namely satisfying needs in the best possible manner.[36] For this reason, all goods suitable for this purpose will be useful to man, but not all of them will be of value to him; not everything that may be used and is useful is therefore valuable, for value is the importance which a useful object acquires by the imminent danger of one's being deprived of it.

There are several specific goods that are of value to all men in nearly all imaginable circumstances, since they serve primarily to satisfy the most important needs, 24 v
but we also find goods that do not meet this requirement at all or at the most in

had been recognized by that arch-defender of an objective (i.e. labour) theory of value, Karl Marx, as of central importance and was violently attacked by him. Cf. Capital (1987), vol.I, p. 157. The example of water is treated at length by Menger himself in the Principles, p. 117 f.

34 Menger (1976), p. 115: 'Value is thus the importance that individual goods or quantities of goods attain for us because we are conscious of being dependent on command of them for the satisfaction of our needs'. The other definitions are suggested by the passages preceding this definition. Menger quotes Condillac in a footnote closely following this passage in the original (p. 296 in the translation).

35 Extensively discussed in Mischler (1857), p. 212 ff.

36 This is the definition of the subject matter of economic science by Menger's predecessor Schäffle (1867), p. 22, where he refers to the fullest satisfaction of needs with a minimum of sacrifices.

37 If this rendering is correct, Menger here contradicts all and every subjective value theory, including his own interpretation. A concept of absolute 'rarity' implies a notion of objective value. In the Principles, Menger himself states (p. 120): 'The value of goods arises from their relationship to our needs, and is not inherent in the goods themselves… Value is thus nothing inherent in

wichtigsten Bedürfnisse dienen, doch wir finden auch solche, die in keinem Falle, oder nur in gewissen Fällen diesen Zweck erfüllen, und daher auch nicht immer von Wert sind. Dieser Begriff aber ist sehr vielen Einflüssen unterworfen.

Wenn der Wert einer Sache auch für alle Menschen vorhanden ist, so ist doch der Maßstab, nach welchem er gemessen wird, ein sehr ungleicher.

Hier haben wir es mit den Unterschieden der Wertmessung zu tun gehabt, die aus der Verschiedenheit der Lage der Menschen und der daraus folgenden unterschiedlichen Anschauung entspringen, doch es gibt noch natürliche Verhältnisse, die aus dem Wesen der Sache selbst[37] folgen und derselben verschiedene Wertschätzung geben; Seltenheit des Gegenstandes erhöht bedeutend seinen Wert, ebenso ist es auch mit der Wichtigkeit des Bedürfnisses, welches damit befriedigt wird.[38]

[35] Mischler (1857), S. 212 ff., diskutiert dies ausführlich.

[36] Dies ist die Definition des Inhalts der Wirtschaftswissenschaften von Mengers Vorgänger Schäffle (1867), S. 22: 'Der Wirthschaftslehrer (hat) ...sein Gebiet... überall da, wo der Mensch in thätiger Beziehung zur Außenwelt steht, mit dem Zwecke, die vollste Befriedigung seiner Bedürfnisse unter geringsten Opfern im gesellschaftlichen Zusammenwirken zu verwirklichen'.

[37] Wenn die Vorlesung richtig wiedergegeben ist, widerspricht hier Menger jeder subjektiven Wertlehre und seiner eigenen Darstellung. Eine absolute Kategorie der 'Seltenheit' spiegelt eine objektive Wertvorstellung. Menger selbst sagt im Wert-Kapitel seiner Grundsätze: 'Der Güterwerth ist in der Beziehung der Güter zu unseren Bedürfnissen begründet, nicht in den Gütern selbst' (S. 85). 'Der Werth ist demnach nichts den Gütern Anhaftendes, keine Eigenschaft derselben' (S. 86). Das war auch in der deutschen Nationalökonomie mindestens seit Hufeland (1807) betont worden.

Auf die objektive Seltenheit als wertbestimmend stellen Adam Smith und vor allem David Ricardo und J.St. Mill ab.

[38] Eine ausführliche Theorie der Wichtigkeit der Bedürfnisse, genauer der 'Dringlichkeit' (eine objektiv–subjektive Theorie des Wertes insofern, als sie für alle Menschen gültig ist), bringt Mengers Lehrer Mischler (1857), S. 208 ff.

certain instances and therefore are not always valuable. This notion is subject to many influences, however.

Even if a thing is of value to everybody, the standards of measurement will differ greatly.

Here we have dealt with the differences in measuring value that result from the diversity of people's situations and their resulting different viewpoints, but there are also natural relationships, derived from the very nature[37] of an object and resulting in diverse valuations of it; both an object's scarcity and the urgency of the need to be satisfied thereby increase its value significantly.[38]

goods, no property of them ...'. This had been emphasised by German economists at least since Hufeland (1807).

38 For objective rarity as value-determining property see Smith and above all Ricardo and J.St.Mill. For an extensive treatment of the importance, or rather urgency, of needs (an objective–subjective theory of value, as it were, because of its universal validity), cf. Menger's teacher Mischler (1857), p. 208 ff.

Politische Ökonomie IV. 1876 Jänner

25 r Dies kann im allgemeinen immer gelten, doch auch in besonderen Fällen kann eine Sache an einem bestimmten Orte unter eigentümlichen Verhältnissen für den Menschen von großem Werte sein, und unter gewöhnlichen Umständen im alltäglichen Leben ist sie ihm ganz wertlos. Z.B. ist ein Glas Wasser in einer quellenreichen Gegend oder in einer Stadt ein ganz wertloser Gegenstand, denn selbst wenn man es ausschüttet, ist der Verlust gleich wieder ersetzt. In der Wüste hingegen wird dieselbe Quantität Wasser das wertvollste Gut sein, für dessen Erhaltung und Erlangung der einzelne alles aufbieten wird, da es ihn vielleicht vor dem Tode schützt.[1]

Dieses Beispiel galt für ein und dasselbe Gut, doch es ist auch eine Tatsache, daß verschiedene Güter verschiedene Werte haben; oft trifft man dies bei
25 v Gegenständen, wo der Charakter der Wertunterschiede uns erstaunt.

Der Grund dafür liegt in der Tatsache, daß die Seltenheit in manchen Fällen, in anderen die Wichtigkeit des Bedürfnisses, das damit erfüllt wird, und in anderen wieder die Quantität, in welcher die Sache vorkommt, den Ausschlag gibt.[2]

Es ist gewiß unstreitig wahr, daß Eisen für den Menschen ein wichtigeres Metall ist als wie das Gold; denn es wird in allen Lagen des menschlichen Lebens gebraucht, und doch hat letzteres einen um so viel höheren Wert.[3] Als den Grund dieser Erscheinung müssen wir die größere Seltenheit des Goldes bezeichnen, und die Schwierigkeit, dasselbe zu erlangen; daher steigt der Wert desselben

[1] Menger behandelt das Thema nunmehr in klassischer Manier, nachdem er es am Ende des vorhergehenden Heftes viel 'moderner' abgehandelt hatte. Das Gegensatzpaar Wasser und Diamanten findet sich bei Smith (1776) I.iv.13 (von 'Diamanten und anderen Schmuckgegenständen' spricht der Kronprinz wenige Absätze weiter unten). Es war das allerdings schon zur Zeit von Smith nicht neu (vgl. die einschlägige Erörterung von R.H. Campbell und A.S. Skinner, in der Glasgow–Edition (1976) des Wealth of Nations: General Introduction, S. 45 f.). Der Topos war von Samuel Pufendorf eingeführt worden, den Menger offenbar nicht unmittelbar gelesen hatte. Er findet sich dann bei Grotius, John Law (den Menger in ähnlichem Zusammenhang in den Grundsätzen, S. 215, Anmerkung, zitiert), Mandeville, Cantillon und Hutcheson (den Menger an derselben Stelle erwähnt). Smith hatte den Wert von Wasser für einen reichen Kaufmann, der sich in den Wüsten Arabiens verirrt hatte, erörtert, allerdings in den Vorlesungen zur Rechtswissenschaft, die Menger wahrscheinlich nicht kannte (vgl. Campbell und Skinner, ebenda).

Menger folgt hier möglicherweise sekundären Quellen. Eine wahrscheinliche Quelle ist Fußnote e) in Rau (1855), S. 167, wo sich die Geschichte eines reichen Reisenden in der Sahara findet, der seinem armen Reisegefährten die Hälfte von dessen Wasservorrat für einen unglaublich hohen Preis abkauft – was freilich nur dazu führt, daß beide verdursten.

[2] Ist dies einmal mehr eine entstellte Wiedergabe von Mengers Vortrag, wobei die dritte Bedingung mit der ersten identisch ist und das Ganze der subjektiven Wertlehre widerspricht?

[3] Der Vergleich von Gold und Eisen folgt wohl Smith (1776) I.xi.c.31.

Political economy IV. 1876 January

This may hold true in general, but in special cases an object may have great value for a person at a certain place in a particular situation, yet be quite worthless to him in the ordinary circumstances of everyday life. A glass of water, e.g., is of no value at all in an area abundant with springs or in a town, since even if it is spilled the loss is made up on the spot. In a desert, however, the same quantity of water will be the most valuable good, and an individual will give anything to acquire and preserve it, since it may save him from death.[1] 25 r

This is an example of the very same good having different values, but it is just as true that different goods have different values; quite often we encounter this in objects where the range of differences in value surprises us. 25 v

The reason is that for some objects value is determined by their scarcity, for others by the importance of the need satisfied, and for still others by the quantity available.[2]

It is undoubtedly true that for man iron is a more important metal than gold, since it is needed in all stations of life, and yet the latter is so much more valuable.[3] We must explain this by the greater scarcity of gold and the difficulty of obtaining it; thus, the value of gold is increased and only a comparatively small number of people will have command over it.

1 Menger returns to a treatment in the classical tradition, after his much more 'modern' treatment at the end of the last Notebook. The water–diamond contrast ('diamonds and other jewellery' will be discussed by the Crown Prince a few paragraphs further on) is given in Smith (1776), I.iv.13. By the time of Smith, however, it was already quite ancient; see the discussion of this topic in R.H. Campbell and A.S. Skinner, eds., The Glasgow Edition of the Works of Adam Smith, vol.I, General Introduction, p. 45 f. The topic had been introduced by Samuel Pufendorf, whom Menger apparently does not know directly. It was then taken up by Grotius, John Law (whom Menger quotes on a related topic, cf. Principles (1976), p. 307), Mandeville, Cantillon and Hutcheson (whom Menger quotes in the same place). Adam Smith had discussed the value of water for a rich merchant lost in the deserts of Arabia, but in the Lectures on Jurisprudence, which Menger probably did not know (see Campbell and Skinner, loc.cit., p. 45).

Menger may be following secondary sources. A likely source would be footnote e) in Rau (1855), p. 167, which relates the story of a rich traveller in the Sahara, who buys half of his poor companion's store of water for an incredibly high price – with the effect that both of them perish.

2 Is this once more a garbled version of what Menger said, the third instance being identical with the first and the whole in conflict with subjective value theory?

3 The comparison of iron and gold may originate in Smith (1776), I.xi.c.31.

und macht den Besitz desselben nur einer kleineren Anzahl der Menschen möglich.

Wie oben schon erwähnt, übt auch die Quantität, in welcher eine Sache
26 r vorkommt, einen großen Einfluß auf deren Wertschätzung aus. Je häufiger ein Gegenstand ist, und je leichter man ihn erlangen kann, desto geringer wird sein Wert sein, denn desto mehr wird sein Besitz allgemein verbreitet sein. Am besten sieht man dies beim Getreide; nach einer guten Ernte sinkt der Wert desselben, nach einer *schlechten* steigt er.[4]

Wichtige Gegenstände, die noch bedeutungsvoll für die Existenz der Menschen sind, verlieren den Wert durch häufiges Vorkommen, dagegen haben noch so unwichtige Gegenstände, die vielleicht nur der Putzsucht einzelner schmeicheln, wenn sie selten vorkommen, einen hohen Wert, wie z.B. Diamanten und andere Schmuckgegenstände.[5]

26 v Den Wert im allgemeinen haben wir als die Bedeutung definiert, welche konkrete Güter dadurch gewinnen, daß bestimmte Bedürfnisse ohne ihren Besitz unvollständiger befriedigt würden. Derselbe kann nun in zwei Arten geteilt werden:

a. in den Gebrauchswert;
b. in den Tauschwert.[6]

Der Gebrauchswert ist jener Wert, den die Güter mit Rücksicht auf die unmittelbare Benützung[7] für ihren Besitzer erlangen, z.B. Kleidungsstücke für denjenigen, der sie benützen will, Brillen für den Kurzsichtigen, astronomische Instrumente für den Astronomen, nicht für den Optiker, der sie verfertigt, oder den Kaufmann, der mit ihnen handelt.[8]

Der Tauschwert ist jener Wert, welchen Güter mit Rücksicht auf die Möglichkeit gewinnen, gegen andere Güter eingetauscht zu werden, z.B. Kleidungsstücke eines Schneiders, soweit sie zum Verkauf bestimmt sind, Brillen für einen
27 r Händler mit normalem Sehorgan, astronomische Instrumente für denjenigen, der sie verfertigt oder mit ihnen Handel treibt etc. etc.

Ein und dasselbe Gut kann sowohl Gebrauchs- als Tauschwert haben, nur ist der eine von beiden der überwiegende. Solange der Gebrauchswert überwiegt, behält man die Sache im Besitze, sobald der Tauschwert zu überwiegen beginnt, veräußert man die Sache.[9]

4 Roscher (1864) gibt in seinem zweiten Paragraphen zum Gebrauchswert, § 103, S. 194, eine ausführliche Darstellung der Wirkung der Ernteschwankungen auf die 'Kornpreise'.

5 Der soeben erwähnte § 103 von Roscher behandelt 'Luxusartikel'.

6 Siehe Smith (1776) I.iv.13; laut Menger (1871), S. 215, Anmerkung, eine 'berühmt gewordene Stelle'.

7 Mengers eigene Definition (1871, S. 215), außer daß der Kronprinz, wie häufig, den deutschen Ausdruck 'unmittelbare Benutzung' wählt statt des lateinischen Lehnwortes 'directe Verwendung'.

8 Menger bringt hier und im folgenden Absatz eigene Beispiele; vgl. 1871, S. 217.

9 Ein, so weit ich sehe, origineller Gedanke von Menger, den er 1871, S. 219-224, geradezu breittritt.

As mentioned above, the available quantity of a thing greatly influences its value. The more there is of a thing and the more easily it is obtained, the less 26 r
its value, since the more common is its possession. The best example is grain; after a good harvest, its value goes down, after a poor harvest it goes up.[4]

Items that are still essential for man's existence lose their value by being abundant; on the other hand, quite unimportant items that may flatter only a few individuals' love of finery are highly valuable if they are rare, e.g. diamonds and other jewellery.[5]

We defined value in general as the significance that specified goods attain 26 v
because, without them, certain needs would be less completely satisfied. Now, value may be of two kinds:

a. use value;
b. exchange value.[6]

Use value is the value that goods acquire if they are immediately useful to their owner,[7] e.g. clothes for the person who wants to dress, glasses for the shortsighted, astronomical instruments for the astronomer (not for the optician who makes them, nor for the merchant who deals in them).[8]

Exchange value is the value that goods attain if they can be exchanged for others, e.g. clothes of a tailor if they are intended for sale, glasses for a merchant with normal eyesight, astronomical instruments for those making them or
dealing in them, etc. etc. 27 r

The same good may have use value as well as exchange value, but one or the other will predominate. As long as use value predominates, a good is kept; when exchange value begins to predominate, it is sold.[9]

4 Roscher (1864), § 103 (the second paragraph on value in use), discusses in extenso the effect of varying harvests on the price of corn.
5 The very paragraph of Roscher (§ 103) deals mainly with luxury consumption.
6 Cf. Smith (1776), I.iv.13, according to Menger a 'famous passage' (see Menger (1976), p. 306).
7 Menger's own definition (1976, p. 228) – apart from the fact that Rudolf avoids the Latin words 'direct' and 'indirect', using words with a German root instead.
8 Here and in the next paragraph, Menger uses his own examples; cf. (1951), p. 229.
9 This is an explanation of exchange very dear to Menger; he discusses it in the Principles over nearly four pages (1976, pp. 231–35). As far as I can see the notion is original with him.

27 v **Über die Lebensfähigkeit des kleinen Gewerbes**[10]

Durch das Zunehmen der Fabriken, durch die Produktion in großen Massen und besonders durch die Arbeitsteilung wird fortwährend die Existenz der kleinen Gewerbsleute untergraben.[11] Man muß diese Tatsache als einen Schaden betrachten, da diese Zunft von kleinen Unternehmern einen soliden, biederen Charakter an sich trägt[12], und durch ihren langen Bestand eine Geschichte[13] aufweisen kann, deren Beginn in sehr frühe Zeiten hineinreicht, die noch jeder anderen Produktion entbehrten und in der der kleine Gewerbsmann der Begründer[14] jeder Fabrikation und jeden Geschäftes war.

Vom Fabriksarbeiter unterscheidet er sich wesentlich dadurch, daß er ein freier Mann ist und sein eigener Herr,[15] der im Schweiße seines Angesichtes die Produkte, die er verfertigt, sein Werk und sein Eigentum nennen kann, und, da er selbst Besitzer eines, wenn auch kleinen, Geschäftes ist,[16] Ordnung und Ruhe in der
28 r Gesellschaft liebt, und dadurch für den Staat und die Regierung angenehmer ist als wie der unruhige[17] bewegliche Fabriksarbeiter.

Darum aber bezeigen die meisten Staaten Bestrebungen zur Erhaltung des kleinen Gewerbes und suchen dasselbe, solange es noch geht, vor den Anforderungen der jetzigen *Zeit*, die Langsamkeit und Kleinlichkeit in keiner Richtung *mehr* duldet, zu schützen.

Doch trotz allen diesen Bestrebungen muß man heutzutage erkennen, daß sich das kleine Gewerbe überlebt hat und sich schwer den großartigen Tätigkeiten der Fabriken gegenüber halten wird.

10 Es erscheint merkwürdig, daß Menger nach der Wertlehre das ganz spezielle Problem der Schwierigkeiten des Kleingewerbes betrachtet. Doch hatte die Wertlehre nur die Fragen der Arbeitsteilung und die (rudimentäre) Theorie der Unternehmung unterbrochen. Smith (1776), I.iii.2, untersucht im Zusammenhang mit der Arbeitsteilung die Frage, welche Betriebsgröße (regional gesehen) jeder Marktgröße entspricht, was naturgemäß zu dem Gedanken anregt, daß das Handwerk durch die moderne Marktintegration verdrängt wird. So wird ein Entwicklungsgesetz über die Zeit aus Smiths regionaler Unterschiedlichkeit der Gewerbe. Menger folgt dabei ganz eng Rau (1855), S. 525 ff.

11 Rau (1855), S. 525, sieht ganz wie hier die Nachteile des 'handwerksmäßigen Betriebes' als Konsequenz der Arbeitsteilung und des Vordringens der 'großen Unternehmungen' (nicht ausdrücklich der Massenproduktion).

12 Rau, ebenda, S. 520: 'Die Handwerksmeister bilden den Kern des Bürgerstandes'.

13 Ebenda, leicht abweichend: 'Der vor Alters gepriesene 'goldene Boden' des Handwerks' (meine Hervorhebung).

14 Ebenda, in etwas anderer Stoßrichtung: 'der leichtere Zutritt zu den Handwerken' ist Ursache des Einkommensrückganges.

15 Ebenda: Vorteile für 'sittliche und geistige Ausbildung'.

16 Ebenda wird betont die hieraus resultierende 'bessere Lage'.

17 Rau, ebenda, S. 521, spricht von 'Leichtsinn..., Rohheit, ... Unsittlichkeit' der Fabrikarbeiter und 'Unordnungen aller Art'. Weiters unter Umständen 'starker Zufluß von Arbeitern' als Problem (S. 520).

On the Viability of Small Businesses[10] 27 v

Increasing numbers of factories, mass production, and especially the division of labour are continuing threats to the small tradespeople.[11] This is unfortunate because the class of small entrepreneurs has a reliable and steadfast character[12] and can point to a long history,[13] going back to very early times when there was no other way of industrial production and when it was the small trader who started each and every factory and business.[14]

He differs from the factory worker essentially because he is free and his own master[15] and may call the products he makes by the sweat of his brow his work and property; and since he owns a business, even if it is small,[16] he loves order and peace in society and thereby is more pleasing to the state and its government than the restless[17] and mobile factory worker. 28 r

For this very reason, most governments try to keep small businesses alive and shield them as long as possible from the demands of the present age that no longer tolerates slowness and pettiness in any way.

But in spite of all such efforts, it seems that the days of small businesses are over now and that they will have a hard time competing with the impressive performance of the factories.

10 It may seem somewhat strange that Menger, after discussing value (the topic, however, having been introduced so as better to elucidate the problems of business enterprises), now jumps to the unrelated topic of small artisan firms. This is not really strange, though, if he tried to stick as closely as convenient to Smith (1776). In I.iii, Smith discusses 'That the Division of Labour is Limited by the Extent of the Market'. He explains at length that 'there are some sorts of industry ... which can be carried on no where but in a great town' (I.iii.2) and goes on to discuss the appropriate size of firms for every market. Menger 'modernizes' regional differentiation – which is taken up later in this same lecture – into a secular trend of development of great social concern in his time: the decline of small-scale handicraft firms. In this, he enlarges on Rau (1855), p. 525 ff.; in fact, one argument after the other can be traced to this source.

11 Rau (1855), p. 525, regards the disadvantages of small artisans' firms as a consequence both of the division of labour and of the rise of large enterprises (not explicitly: of mass production), just as here.

12 Rau, ibid., p. 520.

13 Rau, ibid., p. 520, makes the slightly different point that 'of old' handicraft trades were said to be both reliable and profitable.

14 Rau, ibid., p. 520, again makes a slightly different point: as it has become so easy to start an enterprise as a small artisan, increased competition is a further reason for the declining incomes in this group.

15 Exactly the next argument of Rau, ibid., p. 520.

16 Stressed by Rau, ibid., p. 519, as the cause of a bettered economic situation.

17 Both excess mobility and moral depravity of factory workers are deplored by Rau, ibid., p. 520 f.

Durch das fortwährende große Zunehmen der Kultur haben auch die Bedürfnisse und besonders die Vielartigkeit derselben in großem Maße zugenommen.[18]

Die Menschheit braucht in jedem Gebiete die riesigsten Summen von Produkten, die mit der größtmöglichen Schnelligkeit und Akkuratesse verfertigt sein müssen; diesen Anforderungen können nur Maschinen und Arbeitsteilung entsprechen, beide setzen aber große Unternehmungen voraus.

28 v Die Maschinen arbeiten präzis, ein Stück wie das andere, und durch die große Schnelligkeit, mit der sie arbeiten, werden die Produkte auch billiger.[19]

Der kleine Gewerbsmann konstruiert entweder selbst oder mit höchst primitiven Maschinen dieselben Produkte, aber, in Folge des Charakters seiner Arbeit, ungleich und höchst langsam; da er nur wenige Stücke in einer bestimmten Zeit erzeugt hat und in den Handel bringen kann, verkauft er sie, um sich erhalten zu können, um vieles teurer.

Der große Fabrikant kann sich eine Menge Arbeiter halten, und durch die bis aufs höchste getriebene Arbeitsteilung erzieht er sich Virtuosen in den einzelnen Details, die mit der größten Schnelligkeit und Präzision ihre einfache Tätigkeit Tag für Tag vollführen; durch diesen Vorgang wird in der ganzen Fabrik mit großer Geschwindigkeit produziert und der Absatz an Produkten ist ein großer, und die einzelnen Stücke sind deshalb um billige Preise zu erlangen. Der Vorteil
29 r dieses Systems ist nicht zu verkennen. Rasche Erzeugung, Güte und Gleichheit der Produkte und vor allem Billigkeit sind wichtige Faktoren.[20]

Der kleine Gewerbsmann dagegen kann sich nur einige Gesellen halten, unter die er seine Verrichtungen teilt, langsam natürlich und ungleich arbeitet der einzelne, da er nicht nur eine bestimmte kleine Arbeit stets zu vollführen hat, sondern mit verschiedenen Tätigkeiten überbürdet wird. Durch das Schwerfällige der Produktion ist der Absatz ein geringer, und daher wird der Gewerbsmann gezwungen, seine Produkte teurer zu verhandeln.[21]

Die großen Nachteile sind langsame und ungleiche Erzeugung und Kostspieligkeit. Der Fabrikant, der zum Gange der Tätigkeit in seiner Fabrik viele Rohprodukte kauft, tut dies im großen in bestimmten Zeitabschnitten und hat durch die Größe seiner Unternehmung so viel Kapital, daß er die Rohprodukte in großen Massen einhandelt, gleich verarbeitet, und in ihrer neuen Form mit
29 v bedeutendem Profit verkauft. Durch den Gang des Geschäftes in so großen

[18] Typisch Menger und ohne Vorbild bei dem rein produktionsorientierten Rau; siehe Menger (1871), S. 28.

[19] Rau (1855), S. 528. Daß die Produkte auch besser werden durch Maschineneinsatz, ist eine typische Idee von Rau; siehe insbesondere S. 146: 'vollkommener und werthvoller' (Hervorhebung von Rau).

[20] Die von Menger immer wieder betonte 'Geschwindigkeit' der Fabriksproduktion ist die einzige Aussage, die bei Rau nicht zu finden ist. Natürlich spricht Rau von 'Erniedrigung des Preises' (etwa in § 401).

[21] Wiederholung der schon vorgetragenen und von Smith ausgeführten Effekte fehlender Arbeitsteilung.

With the continued great advances of civilization, needs and their variety have also greatly increased.[18]

In every field, man needs huge quantities of products that must be turned out with utmost speed and accuracy; these requirements can be met only by machinery and by the division of labour, both in turn presuppose large-scale enterprise.

Machines work to precision, all items turn out exactly alike, and through high- 28 v
speed production they also become cheaper.[19]

The small tradesman manufactures the same products either with his own hands or with the most primitive machinery, but because of the character of his work they are not all alike and are turned out very slowly; within a certain period of time he produces and offers only a few items for sale, and to earn his livelihood he sells them much more dearly.

The big manufacturer can employ a large number of workers, and by maximizing the division of labour he trains masters of detail who perform their respective simple tasks day after day with utmost speed and precision; thus, the whole factory produces with great speed, and it sells many products so that the individual items may be obtained at a low price. The advantage of this system cannot go unnoticed. Fast production, high quality and homogeneity of the products,
and especially cheapness are important considerations.[20] 29 r

The small businessman, on the other hand, can only pay a few journeymen to whom he assigns the production tasks. The work is slow and uneven, of course, because the individual worker does not have to perform one unvarying small step, but is overburdened with diverse operations. The cumbersomeness of this production process leads to a small volume of sales and therefore the small businessman must ask a higher price for his products.[21]

Slow, uneven production and high costs are the big disadvantages. The manufacturer buys a large volume of raw products wholesale and at specified intervals to keep his factory going, and because of the size of his enterprise he has enough capital to buy large amounts of raw products which he processes right away and, in their new form, sells at a considerable profit. By operating
on so large a scale, he also gets the raw products more cheaply than if he bought 29 v
them singly or in small quantities.[22]

18 A typical idea of Menger and without precedent in Rau, who only considers supply side factors; see Menger (1976), p. 73.

19 Rau (1855), p. 528. That mechanically produced items are also better is a typical idea of Rau (ibid., p. 146).

20 Only the reiterated idea of the higher speed of production in the factory is not to be found in Rau. Naturally, Rau mentions the reduction in price for the consumer (ibid. p. 528).

21 Repetition of Smith's (1776) arguments on the effects of the division of labour (I.i.).

22 This paragraph and the next follow Rau (1855), p. 526, nearly verbatim. Rau stresses the advantages of bulk purchase and timing. Neither aspect is noticed by Smith.

Dimensionen erhält er auch die Rohprodukte billiger, als wenn er sie einzeln oder in geringer Quantität erwerben würde.[22]

Der kleine Gewerbsmann aber, der, wie schon früher erwähnt, langsam und ungleich, deshalb auch teurer produziert, findet einen sehr geringen Absatz seiner Ware, daher ist auch sein Kapital ein sehr geringes und er ist gezwungen, die Rohprodukte einzeln oder in geringer Anzahl einzuhandeln, was ihn im ganzen teurer zu stehen kommt, als würde er sie in großen Quantitäten einhandeln, was ihm aber im Momente immer unmöglich ist.

Im großen und ganzen kann man *die* kleinen Gewerbs*leute* als eine überlebte *Institution* und Gesellschafts*klasse* betrachten,[23] die durch ihren historischen Ursprung und die lange Dauer ihres Bestandes als eine ehrenvolle biedere Zunft Rechte an der Menschheit haben und die sich in dunklen Zeiten noch durch die
30 r Hebung des Gewerbes verdient gemacht haben. Doch den Anforderungen unseres Jahrhunderts,[24] das in allem Großartigkeit und riesige Dimensionen als Merkzeichen an sich trägt, entspricht eine so langsame und wenig einträgliche Tätigkeit wie die des Gewerbsmannes nicht. In einer Zeit, in der solche Quantitäten von Produkten gebraucht und benötigt werden und wo wirklich nur große Unternehmungen, viele Arbeiter und Maschinen den Ansprüchen Rechnung tragen können, mußten die großen Fabriken, die immer mehr zunehmen, dem kleinen Gewerbe den Todesstoß geben.

Besonders in den großen Städten wird die Existenz desselben immer schwieriger; in kleineren Städten, wo die Arbeitsteilung und große Maschinen zum Zwecke der schnellen Produktion sich nicht rentieren würden, da der Absatz in Folge des kleinen Marktes ein zu geringer ist, und oft mehrere Gewerbe aus diesen Gründen in einem verbunden sind, da kann sich das kleine Gewerbe noch halten.[25]

Doch ebenso wie es fehlerhaft wäre, die Lebensfähigkeit des kleinen Gewerbes
30 v zu behaupten, so unvorsichtig und besonders ungerecht wäre es auch, dasselbe in gar keiner Weise zu unterstützen und als eine schon vollkommen abgemachte Sache zu betrachten. Es ist immer eine traurige Tatsache, wenn ein ganzer Stand

[22] Hier und im folgenden Abschnitt fast wörtlich Rau (1855), S. 526, folgend: 'Hiezu kommen die wirthschaftlichen Vortheile, die der große Unternehmer in Bezug auf Einkauf, Versendung und Absatz besitzt. Er kann Vorräthe seiner Erzeugnisse anlegen und die vortheilhaftesten Gelegenheiten zum Verkaufe aufsuchen oder abwarten, während der Handwerker entweder von Bestellungen abhängt, oder die unbestellten Waaren schnell an den Großhändler verkaufen muß'. Diese Argumente sind bei Smith nicht zu finden.

[23] Rau sagt umgekehrt: 'Man kann ungeachtet der vorhin dargestellten Nachtheile das Aufkommen der Fabriken im Ganzen genommen nicht für ein Uebel halten, wo es nöthig ist, um einem Volke den seiner Bevölkerung und überhaupt dem Stande seiner Güterquellen entsprechenden Antheil an der Betreibung der Gewerbe zu sichern, aber man darf nicht wünschen, daß die Vermehrung der Fabriken rascher erfolge, als es in jener Hinsicht Bedürfniß ist'. Rau (1855), S. 526.

[24] Ein rein Mengerscher Fanfarenstoß – oder gar eine persönliche Note des Kronprinzen?

[25] Smith (1776) I.x.b.35–7, zur lokalen Unterschiedlichkeit der Gewerbe je nach der Art der Städte. Siehe auch I.iii.2.

The small-scale producer, however, as mentioned above, produces slowly and unevenly and therefore at greater cost and achieves only a very small volume of sales; therefore he has very little capital and is forced to buy his raw materials singly or in small quantities, which is more expensive than if he bought them in large quantities, but he cannot do that at any one moment.

On the whole, small business may be considered an obsolete institution and social class,[23] that has certain claims upon humankind because of its historical origins, its long-lived existence as an honourable and steadfast class, and its merits in having improved crafts and trade in dark times. However, the slow and unprofitable activity of the small businessman cannot meet the requirements 30 r
of our century,[24] altogether marked by magnificence and vast dimensions. The big factories, that are ever on the increase, had to deal the death blow to the small business at a time when huge quantities of products are needed and used and when only large-scale enterprises, great numbers of workers, and machinery can truly meet demands.

Especially in the big cities the tradesman finds it increasingly difficult to carry on; the small business can still hold its own in smaller towns where the division of labour and big machinery for fast production would not pay since sales are insufficient because of the small market and where several crafts and trades are often combined in one enterprise.[25]

But just as it would be a mistake to assert the viability of the small business, it would be careless and especially unjust not to support it at all and to regard 30 v
it as altogether a thing of the past. It is always sad when an entire class or profession is doomed, particularly if it has existed diligently and happily for many years, and one should strive to maintain it for as long as possible, especially if it would be an advantage to the state.

23 Rau uses the converse argument, viz. that on the whole factories are good but their increase should not be stimulated; see Rau (1855), p. 526.

24 A flourish by Menger, or even by the Crown Prince himself? Not to be found in the more sedate Rau.

25 Smith (1776), I.iii.2: 'Country workmen are almost every where obliged to apply themselves to all the different branches of industry that have ... affinity to one another. A country carpenter deals in every sort of work that is made of wood: a country smith in every sort of work that is made of iron'. See also Smith (1776), I.x.b.35–7.

oder eine ganze Zunft im Untergange begriffen ist, besonders, wenn sie durch lange Jahre fleißig und glücklich bestanden hat, und man muß trachten, ihren Bestand so lange es geht noch auszudehnen, hauptsächlich, wenn derselbe für den Staat Vorteile mit sich bringt.

Und eben der Staat soll trachten, die kleinen Gewerbsleute dahin zu bringen, daß sie sich durch Vereinigung und gemeinsame Arbeit[26] dem Charakter der großen Unternehmungen nähern; durch diesen Vorgang würde zwar das kleine Gewerbe in seinem eigentlichen Sinne seinen früheren Charakter etwas verlieren, aber da derselbe so unhaltbar ist, gehen diese Bestrebungen nur dahin, die
31 r Gewerbsleute selbst, die meistens biedere, verdiente Männer sind, vor dem Untergange zu retten; spätere Generationen derselben werden von selbst dem Drange der Zeit weichen und in den großen Unternehmungen aufgehen. Die Ratschläge des Staates zur Erhaltung sollen ja eben nur ein Übergangsstadium anbahnen.

Dasselbe soll durch richtige Einführungen[27] die kleinen Gewerbsleute den großen Unternehmungen ähnlich machen, um halbwegs mit denselben konkurrieren zu können.

Ein Mittel wäre die Assoziierung mehrerer Gewerbsmänner in einer Stadt, mit dem Zwecke, durch die gemeinsame Arbeit und die gemeinsamen Geldmittel ihrer Tätigkeit einen größeren Charakter zu geben, nämlich jene Dimensionen in Unternehmungen anzunehmen, die der einzelne nicht, aber mehrere vereint leichter erschwingen könnten.

Der selbständige kleine Gewerbsmann kann sich schwer, fast niemals, Maschinen zu seiner Arbeit anschaffen, und gelingt es ihm selbst, so viel zu ersparen, wird es dann auch nur für den Ankauf sehr primitiver Maschinen genügen,
31 v die wenig Vorsicht und Speisung bedürfen; denn eben das Brennmaterial ist für den kleinen Unternehmer das Kostspieligste. Darum sollten sich mehrere Gewerbsleute vereinigen und durch die Anlage einer gemeinschaftlichen Kassa ihre Schicksale enge verknüpfen und vereinigt den Angriffen der Zeit widerstehen, was sie einzeln nicht mehr leisten können. Sie müßten sich zusammen Maschinen kaufen und die Früchte ihrer Arbeit gleich und friedlich teilen; es müßte im wahrsten Sinne des Wortes eine Gesellschaft werden, die durch einen Vertrag aneinander gekettet ist, und Eintracht wäre die Hauptbedingung, um das Bestehen derselben in den jetzigen ungünstigen Verhältnissen zu ermöglichen.

Auch die Arbeitsteilung, die dem einzelnen, der vielleicht nur ein oder zwei Gesellen hat, fast unmöglich ist, oder doch nur in einem sehr unvollständigen Sinne durchgeführt wird, und dadurch eben zu einem Haupt-Ruine des kleinen

26 Dieser Aufruf zur Bildung von Produktivgenossenschaften fehlt bei Rau.

27 Die 'Ratschläge' des Staates und die 'Einführungen' lassen die Idee Raus anklingen: 'Der Handwerksstand vermag diesen Kampf gegen das Andringen der großen Unternehmungen eher zu bestehen, wenn er sich bemüht, in Kenntnissen und Geschicklichkeiten den Anforderungen der gesteigerten Bildung zu genügen' (1855, S. 526).

The state therefore should strive to induce the small tradesmen to combine and, by joining their efforts,[26] to take on the character of large-scale enterprises; in this way the small business in its proper sense would lose some of its original character, but since that cannot be preserved anyhow, these efforts have only the purpose of saving existing tradespeople – mostly upright, deserving men – from ruin; later generations of them will give way, on their own, to the pressures 31 r
of the times and merge into big firms. Government advice about maintaining this group should be for a period of transition only, to be sure.

Through appropriate measures,[27] the small tradesmen should be made to resemble large-scale enterprises in order to become somewhat competitive.

One way of doing this would be for several tradesmen in the same town to associate, with the goal of increasing the scale of their activities by joint work and joint capital; by operating jointly, their enterprises could more easily attain a size not achievable by a single tradesman.

The independent small businessman can hardly, almost never, buy machines to do his work, and even if he manages to save enough, he will only be able to purchase quite primitive machines needing little attention and fuel; for it is fuel that is the most costly item for the small businessman. Therefore a number of 31 v
such businessmen ought to combine, unite their fates by joint accounting, and together withstand the vicissitudes of the times, which separately they could no longer do. They would have to buy their machinery jointly and divide the fruits of their efforts equally and peacefully; they would have to become a company in the truest sense of the word, chained together by a contract, and unanimity would be the main prerequisite for making such a company viable under the present unfavourable circumstances.

The division of labour, too, which, for a single businessman who employs only one or two journeymen, is nearly impossible or will at least remain in a rudimentary stage and thereby become a main threat to his existence, would

26 Here and below, Menger evidently argues in favour of co-operatives, an idea not to be found in Rau. The co-operative movement for handicraft firms was strong in his time in Austria and Germany.

27 Rau (1855), p. 526, speaks of the need of artisans to educate themselves to the level of industrialists (who, according to him, are 'scientifically educated', p. 525).

32 r Gewerbes wird, müßte, so weit dies möglich ist, durch Assoziation erreicht werden; die einzelnen Meister sollten ihre Gesellen mit sich zur gemeinsamen Unternehmung bringen, und sowohl unter sich als unter diese die verschiedenen Tätigkeiten und Verrichtungen teilen, um eine rasche Produktion zu erreichen.

Als einen Hauptschaden des kleinen Gewerbes haben wir auch den kostspieligen Einkauf der Rohprodukte im kleinen angeführt. Dies könnte wenigstens teilweise gehoben werden, wenn die in einer Gesellschaft vereinigten Gewerbsmänner aus der gemeinsamen Kassa sich Rohprodukte en gros einkaufen würden. Die großen Vorteile wären Billigkeit, größere Ausdehnung und rascheres Pulsieren des Geschäftes.[28]

Auf diese Art könnte ein Versuch zur Erhaltung des kleinen Gewerbes unternommen werden, doch man muß stets vor Augen halten, daß man es in diesem Falle mit einer Frage der Zeit zu tun hat, mit einer Tatsache, die über kurz oder lang hereinbrechen muß.

32 v Hier ist nicht die Gelegenheit zu einer neuen großen Unternehmung, sondern man hat es nur mit der Erhaltung und Unterstützung einer alten, sehr morschen, Ruine zu tun, die über kurz oder lang einbrechen muß.

29.1.1876 Rudolf

[28] Während Rau nur höhere wissenschaftliche Bildung der Handwerker fordert, erörtert Menger hier unabhängig von seiner Quelle die Ideen der Produktivgenossenschaften. Diese sind ja auch ein Beispiel für eine kollektive Nutzung einiger Vorteile der Arbeitsteilung.

have to be achieved as far as possible by association; the masters should bring their journeymen into the joint venture and divide the different operations and duties among themselves and their journeymen to make production speedy. 32 r

We also mentioned the costly purchase of raw products as one of the major disadvantages of the small business. This could be remedied at least partly if these tradesmen, combined in a company, were to buy their raw products wholesale out of a joint account. The main advantages would be cheapness, greater growth in business, and quicker turnover.[28]

In this manner, an attempt could be made to sustain the small business, but one must always remember that this problem is just a matter of time, a fact to be reckoned with sooner or later.

Here, there is no opportunity for any new large-scale undertaking; it is rather a question of maintaining and supporting an old, quite dilapidated ruin that – sooner or later – will inevitably collapse. 32 v

29 January 1876 Rudolf

28 This suggestion of what in fact would be co-operatives – after all an example for a collective attainment of some of the advantages of the division of labour – is Menger's original contribution to this lecture.

Politische Ökonomie V. 1876 Februar

33 r **Über den Ursprung von Geld und Münze**[1]

Seit dem Beginn der historischen Zeit, also seit den ersten Anfängen der Kultur, im weitesten Sinne, haben die Menschen Sachen, die ihnen zur Befriedigung ihrer Bedürfnisse dienen; die Anforderungen der einzelnen aber waren verschiedene, und so entstand durch die ungleiche Hinneigung zu den einzelnen Sachen jenes Maß, das wir mit dem Begriffe Wert bezeichnen. Durch dieses verschiedene Verhältnis der Menschen zu den Sachen entstand ein Vorgang, durch welchen eine Person einen Gegenstand, der für dieselbe von geringerer Wichtigkeit war, für einen anderen, der besser zur Befriedigung ihrer Bedürfnisse diente, hergab, und das nennen wir den Austausch.[2]

Dies ist die erste primitive Grundlage jedes Handels und Verkehrs.

Natürlich war in den ältesten historischen Zeiten dieser Austausch ein sehr
33 v schwerer und willkürlicher, denn die Basis desselben war die persönliche Wertschätzung der Sachen, die natürlich von Launen und Zuneigung beherrscht war.

Als die Menschen auf eine etwas höhere Bildungsstufe gelangten, nämlich in die Zeiten des Trojanischen Krieges und der ersten Geschichte der Griechen, zeigte sich das Bedürfnis nach einem fixen Austauschgegenstande, mit welchem gehandelt werden könne.

Man kann dies als einen Fortschritt in der Entwicklungsgeschichte bezeichnen, als die Willkür des einfachen Tausches verlassen wurde, und die ersten bestimmten Tauschgegenstände eingeführt werden mußten;[3] sie waren durch

[1] Einmal mehr richtet Menger sich in der Abfolge der behandelten Themen nach Smith. Wenn die oben behandelten Probleme der Kleinunternehmen I.iii. (über die 'Schranken der Ausdehnung des Marktes') entsprachen, so kommen wir nunmehr zu I.iv., 'Über Ursprung und Nutzen des Geldes'.

Als deutsche Quellen dienten Menger vermutlich Roscher (1864), II. 3: 'Geld im allgemeinen', §§ 115–26, S. 216–48, und Rau (1855), III.4.2: 'Geld', S. 315–46.

[2] Vgl. Smith (1776) I.iv.l. Menger sieht die Unterschiede zwischen Menschen stärker subjektiv bedingt als Smith. Bei Smith besteht die grundlegende Tauschursache darin, daß die Menschen Verschiedenes erzeugen, für Menger hingegen unterscheiden sie sich in ihren Präferenzen. Darin folgt Menger Roscher (1864), § 116, S. 216, wie auch schon Rau (1855), S. 257, 315.

Auch in Mengers eigenen Grundsätzen wird das Geld nach dem Tausch behandelt, allerdings nicht unmittelbar danach, sondern erst, nachdem dazwischen die Preistheorie und das Thema der 'Absatzfähigkeit' von Waren behandelt wurden, worauf in den Vorlesungen für den Kronprinzen noch nicht eingegangen wurde.

[3] Vgl. Smith (1776) I.iv.2. Menger hatte sich mit diesem Gedanken schon in seinen Grundsätzen

Political economy V. 1876 February

On the Origin of Money and Coins[1] 33 r

Since the beginning of historical time, that is to say of civilization in the widest sense, man has used objects to satisfy his needs; individual requirements differed, however, and from the differing preferences for individual objects the measure we call value was derived. The divergent relationships of men to objects caused a process to be set in motion in which a person gave away an object of lesser importance to him for another that served his needs better; and this is what we call exchange.[2]

This is the first and primitive origin of all trade and traffic.

Of course, in oldest historical times such exchange was very difficult and arbitrary, as it was based on an individual valuation of the objects, naturally 33 v dominated by whims and preferences.

When man reached a somewhat higher stage of civilization, at the time of the Trojan War and in the beginnings of Greek history, the need for a fixed standard of value for trading arose.

An advance in human development occurred when the arbitrariness of simple exchange was abandoned and the first standardized articles of exchange had to be introduced;[3] the growth of individual needs and the consequent expansion of traffic brought this about.

1 Once more, Menger follows Smith in the succession of the topics treated. If the problems of small-scale enterprises just discussed were meant as a treatment of Smith's (1776), I.iii, 'The Limitations of the Extent of the Market', we now come to I.iv., 'Of the Origin and Use of Money'.
As German sources Menger probably used Roscher (1864), II, 3: 'Money in General' (§§ 116–26, pp. 216–48) and also Rau (1855), III.4.2: 'Money', pp. 315–46.

2 Smith (1776), I.iv.l: 'It is but a very small part of a man's wants which the produce of his own labour can supply...Every man thus lives by exchanging'.
Menger, on the other hand, sees the differences of men in more subjective terms than Smith. While with Smith the basic reason of exchange is that men are specialized producers, with Menger they differ in their preferences. In this, Menger follows Roscher (1864), § 116, p. 216, as well as Rau (1855), p. 257, p. 315.
In Menger's own Principles the topic of money also succeeded that of exchange, but not immediately, only after a discussion of price theory and the topic of 'marketability' of commodities in between, topics which have not yet been touched upon in the lectures to the Crown Prince.

das Zunehmen der Bedürfnisse der einzelnen bedingt, und den dadurch wachsenden Verkehr.

Die ersten fixen Tauschgegenstände waren Tiere. Wir finden diese Einführung in den ältesten Zeiten Roms und Griechenlands,[4] es ist die natürliche Folge der Gewohnheiten und Erwerbsquellen jener Zeiten. Ackerbau und besonders
34 r Viehzucht[5] waren in den Anfängen der historischen Zeiten bei allen Völkern Hauptbeschäftigung; ersteres nur bei den gesitteteren Nationen, welche eine Zukunft vor sich hatten, letzteres bildete den ausschließlichen Lebensunterhalt aller nomadischen Stämme.

Darum ist es selbstverständlich, daß die Tiere zum Haupttauschgegenstande wurden, da sie als eine beweglichere Sache leicht aus einer Hand in die andere gehen konnten; auch war bei den Haustieren eine Auswahl nach Größe und Wert möglich, was den Tausch ungemein erleichterte.

So unbestimmt und schwerfällig auch diese Art Tauschartikel war, so kann man es doch als einen Fortschritt gegen die frühesten Zeiten betrachten, in denen jeder Gegenstand zum Tausch und Handel gebraucht wurde; der Gedanke eines fixen Tauschgegenstandes und daher auch der Maßstab zur Wertschätzung war der Fortschritt in der Entwicklung der Menschen.

Mit Zunahme der Kultur bei den Völkern des Altertums mußte die
34 v Schwerfälligkeit[6] dieses Austausches immer mehr hervortreten, besonders bei Volksstämmen, die an den Küsten wohnten, wie viele asiatische Völker und die Griechen; diese konnten schwer mit Tieren über das Meer handeln und mit denselben sich die Produkte ferner Länder kaufen; durch den Handel aber, der rasch zunahm und immer mehr gedieh, entwickelte sich auch bei diesen Völkern besonders schnell Bildung und Kultur.

Darum kamen die Menschen ziemlich früh auf den Gedanken, bestimmten Naturprodukten einen durch Übereinstimmung anerkannten Wert zu geben, und dieselben dann zur Erleichterung des Handels und Einkaufes zu benützen.

Wie schon erwähnt, sprachen viele Gründe für die Abschaffung des Tieres als Tauschgegenstand, besonders zeigte sich der Nachteil des Transportes der

ausführlich befaßt; für ihn ist das Geld die absatzfähigste Ware (vgl. Menger (1871), S. 255 und die nachfolgenden Ausführungen über den gesellschaftlichen Konsens als Auswahlvoraussetzung). Ähnlich spricht schon Roscher (1864), § 116, S. 216, von Geld als der 'gängigsten Ware', während Rau (1855), S. 317, insbesondere die Notwendigkeit des gesellschaftlichen Konsenses hervorhebt.

4 Vgl. Smith (1776) I.iv.3 ('Vieh'); Roscher (1864), § 118, S. 224, der jedoch behauptet, daß die Verwendung von Häuten und Fellen als Geld noch älter sei; der weniger historisch orientierte Rau äußert sich hierzu nicht. Menger hatte das Thema in den Grundsätzen (S. 260 ff.) bereits ausführlich behandelt; er hatte dazu offensichtlich eigene historische und sprachvergleichende Studien angestellt.

5 Roscher (1864), § 118, S. 224, weist im Zusammenhang mit der Verwendung von Vieh als Geld darauf hin, daß solches natürlich das Geld von 'Nomaden und primitiven Ackerbauern' sei; ähnlich Menger (1871), S. 261 f.

6 Menger erwähnt das in den Grundsätzen allgemein, also nicht nur für das Altertum (S. 264: 'lästig').

Animals were the first standardized articles of exchange. They were introduced in early Rome and Greece[4] as the natural consequence of the then existing customs and sources of income. At the beginning of historical time, agriculture and especially pastoralism[5] were the main occupation of all peoples; agriculture evolved only 34 r in the more civilized nations with a future ahead of them, while pastoralism provided the only means of subsistence for all nomad tribes.

Therefore animals necessarily became the main articles of exchange as, being relatively mobile, they could easily pass from hand to hand; in addition, domestic animals could be differentiated by size and value, which greatly facilitated exchange.

Although this sort of exchange article was indefinite and cumbersome, it was an advance over earliest times, when just any object was used for exchange and barter; the idea of a standardized item of exchange and therefore a standard of valuation spelled progress in human development.

With the advance of civilization among the peoples of antiquity, the cumbersomeness[6] of this sort of exchange became ever more apparent, especially 34 v among the tribes living on the coast, like many Asiatic peoples and the Greeks; they found it difficult to trade animals over the sea for the products of far-away countries; but through rapidly expanding and flourishing trade these peoples acquired civilization and refinement especially quickly.

Therefore it occurred to man quite early to ascribe to certain products of nature a value established by agreement and to use them for facilitating trade and purchases.

As mentioned above, there were many reasons for abandoning the use of animals as standardized articles of exchange; their disadvantage became especially

3 Smith (1776), I.iv.2: 'Every prudent man … must naturally have endeavoured … to have at all times by him … a certain quantity of some one commodity or other, such as he imagined few people would be likely to refuse in exchange'. Menger had elaborated on this idea in the Principles with his notion of money as the most marketable commodity (see (1976), p. 259 f. and the subsequent discussion of the social consensus behind its selection). Similarly, Roscher (1864), § 116, p. 216, spoke of 'the most current commodity', while Rau (1855), p. 317, stresses particularly the need for social consensus.

4 Smith (1776), I.iv.3 ('cattle'); Roscher (1864), § 118, p. 224, who suggests, however, that the use of skins and pelts as money is even older; no mention of this is made in the textbook of the less historically inclined Rau. Menger had already discussed the point at length in the Principles (1976), p. 263 ff.). He had evidently done original historical and linguistic research on the topic.

5 Roscher (1864), § 118, p. 224 – in the discussion of cattle as money – points out that it is naturally the money of 'nomads and primitive agriculturalists'; similarly Menger, ibid.

6 A point to be found in Menger, stated as a general principle, and not only for antiquity. See Principles (1976, p. 265: 'discomforts').

Tiere von einem Orte zum anderen,[7] auch waren nicht alle Leute in der Lage,
35 r sich welche zu halten, die Ernährung war kostspielig und der Tod, oder selbst nur Krankheit, konnte den Wert, oft selbst das ganze Vermögen einer Person vernichten; ferner ist der Wert der verschiedenen Tiere ein sehr relativer, und daher bietet dieser Handel großen Spielraum zu Unredlichkeiten aller Art.

Für Jagdvölker und solche, die den Landbau noch in der primitivsten Art betrieben, waren diese Einrichtungen passend, auch für die wilden Völkerschaften der Jetztzeit in den entlegensten Teilen fremder Weltteile kann dieser Handel recht vorteilhaft sein, doch Nationen, die schon vor Jahrtausenden bestimmt waren, die Gründer und später die Träger der Kultur zu sein und die Vorläufer unserer jetzigen Bildung, also der gesamten Zivilisation zu werden, mußten bald diese ursprünglichen Einrichtungen fallen lassen und sich zweckmäßigere Tauschgegenstände erfinden, um Blüte des Handels und regen Austausch der Produkte der einzelnen Länder herbeizuführen, da diese Tätigkeiten Verbindungen
35 v der einzelnen Völker und Reichtum derselben gründen, was die Grundbasis jeder ferneren Entwicklung und Kultur ist.

Bevor wir noch auf die Erfindung des ersten Geldes zu sprechen kommen, muß einiges über die Tauschartikel bei den wilden Völkern gesagt werden. In den anderen Weltteilen sind manche Völker, selbst ganze Rassen, auf jenem Standpunkt der Entwicklung geblieben, den unsere Vorfahren *vor der* historischen Zeit oder im ersten Beginne derselben eingenommen haben.

Manche von diesen Stämmen leben ausschließlich von der Beute, die sie auf ihren Jagden erlegen, oder vom Raube an anderen nachbarlichen Gemeinden. Diese sind wohl noch auf der tiefsten Stufe, da sie bloß von den Ergebnissen ihrer
36 r Räubereien, gerade so wie das wilde Tier, leben; bei solchen Völkern ist der Tausch noch gar nicht oder höchstens nur mit erlegtem Wilde gekannt; doch es gibt auch unter den noch unkultivierten Völkern welche, die sich schon auf einen höheren Standpunkt erhoben haben, als wie der früher besprochene. Die Erwerbsquellen können der beste Maßstab für die Kultur eines Volkes sein; wo die vollkommen ursprüngliche Ernährung durch Jagd aufhört und Landbau, Handel, Tausch mit Rohprodukten, bei vorgeschrittenerer Bildung auch mit schon verarbeiteten Produkten beginnt, dort ist schon ein höherer Grad der Entwicklung zu erkennen.

Auf diesem Standpunkte sind die meisten Völkerschaften der anderen Weltteile. Für Kleinigkeiten, wie unbedeutende Schmuckgegenstände, Feuerwaffen,
36 v europäische Kleidung, Branntwein etc. etc. tauschen sie mit den Europäern die Naturprodukte[8] ihres Landes aus, wie Pelze, Edelsteine, Korallen, selbst Tiere

[7] Merkwürdigerweise findet sich das auf der Hand liegende Argument der relativ billigen Transportierbarkeit von Metallen nur bei Roscher (1864), § 120, S. 229 ff., hier im Zusammenhang mit ausführlichen statistischen Berechnungen von Transportkosten. Bei Menger (1871) findet es sich kurz erwähnt (S. 265).

[8] Das Folgende entspricht einer langen Aufzählung in Mengers Grundsätzen (S. 267–69), die zum Teil nur aus einer ausführlichen Fußnote Roschers (1864, § 119, Anmerkung 12, S. 228 f.) übernommen ist.

obvious when they had to be transported from one place to another;[7] furthermore, not everybody was in a position to keep animals: they were expensive to feed, 35 r
and death or illness could destroy their value and even a person's entire wealth; in addition, the value of the different animals is very uncertain, so trade with them offers numerous opportunities for all kinds of dishonesty.

Such institutions suited hunting tribes and people occupied with agriculture in its most primitive stages; even today, this sort of trade can be quite advantageous to primitive tribes in the most distant parts of the world, but nations that even thousands of years ago were destined to become the founders and later the torchbearers of culture and the precursors of our present intellectual refinement, i.e. of civilization in its entirety, soon had to abandon those original instruments and to invent more expedient articles of exchange in order to bring about a flourishing trade and a voluminous exchange of products among the various countries, for these activities establish communication between peoples and establish their wealth, which in its turn is the basis for all further development and refinement. 35 v

Before we discuss the invention of the earliest money, something has to be said about the articles of exchange among primitive peoples. In other parts of the world some peoples, even entire races, have remained at the stage of development of our ancestors before or in the very beginning of historical time.

Some of these tribes subsist exclusively on their hunting booty or by robbing neighbouring communities. These are at the lowest stage since they live only by the spoils of their pillage, just like wild animals; such peoples are not familiar with barter at all or, at the most, only barter with killed game; but even among 36 r
uncivilized peoples there are those who have attained a higher level than this. The best measure of a people's level of civilization may be its sources of income; a higher stage of development is recognizable when quite primitive subsistence on hunting ceases, and when agriculture, commerce, barter with raw products and, at a higher stage of civilization, with partly finished products begin.

This is the situation of most peoples on other continents. They exchange their countries' natural products,[8] e.g. furs, precious stones, corals, even animals and many other things, for trifles like trinkets, guns, European clothes, brandy, etc. 36 v
etc.; this sort of exchange is still very primitive, since it lacks any established

7 Curiously, the obvious point of the relative cheapness of transport of metals is only made by Roscher (1864), § 120, p. 229 ff., with extensive statistical calculations of transport costs. It was then briefly mentioned by Menger (1976, p. 266).

8 What follows corresponds to a lengthy enumeration in Menger (1976), pp. 269–71, which in part is just copied from an extensive footnote in Roscher (1864), § 119, note 12, p. 228 f.

und viele andere Sachen; diese Art des Verkehrs ist noch eine sehr primitive, da sie jedes fixen Tauschgegenstandes entbehrt, und ohne die geringste bestimmte Wertschätzung und Vergleichung der Werte nur dem Verlangen des Augenblickes folgt.

Bei etwas kultivierteren Naturvölkern finden wir den Gebrauch eines bestimmten Tauschartikels, zur Erleichterung der Kaufgeschäfte, also eine Art Geld. Dies kann man schon als einen großen Fortschritt bezeichnen, da es der Anfang zur Annahme der europäischen Verhältnisse ist.

Oft sind ganz einfache Naturprodukte ausersehen, die Stelle des Geldes zu vertreten, z.B. Muscheln. Es bezeigt dies schon eine höhere geistige Entwicklung und die Fähigkeit, einen richtigen Gedanken zu fassen und denselben durchzuführen.

Einige Stämme in Afrika haben sich diese Art des Geldes erfunden, zahlen
37 r mit einer kleinen Muschelgattung 'Cypraea moneta', von ihnen Kauri[9] genannt, die ziemlich häufig an den dortigen Küsten vorkommt. Nach der Größe wird der Wert bemessen; und so entstehen durch die Größenunterschiede der Muscheln verschiedene Arten des Geldes.

Auf diesen Standpunkten sind die unkultivierten Völker anderer Weltteile, sie sind beiläufig in diesem primitiven Zustand, in dem unsere Vorfahren in den ersten historischen Zeiten waren, nur mit dem Unterschiede, daß diese sich schnell zu höherer Bildung entwickelten, jene aber einen langsam schleichenden Fortschritt durchwandern, dessen unmerkliche Bewegungen und Erfolge die rastlos zunehmende Kultur der gebildeten Rasse nicht wird erwarten können, und daher durch die Ausbreitung ihrer Träger über alle Weltteile jene Völker als ein schwaches Hindernis unfehlbar zu Grunde richten wird.[10]

37 v Kehren wir aber nun nach dieser kurzen Abweichung zum Tauschwesen unserer Vorfahren zurück und verfolgen wir weiters dessen Entwicklung.

Bei den Griechen und Römern kennen wir am besten diesen Entwicklungsgang, da wir am meisten geschichtliche Daten über ihr Leben haben. Die Zeit des ursprünglichen Tauschwesens, nämlich mit Tieren, dauerte nicht sehr lange; bald finden wir die ersten Anfänge des Geldes, zuerst in Form von langen Metallstangen, von denen nach verschiedenen bestimmten Maßstäben einzelne Stücke abgehauen wurden, mit denen dann gehandelt wurde.[11]

So schwerfällig dieses Verfahren auch war, so bildet die Annahme und Erfindung desselben einen großen Fortschritt in der Entwicklungsgeschichte der Menschheit. Es ist das erste Mal, daß Menschen, ganze Völker, einheitlich
38 r beschlossen, eine bestimmte Sache als Tauschgegenstand und Wertmaßstab anzunehmen, um dadurch das Kaufgeschäft zu erleichtern und einzelnen, welche

[9] Nicht in Menger, aber – komplett mit dem für gewöhnlich nicht zitierten lateinischen Namen 'cypraea moneta' – zu finden bei Roscher (1864), ebenda, Anfang Anmerkung 12.

[10] Der Absatz könnte als Probe von Rudolfs eigenem, jugendlich überschwänglichem Stil zu lesen sein.

[11] Smith (1776) I.iv.4; Roscher (1864), § 120, S. 230.

[12] Wiederholung bereits referierter Gedanken.

standard of exchange and simply follows the whims of the moment without any definite valuation and comparison of values.

We find that at a slightly more advanced stage primitive people use some standard article of exchange to facilitate their barter, that is to say: some kind of money. This may be considered a big step forward, since it indicates the beginning reception of European ways.

Often quite simple products of nature are chosen to serve as money, e.g. shells. This signifies a somewhat higher intellectual development and the ability to conceive and realize an actual idea.

Some tribes in Africa invented this sort of money for themselves, paying with small shells of the Cypraea moneta family which they call cowrie[9] and which 37 r
is found rather abundantly on their shores. Their size determines their value; and thus differences in the size of the shells make for different sorts of money.

Such is the situation among uncivilized peoples in other continents; they are more or less at the primitive stage our ancestors reached in earliest historical times, the only difference being that the latter's cultural advance was fast while the former's progress is creepingly slow; the civilized race with its restlessly onward-pushing culture will not be able to wait for the unnoticeable movements and results of such progress and by spreading its own representatives all over the globe will thus undoubtedly ruin those peoples that offer but weak resistance.[10]

After this short digression, however, let us return to exchange as practised 37 v
by our ancestors and look into its developments.

We are most familiar with this development in the case of the Greeks and the Romans, since we know more historical facts about their life than about anybody else. The period of original barter with animals did not last very long; soon we find the first instances of money, at first in the shape of long metal rods from which individual pieces were cut, according to various standards, and then used for trading.[11]

Although cumbersome, the invention and practice of this procedure is a big step forward in the development of mankind. Here, for the first time, men, entire peoples, decided unanimously to accept a specific object as an item of exchange 38 r

9 Not to be found in Menger, but discussed at length – together with the Latin name Cypraea moneta, usually not referred to – in Roscher (1864), § 119, beginning of note 12, p. 228.

10 Rhetoric of the Crown Prince?

11 Smith (1776), I.iv.4; Roscher (1864), § 120, p. 230.

12 Repetition of ideas already stated previously.

nicht im Besitze von Naturprodukten wie Grund und Boden waren, die Möglichkeit zu verschaffen, sich ein Vermögen zu begründen.[12]

Natürlich war auch diese Einführung in ihren ersten Anfängen nicht vollkommen und ließ freien Spielraum zu Ungenauigkeiten aller Art; die Schwerfälligkeit dieses Verfahrens war auch bedeutend, besonders beim Transporte der ziemlich schweren Metallstangen, erschwerend war ebenfalls das Abhauen der einzelnen Stücke, wozu man stets eigene Vorrichtungen bei sich haben mußte; natürlich konnten dabei leicht Willkürlichkeiten und Veruntreuungen stattfinden,[13] was alles dazu beitrug, daß nach kurzer Zeit schon diese Art des Geldes abgeschafft wurde und die ersten Münzen erfunden wurden. Diesen Übergang können wir
38 v abermals als einen Fortschritt betrachten, zwar nicht so bedeutend wie der vorige, der ein ganz neues System begründete, während dieser das bestehende nur verbesserte.

Mit Zunahme des Handels und Verkehrs mußte sich immer mehr die Schwerfälligkeit der unförmlichen Metallstangen fühlbar machen, und so faßten die antiken Völker, die Römer beiläufig 5 Jahrhunderte vor Christi Geburt, den Entschluß, dieselben in bessere kleine Formen zu bringen, so daß sie leicht vom einzelnen bei sich getragen werden konnten.

Auch konnte man nun verschiedene Größen diesem Gelde geben, und nach denselben den Wertmaßstab begründen. So entstanden die ersten Münzen. Die Münze ist das Mittel zur Ermöglichung großen Handels, zur Begründung vom Grund und Boden unabhängigen Reichtums, und der angenommene Wertmaßstab und die Bezeichnung des Wertes aller Dinge. Im ersten Anfang der Annahme
39 r der Münzen wurden dieselben aus Kupfer, noch in ganz roher Form, *gegossen*, später wurden der Wert derselben und andere Zeichen darauf gesetzt, in der Kaiserzeit Roms und bei anderen antiken Völkern, welche Herrscher an ihrer Spitze hatten, kam das Bildnis des Monarchen auf die Münzen.

In den ersten Zeiten, bei Beginne der Münzprägung gab man denselben die Form eines Vierecks, später erst erhielten sie die runde Gestalt eines Kreises; lange Zeit hindurch benützte man nur Kupfer[14] zur Erzeugung des Geldes, mit Fortschritt der Kultur[15] wurden auch aus den edlen Metallen, aus Gold und Silber, Münzen geprägt, welche natürlich einen viel höheren Wert erhielten als die aus
39 v Kupfer geprägten. Die Münzen haben keine weitere Veränderung durchgemacht; etwas verfeinert und schöner gearbeitet, sind sie sonst gerade so wie im Altertum der allgemein anerkannte Tauschartikel.

13 Smith (1776) I.iv.7, spricht von den Nachteilen, insbesondere von den Schwierigkeiten des Wägens und der Qualitätsprüfung; in I.iv.6 werden 'Rohbarren' (oder Stangen) erwähnt; kurze Erwähnung bei Roscher (1864), § 120, S. 230.

14 Smith, I.iv.5,6 und insbesondere I.v.24, bespricht ausführlich und unter zweimaliger Zitierung von Plinius die Verwendung von Kupfer bei den Römern. Roscher (1864), § 119, S. 226, ist nicht dieser Meinung, sondern glaubt, daß Gold und Silber gelegentlich vor Kupfer in Gebrauch kamen.

15 Für gewöhnlich wird festgestellt, daß Gold- und Silbermünzen Zeichen einer höheren Kultur seien. Smith (1776) I.iv.ll; Roscher (1864), § 120, S. 229, erster Satz.

and standard of value to facilitate barter and to give individuals without any natural endowments such as land the opportunity to accumulate wealth.[12]

Naturally, this innovation was not perfect at first and left room for inaccuracies of all kinds; the procedure was also quite cumbersome, especially transporting the rather heavy metal rods; cutting off the individual pieces was troublesome, too, for the appropriate instruments always had to be carried along; naturally, arbitrariness and embezzlements could easily occur in the process,[13] and these led to the abandonment of this type of money and the invention of the first coins. Coins may again be considered a step forward, though not quite as important as the first step, which brought an entirely new system into existence, while coins merely improved an existing one. 38 v

With expanding trade and traffic the cumbersomeness of the unwieldy metal rods must have become more and more noticeable, and so the ancients, e.g. the Romans about five centuries BC, decided to give them a better, small shape so that they could easily be carried around by a person.

In addition, this money could be made in different sizes, and the size could establish the value. Thus, the first coins came into existence. Coins are the prerequisite for a large volume of trade and for the accumulation of wealth independent from landed property, and they are the standard measure and denomination of all material value. When coins first came into use, they were cast of copper in quite rudimentary shape; later their value and other markings 39 r
were stamped upon them; in the Roman Empire and in the case of other ancient peoples who were governed by individual rulers, the likeness of the monarch was stamped upon the coins.

In earliest times, when metal was first coined, the coins were given a square shape; only later were they shaped round like a circle; for a long time, only copper[14] was used for minting coins; as civilization advanced,[15] precious metals, gold and silver, were also made into coins that, of course, were of much higher value than those made of copper. Apart from that, coins have not changed any further; somewhat refined and more beautifully made, they still constitute the 39 v
generally accepted means of exchange, just as in antiquity.

13 Smith (1776), I.iv.7, discusses the inconveniences, but in particular that of weighing and assaying; I.iv.6 mentions ‘rude bars’; briefly discussed in Roscher (1864), § 120, p. 230.

14 Smith (1776), I.iv.5,6 and especially I.v.24, remarks at length on the use of copper by the Romans, quoting Pliny twice. Roscher (1864), § 119, p. 226, is not of this opinion, thinking that gold and silver were in some instances used before copper.

15 It is commonly stated that gold and silver coins are signs of higher civilization: Smith (1776), I.iv.11; Roscher (1864), § 120,p. 229.

Das Geld überhaupt verlangt aber große Vorsicht und Genauigkeit in der Erzeugung, eine Münze muß in Gestalt, Gewicht, Gehalt des Metalles und daher Wert gleich sein der anderen, denn große Übelstände können aus einer unrichtigen Münzprägung entstehen, da die einzelnen Mitglieder des Staates ihr Vertrauen in den richtigen Wert ihres Geldes setzen. Zu großer Gehalt des edlen Metalles würde zur Einschmelzung der Münzen führen,[16] zu geringer wäre ein Verlust der einzelnen Staatsbürger und ein Betrug des Staates an denselben. Auch soll eine Regierung strenge darauf sehen, daß keine Falschmünzerei
40 r überhand nehme, denn außer der großen Immoralität und dem verbrecherischen Charakter dieser Tat zieht sie auch praktische Benachteiligungen einzelner sowie des Staates nach sich.

Doch vor allem müssen wir als Hauptbedingung und Notwendigkeit ein redliches Verfahren in Prägung der Münzen von seiten der Lenker der Staaten bezeichnen.[17] Jede Moralität und Möglichkeit einer allgemeinen Gerechtigkeit hört auf, wenn der Regent, statt als Muster und Beschützer des gesicherten Rechtslebens rein vor den Augen der Menschen *zu stehen*, selbst seine eigenen Untertanen durch falsche Münzprägung betrügt.

Nebst dem, daß so eine Handlungsweise jedes moralische Gefühl des Rechts untergräbt, nimmt es im In- und Auslande das Vertrauen zur Regierung, hindert dadurch den Verkehr und führt Armut herbei.

40 v Der Monarch, der durch solche Mittel sich zu helfen sucht, untergräbt sich seine Stellung selbst und sinkt zum gewöhnlichen Betrüger herab.

In den jetzigen Zeiten geschieht so ein schweres Vergehen nicht mehr, doch das sogenannte biedere Mittelalter und der Beginn der Neuzeit weisen genug solche Beispiele auf.

Wien, den 9. Februar 1876 Rudolf

[16] Rau spricht ausdrücklich davon, daß der Münzwert stets nahe beim internationalen Preis des entsprechenden Edelmetalls liegt, widrigenfalls die Münzen eingeschmolzen würden. Vgl. Rau (1855), S. 328.

[17] Die moralischen Lehren, die hier zu ziehen sind, finden sich weder bei Smith noch bei Rau oder Roscher; sie zeichnen Mengers Unterricht des Kronprinzen aus.

In general, producing money requires great care and accuracy; in shape, weight, metal content, and value one coin must be exactly like any other for great problems can arise from inaccurate coinage, since the members of the state trust that money has the right value. If there were too much of the precious metal in the coins, they would be melted down;[16] if there were too little, the individual citizen would suffer a loss and government would have cheated him. Government should also take great care to keep counterfeiting under control for, apart from its grave immorality and criminal character, it causes real damage to individuals and to the community as a whole. 40 r

But above all else, we must regard honesty on the part of the rulers of states as the main and necessary prerequisite in coining.[17] Morality and the possibility of general justice come to an end when the ruler deceives his very subjects by false coinage instead of appearing immaculate to the eyes of the world, a symbol and protector of law and order.

In addition to undermining all moral sense of right and wrong, such action destroys confidence in the government at home and abroad, thus impeding trade and leading to poverty.

The monarch who has recourse to such methods undermines his own position 40 v
and sinks to the level of a common swindler.

At present such grave offences no longer occur, but the so-called honest Middle Ages and the beginnings of the Modern Age provide enough pertinent examples.

Vienna, 9 February 1876 Rudolf

[16] Rau explicitly discusses the constant closeness of the value of coins to the international price of precious metals and their being melted down otherwise; cf. Rau (1855), p. 328.

[17] The moral lessons to be drawn can be found neither in Smith nor Rau nor Roscher; they are specific to Menger's teaching of the Crown Prince.

Politische Ökonomie VI. 1876 Februar

41 r **Über den Nutzen der staatlichen Beeinflussung der Volkswirtschaft und die Grenzen derselben (I)**

Für den einzelnen, wie für den Staat liegt in der Befriedigung der Bedürfnisse das höchste Interesse; mit Befriedigung der notwendigsten *Bedürfnisse* steigt ihre Anzahl, und mit dem Steigen dieser zeigt sich das Zunehmen der Kultur im allgemeinen.[1] Der Staat, wie das einzelne Mitglied desselben, haben die nämliche Quelle zur Erreichung jener Mittel, mit denen die Befriedigung der Bedürfnisse, daher auch der Reichtum, die Hauptbedingung jeder Machtentfaltung nach außen erlangt wird.

Ich meine nämlich den Fleiß und die Wirtschaftlichkeit der Bürger:[2] Sparsamkeit, Arbeit und reeller Erwerb sind wahre Bürgertugenden, die eine solide Basis zu einem großen Aufschwung der materiellen wie der geistigen Kultur bilden.

Da der Staat ja nur die Gesamtheit aller seiner Bürger in einem Begriff zusammengefaßt, wie eine Person ist, so kann weder das Ganze blühen ohne
41 v die Blüte der Teile, noch diese gedeihen, ohne jenes zu fördern.

Dies muß vor allem dem Folgenden vorausgeschickt werden, damit kein trennender Begriff den Staat und seine Bürger nebeneinander als verschiedene Ganze, sondern stets als einen Körper,[3] bestehend aus vielen Atomen, erscheinen lasse.

[CM am Rand: *1. Jeder Mensch hat ein großes Interesse am Erfolg seiner Wirtschaft.*[4]]

1 Etwas anders hatte Menger (1871) im Abschnitt I, § 5 'Über die Ursachen des fortschreitenden Wohlstands der Menschen' argumentiert: 'Je weiter die Menschen ... fortschreiten, um so vielfältiger werden die Güterarten'. Dies wird eher als ein Erkenntnisproblem der möglichen Produktions- und Konsumtechnologien geschildert denn als Problem der Ausdehnung der Bedürfnisse (S. 28 f.).

2 Rau (1854), S. 4 (siehe Zitat in Fußnote 4 unten). Weiters schon Smith (1776) IV.ii.9.

3 Roscher (1864), §§ 12–15, S. 21–27, bezeichnet die Volkswirtschaft als einen Organismus und diskutiert, inwieweit sie 'mehr (ist) als ein bloßes Nebeneinander vieler Privatwirthschaften' (S. 21).

4 Rau (1854), S. 4: 'Es ist aber zu 1) der Eifer der Einzelnen, ihr Vermögen zu erhalten, zu vermehren und zu Genüssen (persönlichen Gütern) zu verwenden, die Haupttriebfeder in der Volkswirthschaft..., aus welchen ein angestrengter Fleiß, Nachdenken, Aufsuchen der besten Erwerbsgelegenheiten und Verlangen nach den hiezu dienlichen Kenntnissen von selbst hervorgehen'. Sinngemäß ähnlich Smith.

Political economy VI. 1876 February

On the Benefits and Limits of Government Intervention in the Economy (I) 41 r

The individual, like the state, is above all interested in satisfying needs; as the essential needs are satisfied, the number of needs increases, and increasing needs signal the general advance of civilization.[1] The state looks to the same source as its individual members for acquiring the means for satisfying needs and attaining wealth, the main prerequisite for any external display of power.

I am referring to the industry and economy of citizens;[2] thrift, work, and earning a living in an honourable way are genuine civic virtues that provide a reliable foundation for a major upswing of material and immaterial culture.

As the state is but the sum total of its citizens and, considered as a whole, is like a person, the whole cannot flourish without the flowering of the individual parts, nor can these parts prosper without benefit to the whole. 41 v

This has to be set down as a premise so that no one should conceive of the state and its citizens as different entities, living side by side, but rather as one organism,[3] made up of many atoms.

[CM in the margin: 1. Everyone takes great interest in the results of his economizing.[4]]

1 In his Principles I, § 5, 'The Causes of Progress in Human Welfare', Menger had argued somewhat differently: 'The further mankind progresses in this direction, the more varied become the kinds of goods' (p. 73). This is presented as a problem of discovering the feasible production and consumption technologies rather than of an expansion of needs.

2 Smith (1776), IV.ii.9: 'The annual revenue of every society is always precisely equal to the exchangeable value of the whole annual produce of its industry, or rather is precisely the same thing with that exchangeable value'. Rau (1854), p. 4, elaborates on this.

3 Roscher (1864), §§ 12–15, pp. 21–27, speaks of the economy as an organism and discusses to what extent it be 'more than mere coexistence of many private economic units'.

4 Rau (1854), p. 4: 'The eagerness of everyone concerned to maintain and increase their wealth and to use it in consumption (for personal goods) is the main driving force in the economy…; from these there will automatically follow: concentrated assiduity, thought, search for the best opportunities for making an income, and the desire for the requisite knowledge and skills'. The same ideas may be found in Smith.

In jedes Menschen Brust wohnt der Drang nach Begründung eines gesicherten, ruhigen Haushaltes und einer Familie.[5] Aber selbst bei den wenigen, die dieser natürlichsten Bestimmung nicht folgen wollen, ist deshalb die Lust nach Erlangen der nötigen Mittel zum angenehmen Leben darum doch keineswegs ausgeschlossen. In jedem Falle ist die Befriedigung der Bedürfnisse ein Hauptziel jedes Menschen,
42 r auf das man die meisten Tätigkeiten und Bestrebungen des Lebens zurückführen kann.

Die Bedürfnisse sind freilich sehr verschieden, doch mit der Befriedigung der kleineren wächst ihre Anzahl und Größe,[6] die endlich der Reichste selbst zu befriedigen nicht imstande ist.

Ein großer Feind steht diesen Bestrebungen aber entgegen, das ist der Leichtsinn, der dazu treibt, daß die Genußsucht des Augenblickes die Früchte der Arbeit verzehre; das ist eine Krankheit, an der einzelne, ganze Stände, und oft periodenweise selbst Völker darben.[7]

Das Gegenteil dieses krankhaften Zustandes ist die gesunde Wirtschaftlichkeit des wahren Bürgertums, die darin besteht, daß die Früchte des Erwerbes zur Befriedigung der dringendsten Bedürfnisse mit Hintansetzung der minder wichtigen benützt werden, und selbst da wieder so vorgegangen wird, daß möglichst viele Bedürfnisse mit möglichst wenig Mitteln befriedigt würden, damit ein Teil des Einkommens als Basis für neuen Erwerb übrig bleibe.[8]

42 v Man kann also sagen, daß die wirtschaftlichen Bestrebungen enge verknüpft sind mit dem ganzen Leben der wahren Bürger, sie sind seine vorzüglichen Sorgen
43 r und der Ausgangspunkt aller seiner Tätigkeiten.[9] Wenn diese ihm gelingen, schreitet er auf dem festen Boden eines gesicherten Haushaltes zur Erfüllung seiner Pflichten als guter Staatsbürger, und beginnt erst dann zum allgemeinen Wohle mit Hilfe seines Vermögens zu arbeiten.

Aber auch der Staat, der als Gesamtheit der Teile, durch die Stärke derselben, selbst stark wird, muß, um seinen großen Zweck zu erfüllen, was er nur durch Reichtum in vollem Maße tun kann, die wirtschaftlichen Bestrebungen der Bürger und ihr Gedeihen als die Quelle des seinigen betrachten und beschirmen.[10] [CM

[5] 'Das Streben, weise im Genuß zu sein, Ersparungen zu machen, hängt ferner nicht allein mit dem Erwerbseifer der Menschen, sondern auch mit seiner Liebe zu seinen Kindern und seiner Familie zusammen … der Mann ist haushälterisch, weil er für seine Familie zu sorgen hat': Mischler (1857), I, S. 177.

[6] 'Die Entwicklung der Bedürfnisse hat keine Gränze". Mischler, ebenda, S. 181.

[7] Etwa Roscher (1864), § 222, S. 455 ('Wie es verschwenderische und sparsame Individuen gibt, so auch Völker').

[8] Dieser Optimierungsgedanke ist eine von Mengers Hauptaussagen in seinen Grundsätzen (1871), S. 86 ff. Er ist jedoch vorgebildet bei seinem Lehrer Mischler, der auf dieser Seite offensichtlich herangezogen wird; siehe Mischler (1857), I, zur Bedürfnishierarchie S. 208 und insbesondere S. 231 f. zu dessen rudimentärem sogenanntem 2. Gossenschen Gesetz für Tausch und Produktion. Siehe ausführlicher Streissler (1990a), S. 45.

[9] Die letzten vier Absätze sind weitgehend – im Kern an Smith angelehnte – Wiederholungen von bereits Gesagtem (vgl. S. 28 und S. 36).

[10] Rau (1855), S. 5: 'Volks- oder Nationalvermögen, d.h. der Inbegriff aller im Vermögen der

In his innermost being, man feels the urge to establish a well-secured, peaceful household and a family.[5] But even the few who do not want to pursue this most natural course do not lack the desire for obtaining the means necessary for a pleasant life. In any case, satisfying needs is a major aim of man, to which most of his activities and endeavours in life refer.

42 r

The needs are of very different kinds, of course; but in satisfying the smaller ones, their number and size increases so that eventually not even the richest man is able to satisfy them.[6]

Recklessness, though, is a strong adversary of these endeavours and causes the craving for momentary pleasures to consume the fruits of labour; this is a malady that befalls individuals, entire classes of society, and at times even whole nations.[7]

The opposite of this pathological state is the healthy economy of the true citizen that consists of employing the fruits of labour in satisfying the most urgent needs while ranking the less important ones below, and even this is done so that the greatest possible number of needs is satisfied with a minimum of resources, and a part of income can be set aside as a basis for further earnings.[8]

Thus, economic endeavours are tied up with the entire life of the true citizen, 42 v
they are his foremost concern and the starting point for all his activities.[9] If a
person is successful, he will attend to his duties as a good citizen, settled in his 43 r
well-established household, and only then begin to work for the common good with his assets.

But the state, too, grows strong as the sum of its parts, by virtue of their strength; to accomplish its major purpose, fully realizable only through wealth, it must pay attention to and protect the economic efforts and welfare of its citizens as the source of its own wealth.[10] [CM in the margin: The state, too, is greatly interested in individual economic performance, since its own wealth is rooted in that of the individuals.]

5 The family as an incentive for a man's economy is found in Mischler (1857), I, p. 177.

6 Mischler, loc. cit., p. 181, comments on the illimitable development of needs.

7 See Roscher (1864), § 222, p. 455: 'There are thriftless and thrifty individuals; the same is true of nations'.

8 This process of optimization is one of Menger's main ideas in the Principles, p. 121 ff. It was anticipated, however, by his teacher Mischler, who is evidently referred to here. Cf. Mischler (1857), I, on the hierarchy of needs, p. 208, and especially p. 231 f., for rudiments of 'Gossen's Second Law' in exchange and production. This is treated in detail in Streissler (1990a), p. 45.

9 These last four paragraphs (on the whole taken from Smith) mostly repeat what had already been said above; cf. pp.29 and 37.

10 Rau (1855), p. 5, points out that private and national wealth are not opposites, but that national wealth is the sum of all private wealth within a state – an idea audibly echoing Smith.

am Rand: *Auch der Staat hat ein hohes Interesse an den wirtschaftlichen Erfolgen des einzelnen, weil sein Reichtum in jenem der einzelnen wurzelt.*]

Ein Staat, dessen Mitglieder durch Sparsamkeit und Fleiß ziemlich gleich verteilte Wohlhabenheit[11] erlangt haben, wird zur Lösung jener Fragen, welche die Gesamtheit durch die Mittel aller beantwortet, mit größerer Macht auftreten können.

Natürlich muß die Regierung, welche als Vertretung des Ganzen, als Haupt für die Angelegenheiten des übrigen Körpers sorgt, mit den Kräften desselben wirtschaften; denn Fleiß der einzelnen und Wirtschaftlichkeit im kleinen hilft dem Ganzen nichts, wenn die Regierung mit den Mitteln der Teile unwirtschaftlich verfährt und dadurch stets in Geldnöten ist.[Am Rand: Darum liegt in den wirtschaftlichen Erfolgen des einzelnen der Grundstein zum Gedeihen des Ganzen und eine Garantie des Gelingens der großen Ziele des Staates.[12]]

43 v Darum ist der Staat der Schutz der Teile, und durch die Leistungen von jenem sorgen diese für ihre eigenen Interessen; es zahlen die Untertanen die Steuern nicht wie Auflagen eines fremden Herrn, sondern als Abgaben an das eigene Ganze und in demselben zugleich an sich selbst. Wer dem Staat mehr leisten kann, dem leistet auch der Staat mehr.[13] Wie der Schutz des Staates und oft nur das Bewußtsein seiner Aufmerksamkeit den Bürgern Sicherheit und Vertrauen
44 r einflößt, so ist ebenfalls die wirtschaftliche Tätigkeit dieser die Hauptmacht des Staates.

Somit ist es eine Pflicht des Staates, die wirtschaftlichen Bestrebungen seiner Bürger zu unterstützen, um durch die Hilfe, die er diesen leistet, das Gedeihen des Ganzen zu heben.

So wahr und notwendig auch dieser Grundsatz ist, kann er doch zum Nachteile jener durchgeführt werden, deren Wohl er bezwecken soll. Besonders bei einem in der Kultur sehr vorgeschrittenen Volke muß die Regierung mit großer Vorsicht bei der Unterstützung der wirtschaftlichen Tätigkeiten einzelner vorgehen, um ja nicht in den großen Fehler der Bevormundung zu verfallen.

Bei einem noch unkultivierten Volke kann das Haupt des Staates durch eigenes Eingreifen die vollkommen darniederliegende Volkswirtschaft zu heben

Staatsbürger befindlichen sachlichen Güter. Privat- und Volksvermögen sind daher nicht einander entgegengesetzt, sondern das zweite ist die Gesammtheit des ersten innerhalb eines Staates'. Der Gedanke selbst entspricht deutlich der Grundkonzeption Smiths (1776).

11 Roscher (1864), § 205, S. 423 (mit Berufung auf J.J. Rousseau und schon Aristoteles): 'Zur wirthschaftlichen Blüthe eines Volkes kann darum eine Harmonie der großen, mittleren und kleinen Vermögen die unentbehrliche Voraussetzung heißen'. Siehe §§ 201–4 bei Roscher.

12 Rau (1855), S. 13: 'Für die Wohlfahrt eines Staates (ist es) keineswegs gleichgültig, ob das Volk sich in einem günstigen oder ungünstigen Vermögenszustande befindet, vielmehr bringt ein guter Erfolg der Volkswirthschaft für das Staatsleben große Vortheile und muß daher von der Regierung eifrig erstrebt werden'. Rau (1854), S. 1: 'Der Wohlstand des Volkes gehört demnach... unter die Staatszwecke'.

13 Smith (1776) V.ii.b.3, zur Höhe der individuellen Steuerbeiträge.

A state whose members have, by thrift and industry, attained a condition of fairly equally distributed prosperity,[11] will be able to exert greater power when dealing with problems that it can solve by employing the resources of all.

Of course, as representative of the body politic, as the head responsible for its activities, the government has to employ society's energies in an economic manner; for industriousness and economy at the individual level are of no use to society as a whole if government uses its resources uneconomically and thus is always short of money.[12] [In the margin: Therefore individual economic success is the cornerstone of society's prosperity and a guarantee for realizing the major ends of the state.]

Therefore the state protects the individuals in it and, by virtue of its performance, 43 v
the individuals pursue their own interests; the subjects pay taxes not like dues to a foreign overlord, but rather as contributions to their own body politic and thus to themselves. The man who can give more to the state will also be given more by the state.[13] Just as protection by the state and even an awareness of its attention make the citizens feel secure and confident, their economic activities are the staying power of the state. 44 r

Thus, it is a duty of the state to promote the economic efforts of its citizens and raise the level of general prosperity by the support that it gives them.

Though this principle is true and necessary, its application may nevertheless be disadvantageous to those for whose well-being it is intended. Especially when a people has reached an advanced stage of civilization, its government has to act with the greatest discretion when promoting individual economic activities so as safely to avoid the grave mistake of acting like a guardian.

When a people is still uncivilized, the head of state may attempt to activate the sluggish economy on his own initiative; but where trade and commerce flourish because of a people's industry and education, the state can greatly harm the

11 Roscher (1864), § 205, p. 423, quotes Rousseau and Aristotle to the effect that the indispensable prerequisite for the flowering of a national economy is the 'harmony' between big, medium and small-scale wealth.

12 Rau (1855), p. 13. Also Rau (1854), p. 1: 'The economic wellbeing of the people is ... among the purposes of the state'.

13 Smith (1776), V.ii.b.3: 'the subjects of every state ought to contribute towards the support of government, as nearly as possible, in proportion to their respective abilities; that is in proportion to the revenue which they respectively enjoy under the protection of the state. The expence of government to the individuals of a great nation, is like the expence of management to the joint tenants of a great estate'.

suchen; doch, wo durch Fleiß und Bildung das Gewerbe und der Handel blühen,
44 v kann der Staat durch *allzugroße* Einmengung in die Interessen der Bürger ungemein schaden, während er durch Zulassung eines freien Spielraumes und Hilfe nur in jenen Fällen, wo die Kraft der einzelnen zu schwach ist, am sichersten die volkswirtschaftlichen Interessen *fördert.*[14]

Die Verantwortung und Sorge für das eigene Wohl und das der Familie ist ein mächtiger Stachel zu Arbeit und Fleiß und wird durch die Erfüllung dieser Aufgaben zur reinsten Freude und zum wahrsten Stolze des freien Bürgers;[15] wälzt nun der Staat einen Teil dieser Sorgen auf sich, so wähnt der einzelne sich bevormundet und nicht frei, selbst in jenen Angelegenheiten, die seine eigensten Interessen betreffen; der Stolz, der in der unabhängigen Erhaltung der Seinigen ohne fremde Hilfe liegt, und das Bewußtsein, allein den schweren Kampf ums Dasein zu bestehen, sind die höchsten Güter eines gebildeten Bürgers, in diesen fühlt er sich dann durch den Staat verletzt, und es schwindet mit der Sorge die Freude und der Stachel zur Arbeit;[16] dadurch erreicht nun die Regierung das Gegenteil von dem, was sie erzielen wollte.

45 r Auch vollkommen praktische Gründe sprechen dagegen. Es ist unmöglich, daß die Regierung die Interessen aller Bürger kennt, und um denselben wirklich zu helfen, müßte sie die so verschiedenen Bestrebungen der einzelnen jede einzeln berücksichtigen. Denn ein schablonenhafter Vorgang, der, wo er auch angewendet

14 Ausführlichere Wiederholung aus Heft I; siehe Anfang S. 1v; Mengers zentraler Gedanke in Weiterführung von Rau (1855), § 16.

15 Dieser Satz folgt fast wörtlich Mengers Lehrer Mischler (1857), S. 16 f. In § 8, 'Princip des Fleißes', hält Mischler, teilweise gesperrt gedruckt, fest: 'So ist die Sorge für das eigene Wohl eine der mächtigsten Triebfedern menschlicher Thätigkeit... Sie spornt die Thatkraft, weckt die Energie, fördert die geistige Entwicklung'. Auf der folgenden Seite heißt es: 'Die Sorge für das eigene Selbst (wird) erweitert, verstärkt und veredelt in der Sorge für die Familie und als solche wieder berechtigt durch die Liebe zur Familie, als Sorge für das Wohl der Familie'.

Im folgenden argumentiert jedoch Mischler ganz konträr zu Menger. Er führt den 'Flor des Gemeinwesens' ein: 'Indem die Anwendung des Erwerbseifers jetzt in der Schranke bleibt, die durch die Pflicht für Familie und Gemeinde gezogen ist, wird es (sic) noch mehr veredelt durch den gemeinnützigen Charakter, den es annimmt, durch das Gepräge des Gemeinsinns, der Bürgertugend'. Bei Menger ist umgekehrt der Staat zu beschränken in einer Weise, die 'Individualität und freie Entwicklung' erhält. Mischler (1857) schließt seine Ausführungen mit der gesperrt gedruckten Feststellung (S. 18), die Menger ganz unterdrückt: 'Je mehr der religiöse Sinn gepflegt wird, desto stärker wirkt der in der Erkenntnis der religiösen Pflichten und in dem Streben, sie zu befolgen, liegende Hebel als Triebfeder des Handelns, desto glücklicher lebt der Einzelne, die Familie, die Gemeinde, die bürgerliche Gesellschaft'.

16 Dieser Absatz und teilweise die nächsten entsprechen auch in etwa der ausführlichen Ableitung zunehmender wirtschaftlicher Interaktion mit der Notwendigkeit einer weitergespannten Gütervorsorge bei Hermann (1870), S. 7–44. S. 9: 'Arbeit ist Lebensaufopferung'. S. 15: 'Der Egoismus der Selbsterhaltung der Eltern wird durch die Liebe zu den Kindern gebrochen'. S. 38: 'Die Einzelwirthschaften (verbinden) sich in so vielen Richtungen und so unaufhörlich zu einer Gesamtthätigkeit, daß man mit Recht von Wirthschaft eines Volkes sprechen mag'. S. 43: 'Es wurde zugleich gezeigt, daß ein Volk im Ganzen kein wirthschaftliches Subjekt bildet, sondern daß alle Bedürfnißbefriedigung in demselben der Sorge von Einzelwirthschaften überlassen ist'.

citizens' interests by interfering too much, while it will most definitely promote the interest of the national economy by allowing scope for individual action 44 v
and lending support only in cases where an individual's strength is insufficient.[14]

Being responsible and caring for the well-being of one's self and family is a powerful incentive for work and industry, and the discharge of these duties becomes the purest joy and truest pride of the free citizen; now, if the state seizes some of these responsibilities, the individual will feel imposed upon and not free, even in such matters as pertain to his most personal interests;[15] the pride he takes in providing for his family on his own without anybody's help and the knowledge that he is able, on his own, to master the great struggle for existence are the most precious goods of an educated citizen; if the state relieves him of these, he will feel hurt, and his enjoyment of and incentive to work will disappear along with the responsibility;[16] thus, government will achieve the opposite result from what it intended.

Furthermore, quite practical reasons speak against this. Government cannot 45 r
possibly know the interests of all citizens, and in order to help them it would have to take account of each of the diverse activities of everybody. For any sort of blueprint that hampers individuality and its free development, no matter where it is applied, would be quite unsuitable here.

14 Enlarged repetition from Notebook I, see p. 1v; Menger's central idea is developed from Rau (1855), § 16.

15 This sentence closely follows Menger's teacher Mischler (1857), p. 16 f. In his § 8, 'The Principle of Industry', Mischler calls the care for one's own well-being one of the mainsprings of human activity, stirring and increasing physical energy and promoting intellectual development (p. 16). This self-interest is then enhanced, enlarged and ennobled by the care and love for one's family (p. 17).

From then on, however, Mischler follows a different line of argument from Menger. From the interest in his family, the individual is supposed to go on to take a noble interest in the common good and become public-spirited. Menger, on the other hand, advocates restrictions on the state so as to ensure 'unhampered individual development'. Mischler's concluding plea for the observance of religious duties and his praise of religion as the prerequisite to a happy conduct of individual and public affairs is not echoed by Menger.

16 This paragraph and parts of the following ones correspond to Hermann (1870), pp. 7–44, where he speaks of work as life-long dedication and sacrifice (p. 9) and suggests that the love of their children breaks the egoism and self-preserving drives of the parents (p. 15). Although the ever increasing economic interaction of individuals ere long becomes such that one may duly speak of the 'economy of a people', this people as an entirety should never be regarded as one economic agent – for the satisfaction of needs within this economy will always rest with the individual economic agents.

wird, die Individualität und die freie Entwicklung derselben untergräbt, wäre in diesem Falle vollkommen unanwendbar.

Einrichtungen, die noch so sorgsam ausgedacht und gut gemeint sind, werden dennoch gewiß nicht auf alle Bürger passen, da nur der einzelne genau seine Interessen und die Mittel, sie zu *fördern*, kennt.

Unzählige Einflüsse, die bei jedem Menschen verschieden sind, beherrschen seine Tätigkeiten, und er allein kennt die Mittel, diese Ziele zu erreichen; daraus entspringt, durch die freie Entwicklung der Individualität ermöglicht, eine große Vielseitigkeit der Tätigkeiten, welche einen hohen Grad der Kultur erzeugt. Der einzelne Bürger weiß am besten, was ihm von Nutzen ist,[17] und wird, da er für sein eigenstes Interesse arbeitet, den größten Fleiß entwickeln.[18] Als einen nennenswerten Antrieb zur Arbeit muß man *ferner* in einem kultivierten Staate das Bewußtsein der Mitwirkung zur Hebung des allgemeinen Wohlstandes
45 v durch die eigenen Bestrebungen betrachten. Dieses sittliche Moment entsteht *aber* nur bei vorgeschrittener Bildung, durch eine freie Entwicklung der Individualität.

Wo diese Verhältnisse bestehen, wird das ganze Land gedeihen, die Kultur, gepflegt von zufriedenen, selbstbewußten und fleißigen Männern, blühen und zunehmen; dies wird aber entstehen durch die Freiheit der einzelnen Bürger in ihren wirtschaftlichen Bestrebungen, dann haben diese das größte Interesse an ihrer eigenen Wohlfahrt, und dadurch an der des Staates; wollte aber die Regierung das fehlerhafte Verfahren der Bevormundung verfolgen und den Bürger in seinen privativsten Angelegenheiten überwachen, um ihm zu helfen, in Wirklichkeit aber zu schaden;[19] da müßte die Beamtenwelt als Organ der Regierung die wirtschaftlichen Bestrebungen leiten und in die Tätigkeiten der einzelnen eingreifen.

Die Verschiedenartigkeit der Arbeiten, welche durch die Verschiedenheit der Individualitäten entsteht, und durch diese Vielseitigkeit den Fortschritt in jeder Hinsicht fördert, würde durch *eine alles umfassende* Überwachung der Beamten
46 r vollkommen untergraben werden. Der eifrigste Beamte selbst ist nur ein blindes *Werkzeug* einer großen Maschine, der schablonenmäßig alles gleich nach Paragraph und Vorschrift behandelt und weder den Anforderungen der Fortschritte der Zeit noch der Vielgestaltigkeit der praktischen Verhältnisse Rechnung zu tragen weiß.

[17] Smith (1776) IV.ii.10.

[18] Roscher (1864), § 81, S. 148: 'Sonst aber [d.h. wenn es sich nicht um 'Engel' oder Mitglieder einer 'musterhaften' Familie handelt] wird in der Regel jeder Theilnehmer der Gütergemeinschaft möglichst wenig arbeiten, möglichst viel genießen wollen. Bei einer Gemeinschaft von 100.000 Mitgliedern wäre jedes einzelne am Resultate seines Thuns oder Lassens nur zu 1/100.000 interessirt, d.h. so viel wie gar nicht!'

[19] Rau (1854), S. 9: 'Die Volkswirthschaftspflege gehört... zu den fördernden... Regierungszweigen ... und muß mit großer Behutsamkeit, öfter helfend und anregend, als zwingend verfahren'.

However carefully designed and well-meant institutions may be, they will never suit everybody, since only the individual himself knows exactly his interests and the means to promote them.

Innumerable influences, different for everyone, dominate man's activities, and only the individual knows the means for gaining his ends; from unhampered individual development there results a wide range of activities that permit an advanced stage of civilization to be reached. The individual citizen knows best what is of use to him[17] and he will be most industrious when working for his own personal ends.[18] In a civilized country, the knowledge that personal efforts contribute to increasing the general welfare must also be mentioned as a considerable incentive to work. This ethical impulse, however, appears only at an advanced stage of civilization, brought about by the free development of the 45 v
individual.

In this sort of situation the whole country will prosper, culture will flower and advance, tended by content, self-confident and industrious men; this will come about, though, by virtue of the freedom that individual citizens enjoy in their economic endeavours, for then they have the greatest interest in their own well-being and thereby in that of the state; but if government were to take the erroneous course of paternalism and of controlling the citizen's most private affairs with the intent of helping, though actually harming, him, the bureaucracy as an agent of government would have to take charge of economic affairs and interfere with individual activities.[19]

The variety of work performed follows from the variety of individuals and, by its very manifoldness, promotes progress in every way; it would be altogether lost with comprehensive bureaucratic controls. Even the most devoted civil servant is but a blind tool within a big machine who treats all problems in a stereotyped 46 r
manner according to regulations and instructions and can cope neither with the requirements of contemporary progress nor with the diversity of practical life.

17 Cf. Smith (1776), IV.ii.10: 'What is the species of domestick industry which his capital can employ, and of which the produce is likely to be of the greatest value, every individual, it is evident, can, in his local situation, judge much better than any statesman or lawgiver can do for him. The statesman, who should attempt to direct private people in what manner they ought to employ their capitals, would not only load himself with a most unnecessary attention, but assume an authority which .... would nowhere be so dangerous as in the hands of a man who had folly and presumption enough to fancy himself fit to exercise it'.

18 Roscher (1864), § 81, p. 148, in his discussion of the drawbacks of communal property, where the free-rider problem is explicitly stated.

19 Rau (1854), p. 9, on economic policy as one of those government activities that 'consist in encouragement'; economic policy ought 'to proceed with great discretion, by helping and stimulating more often than by using force'.

Und darum kann man einen Vorgang in Betreff wirtschaftlicher Bestrebungen für unmöglich halten, der, alle Interessen der einzelnen außer acht lassend, nach einem Muster und einer Vorschrift vorgeht. Wer anders sollte diese eigensten, für ihn wichtigsten Bestrebungen durchführen als derjenige, der darin den Kampf um seine und seiner Familie Existenz erblickt.

Freiheit und Selbstverantwortlichkeit der Bürger in ihren wirtschaftlichen Bestrebungen sind die Grundfesten der allgemeinen Entwicklung eines Staates; darum muß dieser diese Hauptprinzipien ermöglichen und schützen. Durch das Gegenteil, durch das Bevormundungssystem, schwächt und untergräbt er seinen
46 v eigenen Fortschritt und versündigt sich an den natürlichsten Rechten seiner Bürger.

Der Staat, wie schon früher erwähnt, ist nur die Gesamtheit der Teile und bildet mit denselben ein Ganzes. Das Gedeihen jener ist seine Blüte, und darum muß die Regierung, als die Vertretung des Ganzen in allen Angelegenheiten, besonders die wirtschaftlichen Bestrebungen der Bürger berücksichtigen, da sie ja die Quelle allen Reichtumes und daher auch der Machtentfaltung des Staates sind.

Es muß das höchste Interesse einer weisen Regierung in Anspruch nehmen, auf welche Art sie, ohne zu hindern, fördernd ihren Einfluß auf das Gedeihen der Volkswirtschaft betätigen kann.

Wie schwer dies in den gewöhnlichsten Verhältnissen ist und wie leicht aus der Hilfe Bevormundung und aus dieser Einschränkung der persönlichen Freiheit wird, wurde im vorhergehenden besprochen. Doch trotzdem gibt es Fälle im Leben der Staaten, wo dem Gedeihen der wirtschaftlichen Bestrebungen einzelner
47 r sowie mehrerer Bürger sich solche Hindernisse in den Weg stellen, deren Beseitigung die Kraft der Regierung erheischt, da die Mittel der einzelnen unmöglich dazu ausreichen würden.[20]

Wir haben es hier mit anormalen Fällen zu tun, denn nur diese gestatten das Einschreiten des Staates, in den normalen Situationen des volkswirtschaftlichen Lebens werden wir so ein Verfahren stets für schädlich erklären müssen. [In Bleistift am Rand:?]

Meistens sind es so mächtige Erscheinungen, daß sie entweder den Erlaß eigener Gebote, was natürlich nur der Staat tun kann, oder einen solchen Aufwand von

20 Rau (1854), S. 7 f., nennt unter den wirtschaftsfördernden Aufgaben des Staates: '1) Belehrung, wo die Kenntniß der Bürger über gewisse gewerbliche Angelegenheiten mangelhaft ist; 2) Ermunterungen, um den Gewerbefleiß zu solchen Unternehmungen hinzulenken, zu denen der Erwerbseifer noch nicht hinreichend antreibt; ... 3) Hinwegräumung von Hindernissen, welche von den Einzelnen nicht gehoben werden können, weil dazu überhaupt eine Vereinigung vieler Kräfte, oder insbesondere die Hülfe der Staatsgewalt erfordert wird; 4) Errichtung, Pflege und Leitung oder Beaufsichtigung verschiedener Hülfsanstalten, welche durch die Mitwirkung der Regierung erst ihre volle Nützlichkeit erreichen.' Menger ignoriert die staatliche Lehraufgabe unter l), folgt jedoch voll den Positionen 2) bis 4), wobei 3) und 4) Smith entsprechen (bei Smith ist keine 'Ermunterung' erforderlich). Siehe insbesondere Smith (1776) IV.ix.5l, zur 'dritten Aufgabe des Souveräns', der Errichtung öffentlicher (Infrastruktur-) Einrichtungen.

Therefore one may consider it impossible that all economic activities be treated in a stereotyped way, following one and the same rule with utter disregard for individual interests. Who else should pursue these personal interests but the person for whom this represents the struggle for his and his family's existence.

Freedom and self-reliance in the economic efforts of citizens are the foundation of the overall development of a state; therefore the state has to realize and defend these fundamental principles. By its opposite, by paternalism, it spoils and hinders its own progress and infringes upon the most natural rights of its citizens. 46 v

The state, as mentioned above, is but the sum of its parts and with them constitutes a whole. It flourishes if and when they prosper and therefore the government, which in all matters represents the whole, must take account especially of the economic efforts of the citizens, for these are the source of all wealth and thereby also of the power of the state.

It must be of the greatest interest to a wise government to find out how it can favourably affect the performance of the economy without hindering anyone.

Above, we discussed how difficult this is even in the most ordinary circumstances and how easily support may turn to paternalism and thus curtail personal freedom. Nevertheless, there are instances in the life of a state when the economic performance of individuals or of groups of citizens runs up against obstacles that require the government's powers to remove them, since individual resources 47 r would not possibly be enough.[20]

We deal with abnormal situations here, since only these justify government interference; in everyday economic life we shall always have to denounce such action as harmful. [In the margin, in pencil: ?]

For the most part, these are such powerful phenomena that they either require special laws, which, of course, only the state can pass, or involve such high costs – because of the size of the obstacle – that government support becomes indispensable.

20 As the first concern of government Menger thus names Smith's 'third duty of the sovereign'. Cf. Smith (1776), IV.ix.51: 'Thirdly, the duty of erecting and maintaining certain publick works and certain publick institutions, which it can never be for the interest of any individual, or small number of individuals, to erect and maintain; because the profit could never repay the expence to any individual or small number of individuals, though it may frequently do much more than repay it to a great society'. This is elaborated in Rau (1854), p. 7 f: in addition to Smith's concerns, this author stresses 'instruction' in commercial matters (not taken up by Menger) and 'exhortation' to pursue certain activities (taken up by Menger).

Kosten, wegen der Dimension*en* des Hindernisses erheischen, *daß sie* unbedingte Hilfe der Regierung benötigen.

In solchen Momenten würde die Durchführung bis ins Extrem des Prinzips der Selbstverantwortung und Selbstüberlassung der Bürger in ihren wirtschaftlichen Bestrebungen den ärgsten Schaden für diese und dadurch auch für den Staat herbeiführen. Die Kunst der Regierung liegt eben darin, den richtigen Augenblick
47 v zu erkennen, wo der größte Fleiß und die edelste Aufopferung der Bürger dem Drucke des hereinbrechenden Unheils erliegt; hier kann man das Eingreifen des Staates keine hindernde Bevormundung der eigenen Interessen der Bürger, sondern die notwendige Rettung derselben nennen.

Kein Mittel steht zum Beispiel dem *einzelnen* Land- *und Forst*wirt zur Hand, der Einschleppung von Viehseuchen entgegenzutreten, oder das Überhandnehmen der Reblaus oder des Borkenkäfers zu verhindern.

Der Staat aber kann leicht gegen die Viehseuche, durch eine Viehkontumaz, einen Kordon ziehen, oder die Einfuhr fremder Reben verbieten, auch kann er
48 r großartige Maßregeln gegen den Borkenkäfer ergreifen, indem er größere Waldungen, in denen derselbe wütet, ausschlagen läßt und den Eigentümern den Schaden ersetzt. Alle diese Mittel kann ein einzelner niemals anwenden, da sie meistens über *einen* Besitz hinaus sich erstrecken und also nur durch die Gesamtheit, den Staat, angeordnet werden dürfen.[21]

Bei den Handelsbeziehungen zu auswärtigen Staaten tritt uns derselbe Fall der unbedingten *Notwendigkeit der* Hilfe der Regierung entgegen; der Industrielle ist bestrebt, seine Waren in fremde Länder zu exportieren, wodurch er sowohl wie der Staat Nutzen hat, denn Handel und Verkehr fördern im hohen Maße die Volkswirtschaft; doch der einzelne Bürger kann unmöglich seinen Produkten in einem fremden Staat Einlaß verschaffen, er als ein Sandkorn dieses Riesenberges des gesamten Volkes verschwindet in diesen großen Interessen, hier muß die Gesamtheit zum Wohle der Teile wirken, und die einzelnen Staaten müssen in diesem Falle wie Personen untereinander ihre Interessen verhandeln; da werden
48 v Handelsverträge geschlossen, welche die Handelsinteressen der einzelnen *fördern* und dadurch die Blüte des Staates in einem der wesentlichsten Punkte *begründen*.[22]

21 Rau (1854), S. 200, nennt für die Bodenpolitik zwei Gründe: 'Ein Beistand der Staatsgewalt (ist) erforderlich... namentlich 1) wenn die Unternehmung nur im Großen, nach einem einheitlichen Plane ... auszuführen ist, oder wenn 2) die Rechte einzelner Grundeigenthümer die Anwendung der zweckmäßigsten Mittel verhindern.'

22 Rau (1854), S. 320: 'Für den Handel zwischen zwei Ländern kann durch Übereinkunft beider Regierungen den beiderseitigen Kaufleuten eine Milderung oder Befreiung der bestehenden Beschränkungen, sowie manche andere Erleichterungen ihrer Unternehmungen verschafft werden. Solche Handelsverträge... haben dem auswärtigen Handel viel genützt, ihm neue Richtungen eröffnet und eine Annäherung an seine Freigebung bewirkt'. Charakteristischerweise erwähnt Menger überhaupt nicht die folgenden Warnungen vor negativ wirkenden Handelsverträgen sowie die langen Ausführungen von Rau zur Zollpolitik, obwohl diese weitgehend liberal inspiriert sind. Siehe zu Handelsverträgen im gleichen Sinne Smith (1776) V.i.e.2 und 4 sowie IV.vi.

If, under such circumstances, the principle of individual responsibility and self-reliance of citizens in economic matters were to be carried to its extreme, it would be most harmful to them and thereby to the state. The very art of government consists of realizing the precise moment when the greatest diligence and most valiant sacrifice of citizens may yield to impending disaster; in such cases, 47 v
government interference must not be seen as paternalistic obstruction of the citizens' personal interests, but rather as their necessary rescue.

The individual farmer or forest-owner, for example, can do nothing to prevent cattle plagues from being brought into the country or to stop Phylloxera or the bark-beetle from spreading.

The state, however, can easily take measures to contain a cattle plague, by ordering a quarantine, or it can prohibit the import of vines from abroad; it can also fight the bark-beetle on a large scale by ordering sizeable tracts of infested 48 r
forest to be cut down and refunding the owners for the damage. All these measures can never be adopted by an individual, as they usually extend over more than one private property and therefore can only be ordered by the community, by the state.[21]

In trade relations with foreign countries we encounter an analogous situation where support by the government is indispensable; the industrialist seeks to export his products to foreign countries, this being advantageous to him and to the state, since trade and commerce greatly boost the performance of the national economy; but the individual citizen with his products cannot possibly gain access to a foreign country; among all the big interests, he disappears like a grain of sand in the huge mountain of an entire people; here the whole must act for the benefit of its parts, and the several states must negotiate their interests just like individual persons; commercial treaties are signed which promote individual trade interests and thereby cause a state to prosper in one of the most essential areas.[22] 48 v

21 This follows the somewhat more explicit treatment in Rau (1854), p. 200.

22 Smith (1776), V.i.e.4: 'The protection of trade in general has always been considered as essential to the defence of the commonwealth, and upon that account, a necessary part of the duty of the executive power'. Also V.i.e.2: 'Some particular branches of commerce, which are carried on with barbarous and uncivilized nations, require extraordinary protection'. In IV.vi., Smith speaks 'Of Treaties of Commerce'. Rau (1854), p. 320, on commercial treaties is evidently a proximate source of this passage. Note that Menger – in contrast to Smith or Rau – does not even mention import tariffs.

In solchen Fällen, wie diesen letzterwähnten, ersieht man am besten, welchen großen und schönen Spielraum der Staat zu Eingriffen in die wirtschaftlichen Bestrebungen der einzelnen hat, ohne im mindesten sich der Bevormundung oder Einschränkung der Freiheit derselben schuldig zu machen. [CM am Rand: Einflicken]

Wo die Volkswirtschaft, als die Hauptquelle der Entwicklung für das Volk, durch positive Förderungsmittel gehoben werden kann, welche aber die schwache Kraft der einzelnen nicht zu schaffen in der Lage ist, soll es der Staat tun, dies ist eine der wichtigsten Aufgaben seiner Vertreter; in der Erkenntnis des richtigen Augenblickes und in der Wahl der wirksamsten Mittel besteht die Kunst des Regierens in volkswirtschaftlichen Dingen.

49 r [Auf der 3. Umschlagseite des Heftes mit Anweisung 'Einflicken': Wir haben nun den ersten Fall in Betracht gezogen, wo der Staat, ohne eigentliche Bevormundung der Bürger in die Wirtschaft derselben fördernd eingreifen kann, wir übergehen jetzt zu einer anderen Gruppe von Fällen.]

Such instances as the ones just mentioned make one realize most clearly the wide and welcome latitude within which the state can intervene in individual economic efforts without becoming at all guilty of paternalism or infringements on personal freedom. [CM in the margin: insert]

Government should step in where the national economy – the foundation of a people's development – can be improved by positive measures of support which the feeble power of individuals could not bring to pass; this is one of the most important tasks of its representatives; in economic matters the art of government consists in determining the right moment and the most effective means.

[On the inside of the back cover of this notebook, with the instruction 'insert': 49 r
So far, we have considered the first case, i.e. where the state can beneficially intervene in the economic activities of its citizens without actual paternalism; we shall now turn to another set of cases.]

Politische Ökonomie VII. 1876 Februar

Über den Nutzen der staatlichen Beeinflussung der Volkswirtschaft und
50 r die Grenzen derselben (II)

Also nicht bloß zur Beseitigung von Übeln, sondern auch bei Gründung von Unternehmungen, die auf die wirtschaftlichen Bestrebungen fördernd einwirken, aber wegen ihrer Dimensionen die Mittel einzelner und selbst privater Gesellschaften übersteigen, muß der Staat zum Wohle aller in die Volkswirtschaft positiv einwirken.

Es sind dies keine *bevormundenden* Eingriffe in die Bestrebungen der Bürger, sondern ganz im Gegenteile die Mittel, um dieselben zu fördern, außerdem sind es wichtige Momente für die großen Zwecke des ganzen Staates, die demselben den Stempel der Kultur aufdrücken.

Besondere Beispiele für diese Art von Unternehmungen als *dauernde* Zeugnisse der Sorge des Ganzen für das Wohl der Teile, und dadurch für die eigene Macht desselben, sind wichtige Landstraßen, Eisenbahnen *und Kanäle*, die den Verkehr[1] und im selben Maße auch den allgemeinen Wohlstand heben und zugleich Hauptbedingungen fürs Gedeihen eines modernen Staates sind/bilden.

50 v Auch der Bau von Schulen[2] ist ein schönes Gebiet für den Staat zur Kundgebung seiner Sorgen ob des Gedeihens der wirtschaftlichen Bestrebungen seiner Bürger.

Dem einzelnen Bürger, der sein Leben in steter Arbeit, im fleißigen, redlichen Gewinne zum Zweck der Gründung einer glücklichen Familie, getragen von wahrem Patriotismus und echter Bürgertugend, zugebracht hat, ist es eine der ersten Sorgen, in seinen Söhnen würdige Nachfolger und brave Männer zu erblicken, die mit einem den jetzigen Zeiten angemessenen Wissen ausgerüstet sind. Der Tag ist für ihn mit Arbeit ausgefüllt, und er erfühlt, daß es ihm an Zeit und oft auch an dem Wissen gebricht, seinen Sohn so auszubilden, daß er, gebildeter wie er und um die Fortschritte der Kultur, die seit seiner Jugend gemacht wurden, bereichert, seinen Beruf einstens übernehme.

1 Folgt eng Smith (1776), V.i.d.l.

2 Menger empfiehlt nur den Bau von Schulen, nicht jedoch den staatlichen Betrieb des Unterrichtswesens. Das ist umso erstaunlicher angesichts der Tatsache, daß die Lehrer in dem damals bereits sehr ausgebauten öffentlichen Schulwesen in Österreich die zahlenstärkste Gruppe der Beamten waren. Ähnliche Vorbehalte in bezug auf das Schulwesen schon bei Smith (1776), V.i.f.55.

Political economy VII. 1876 February

On the Benefits and Limits of Government Intervention in the Economy (II) 50 r

Government thus has to intervene in economic life for the benefit of all not only to redress grievances, but also to establish enterprises that promote economic efforts but, because of their size, are beyond the means of individuals and even private corporations.

These are not paternalistic measures to restrain the citizens' activities; on the contrary, they furnish the means for promoting such activities; furthermore, they are of some importance for those great ends of the whole state that make it appear civilized and cultured.

Important roads, railways and canals that improve the general well-being by improving traffic and communication are special examples of this kind of enterprise and lasting evidence of the concern of the state for the well-being of its parts and thereby for its own power;[1] at the same time, they are/constitute major prerequisites for the prosperity of a modern state.

The building of schools,[2] too, is a suitable field for government to prove its 50 v
concern with the success of its citizens' economic efforts.

The individual citizen who has spent his life working steadily, diligently, and honestly making a living to found a happy family and who is motivated by true patriotism and genuine civic virtues, is most eager to see his sons grow into worthy successors and upright men, equipped with knowledge that is adequate for present times. He spends his day working and senses that he lacks the time and often also the knowledge to educate his son so that the latter – better trained than himself and better off for the advances of civilization achieved since his own youth – could eventually step into the father's trade.

1 Smith (1776), V.i.d.l, recommends 'the erection and maintenance of the publick works which facilitate the commerce of any country, such as good roads, bridges, navigable canals, harbours'. Menger omits bridges and harbours, while adding railways.

2 Note that only the building of schools is recommended here, not the public maintenance of teachers (a typical and large part of public expenditure in Austria), about which Smith had had some reservations. Cf. Smith, V.i.f.55: 'The publick can facilitate (popular education) by establishing in every parish or district a little school, where children may be taught for a reward so moderate, that even a common labourer can afford it; the master being partly, but not wholly paid by the publick'.

In den gewöhnlichen Unterrichtsanstalten[3] sieht er seinen Sohn zum gebildeten Mann heranwachsen, dem jede andere Laufbahn offen steht,[4] der aber schwerlich in das Nest zurückkehrt, aus dem er ausgeflogen, und kaum den Beruf seines Vaters ergreifen wird.

51 r Darum ist es für ihn eine der größten Wohltaten, wenn der Staat in jenen Sorgen, die ihn vielleicht oft am meisten bekümmern und gegen die er keine Mittel hat, durch die Gründung von Landwirtschafts- oder Gewerbe-Schulen[5] hilfreich entgegenkommt.

Doch gerade diese Anstalten vereinigen auch für die Gesamtheit einen großen Vorteil neben dem, den sie den Bestrebungen einzelner gewähren; denn die Volkswirtschaft, als einen der Hauptzweige der Bildung für den kultivierten Teil der Bevölkerung, findet man neben den großen Opfern, die für die anderen Wissenschaften gebracht werden, so wenig praktisch gelehrt;[6] und so leicht kann das Volk, das doch größtenteils seinen wirtschaftlichen Bestrebungen die größte Aufmerksamkeit widmet, in denselben veralten, und der Stillstand in diesem Zweige der Kultur wird sich wie in keinem anderen für das Gedeihen des ganzen Staates fühlbar machen.

Darum ist die Gründung von solchen Schulen eines der Hauptmittel des
51 v Staates, durch welches er sein Interesse an dem Glücke der Teile, für diese und sich selbst gleich segensreich, bezeigen kann, ohne daß man ihm auch in diesem Falle den Vorwurf der Bevormundung machen kann.

Den einzelnen Zweigen der praktischen Volkswirtschaft kann der Staat gleichfalls hilfreich durch positive Förderungsmittel zur Hand gehen, natürlich nur in solchen Dingen, die den Bürgern Nutzen gewähren, aber die Mittel des einzelnen übersteigen: sie haben eigentlich den Zweck, als Eigentum der Gesamtheit ein für alle Teile nützliches Gemeingut zu werden.

Dies ist z.B. der Fall, wenn der Staat der Landwirtschaft und besonders der Viehzucht durch den Ankauf hervorragend geeigneter Zuchttiere helfen will, deren Preis über die Mittel der meisten hinausreicht,[7] und dadurch, daß sie zum Eigentum
52 r des Staates wurden, ihren Zweck, allen gleich zu dienen, am besten erfüllen.

[3] Die nächsten vier Absätze folgen sehr eng Rau (1854), S. 39, wo 'Die Geschicklichkeit der Arbeiter' zurückgeführt wird auf 'Volks- (Elementar-)Schulen' als Bildungsgrundlage einerseits, auf berufsbildende 'besondere Schulen' andererseits.

[4] Smith (1776), V.i.f.52, sieht in der Bildung für die breite Bevölkerungsmasse eine wichtige Staatsaufgabe, wobei §§ 49 und 50 – teilweise ähnlich moralisierende – Begründungen enthalten.

[5] Rau (1854), S. 39, spricht einerseits von 'Schulen für Landwirthschaft, Forstwesen…', andererseits von 'Arbeits- oder sogenannten Industrieschulen, in denen der gewöhnliche Schulunterricht mit der Unterweisung und Uebung in Handarbeiten verbunden wird'.

[6] Smith (1776), V.i.f.46, spricht sich für praktisch orientierte Schulbildung und gegen jeden Scholastizismus aus.

[7] Rau (1854), S. 340: 'Die Rindviehzucht verdient eine sorgfältigere Beförderung von Seiten der Staatsgewalt, als sie gewöhnlich erhält, weil mittlere und kleine Landwirthe, sich nicht selbst mit guten Zuchtstieren versorgen können … und die Wahl der besten Stämme (Schläge, Rassen) auf den Gewinn der Landwirthe großen Einfluß ausübt'. Bemerkenswert ist, daß

In the ordinary schools[3] he will see his son grow into a well-educated man to whom any career is open,[4] but who is not likely to return to the nest he has left and take up his father's trade.

It is of the greatest possible benefit to him therefore if the state establishes 51 r
agricultural or vocational training institutions[5] and relieves him of worries that often weigh most heavily on him, but about which he can do nothing.

These very institutions are of great advantage to the community, too, apart from their beneficial effect upon individual efforts; although it provides one of the major fields of training for the educated part of the population, the national economy hardly figures as a subject of practical instruction, while great sacrifices are made for the other sciences;[6] and while a people may, for the most part, pay the closest attention to its economic activities, these may yet become obsolete, and stagnation in this area of civilization will be felt like none other as far as general prosperity is concerned.

Therefore the establishment of such schools is one of the best ways for the
state to prove – without undue paternalism – its interest in the happiness of its 51 v
component parts, a happiness equally beneficial to them and to itself.

The state may also well support the various sectors of the national economy by actual subsidies, of course only when it is useful to the citizens but surpasses their individual means: strictly speaking, such subsidies are intended to become a useful public good, owned by the community as a whole.

This will occur, for example, if the state wants to promote agriçulture and especially cattle breeding by purchasing prime quality breeding animals whose price exceeds most people's means;[7] by becoming public property, the animals
best serve their purpose: to serve all alike. 52 r

3 The next four paragraphs closely follow Rau (1854), p. 39, interspersed with ideas possibly taken from Smith. Rau distinguishes the complementary functions of elementary schooling and of vocational schools, in the same way as Menger.

4 Cf. Smith (1776), V.i.f.52: '… the education of the common people requires, perhaps, in a civilized and commercial society, the attention of the publick more than that of people of some rank and fortune'. Reasons are given in 50. In 49, it is also pointed out that government education may be necessary 'to prevent the almost entire corruption and degeneracy of the great body of the people'.

5 Rau (1854), p. 39 ff., considers both agricultural schools and vocational training for industrial employment.

6 Smith (1776), V.i.f.46, seems to think it appropriate to have a modern education, one for which there is 'some demand' and which conforms to the 'circumstances of the times'. He is highly sceptical of any scholasticism.

7 Closely following Rau (1854), p. 340. Rau speaks of breeding bulls ('Zuchtstiere', sounding very much like the German word for breeding animals, viz. 'Zuchttiere', which the Crown

In dieser, in allen vorangegangenen Beispielen erwähnten Weise soll der Staat selbst tätig in das wirtschaftliche Leben seiner Bürger eingreifen. Hier sind diese Eingriffe keine Bevormundungen, Überwachungen und daher Hindernisse, sondern der segensreiche Schutz, die Vertretung und die Hilfe der Gesamtheit zu seinem und der Teile größten Glücke.

In solcher Weise muß *also* der Staat seinen guten Einfluß geltend machen, um jene Hindernisse zu überwältigen, oder *jene* Mittel zu schaffen, die von ihm leichte Mühe fordern, aber den Kräften der einzelnen unmöglich wären.

Neben *diesen Maßregeln zur Beseitigung der Hindernisse einer blühenden Volkswirtschaft und den* positiven Förderungsmitteln derselben gibt es noch eine Art nutzbringender Einflußnahme, wo der Staat *zum Schutz der Gesamtheit* gegen schädliche Bestrebungen einzelner in deren *wirtschaftliche Verhältnisse* mit mächtiger Hand eingreift.

52 v Hier tritt uns nicht die sorgsame Unterstützung der Bürger in jenen Fällen, wo ihre Kräfte zu schwach sind, ihre *wirtschaftlichen Ziele zu erreichen*, entgegen, sondern *eine Beschränkung der gemeinschädlichen Bestrebungen einzelner*. Diese Maßregel zieht ebenso segensreiche Folgen nach sich, wie die früher erwähnten Beispiele der Hilfe aller für die Teile. Wir haben es nun mit einem Falle zu tun, der an Willkür und Störung der Bürger in ihren wirtschaftlichen Bestrebungen erinnert. Für einzelne werden diese Maßregeln des Staates auch zu Hemmnissen in ihren Bestrebungen, aber nur dann, wenn dieselben dem Wohle aller zuwider laufen.

Wenn der Egoismus einzelner und ihre Gewinnsucht den Interessen vieler ein Hindernis bietet, ist der Moment gekommen, in dem der Staat die gleichen Rechte aller wahren soll, und *zum Wohle des Ganzen* kräftig in die Tätigkeiten des einzelnen eingreifen und dessen Egoismus in die gesetzlichen Schranken weisen muß. Dies sind meistens für den Staat schwierige Fälle, besonders, wenn
53 r das Interesse des einzelnen auch scheinbar die momentanen Interessen vieler fördert, in Wirklichkeit aber sie vielleicht für lange Zeiten hinaus schädigen würde.

Leicht erhält die Regierung dann den Ruf der Einmengung in die wirtschaftlichen Bestrebungen der Bürger, und ebenso leicht verfällt sie in diesen Fehler, wenn sie mit ihrer Einmengung, was der äußerste letzte Schritt sein muß, zu früh beginnt, bevor sie sich noch völlig von der unbedingten Notwendigkeit dieser Maßregel überzeugt hat.

Und trotzdem kann eben durch diese Art der Hilfe, wenn sie richtig angewendet wird, oft am meisten geholfen werden; denn der Schaden, den der einzelne durch *eigennütziges* Verfahren in seinen wirtschaftlichen Bestrebungen auf Kosten anderer anrichten kann, ist ein gewaltiger, der oft über den Moment hinaus auch auf spätere Zeiten schädlich wirken kann.

Menger unter den vielen möglichen Stoßrichtungen der Agrarpolitik, die Rau herausarbeitet, nicht einmal die Trockenlegung von Sümpfen oder eine Bewässerung erwähnt (Rau, ebenda, S. 200 f.).

In this way, as mentioned in all of the cases above, the state shall actively intervene in the economic life of its citizens. Such intervention spells neither paternalism nor the exercise of control and thus a handicap, but wholesome protection and the representation and support of the community for the greatest happiness of the whole and its parts.

In this way then the state must assert its benign influence to overcome any obstacles or furnish the resources it can easily raise on its own but which cannot be raised by individual efforts.

In addition to the actual subsidies and to these measures for removing obstacles to prosperity in an economy, there is still another kind of useful intervention, namely when the state interferes powerfully with the economic activities of certain individuals in order to protect the community against their detrimental schemings.

This is not a case of caring support of citizens too weak to attain their 52 v
economic ends, but of restraining individual actions that are detrimental to the community. The effects are just as beneficial as in the previous examples of how the state aids its members. But now the situation suggests arbitrariness and interference with the economic activities of citizens. The pertinent measures taken by the state will indeed obstruct some people's actions; but only when these run counter to the common good.

If and when the egoism and greed of a few become an obstacle to the interests of the many, the time has come for the state to defend the equal rights of all and, for the benefit of society, to interfere forcibly with the activities of an individual and put his egoism in its legally defined place. For the most part, these are difficult cases for the state, especially if the interest of the individual seems to promote the temporary interests of many, though in reality it would harm them in the 53 r
long run.

Government is then easily denounced for interfering with the economic activities of citizens; just as easily it may make a mistake if its intervention, which must be the very last step taken, occurs before it has made sure of the absolute necessity of this measure.

And yet, often this sort of remedy can be most useful when properly administered; for the damage that an individual can do by selfishly pursuing his economic interests at other people's expense is enormous and – over and above the concerns of the moment – often may have long-term detrimental effects.

Prince uses). The purchase of breeding bulls, of course, makes more sense.

Surprisingly, Menger does not mention any of the other measures of public agricultural policy suggested by Rau in the latter's hundreds of pages, not even irrigation or draining.

Zu solchen Übeln ist *beispielsweise* den Fabriksherren Gelegenheit gegeben,
53 v weswegen auch der Staat besonders ihre Arbeiter vor zu schlechter und ihrem Wohle nachteiliger Behandlung schützen muß.[8]

Es ist natürlich ein Hauptinteresse des Staates, daß ein so großer Teil seiner Bevölkerung und gerade einer der Haupt*faktoren* im großen Ganzen, nämlich die Arbeiter, nur durch die Willkür einzelner Reicher zum bloßen Wohle dieser, bei ihrer ohnedies *kümmerlichen Lebensweise* nicht noch neue Leiden hinzugefügt bekommen. Der Gesamtheit muß es stets darum zu tun sein, den allgemeinen Fortschritt der Kultur zu erhalten, deshalb darf weder der Staat durch eigene Maßregeln ein Hindernis dieser großen Entwicklung in den Weg legen, noch darf er eine Hemmung durch die egoistischen Bestrebungen einzelner dulden, da durch diese oft das Glück jetziger sowie folgender Generationen untergraben werden kann.[9]

Besonders begegnet uns dieser Fall, *wie bereits erwähnt*, bei Fabriken; hier hat der Fabriksherr die Gelegenheit, durch Milde, Wohlwollen und gute
54 r Behandlung die Bildung des Geistes, wie des Gemütes vieler zu *befördern* und sie dadurch zu braven Staatsbürgern zu machen;[10] während er durch rauhe Behandlung, durch Überbürdung mit Arbeit, die ohnedies auf einer tiefen Stufe stehenden Arbeiter vollkommen verwildern kann, so daß aus ihnen die wahre Hefe des Volkes entsteht. So wachsen dann die sogenannten Proletarier und Kommunisten heran, die das Werk der schlechten Behandlung der Reichen sind und nun zu ihrem Gespenste wurden.

Selbst auf das körperliche Gedeihen der Arbeiterbevölkerung können die Fabriksherren einen entscheidenden Einfluß nehmen;[11] und eben in diesem Punkte muß der Staat aufmerksam das Leben in den Fabriken verfolgen, um eine Degenerierung des Arbeiterstandes durch Überbürdung mit Arbeit zu verhindern. Daher wird es den Fabriksbesitzern nicht gestattet, ihre Arbeiter über ein

8 Siehe Smith (1776), I.viii.12,13, zur Kritik an den Arbeitgebern. Die nächsten 10 Absätze folgen insbesondere Rau (1854), II, S. 52–63.

9 Zusammenfassung des Grundgedankens von Rau (1854), II, Kapitel 'Pflege der Gewerke' (sic), S. 1–143. Rau sagt auf S. 1: 'Dieselben kommen…größtentheils miteinander überein. Daher ist die Regierung der Mühe überhoben, für jedes einzelne Gewerk auf ähnliche Weise zu sorgen, wie es bei den Zweigen der Landwirthschaft Bedürfniß ist'. Gewerbefreiheit in der Industriepolitik wird also mit den geringeren externen Effekten begründet. 'Gewerbefreiheit ist, den Erfahrungen mehrerer Länder zufolge, zwar von manchen ungünstigen Erscheinungen nicht frei, jedoch im ganzen überwiegend vortheilhaft gewesen' (S. 23).

10 Rau (1855), S. 523, hält fest: 'Die Uebelstände, welche in moralischer und wirthschaftlicher Hinsicht aus einer großen Ausdehnung des Fabrikswesens entstehen, und wegen des Daseins vieler vermögensloser, leicht aufzureizender Lohnarbeiter selbst die Sicherheit im Staate bedrohen können, lassen sich durch viele Erfahrungen nachweisen… Indeß sind jene Uebel wenigstens zum Theile vermeidlich, indem, abgesehen von dem, was die Staatsgewalt zur Besserung der Arbeiter thun kann, das fleißige, haushälterische und gesittete Verhalten der letzteren, unter dem Einfluß guter Volksschulen, eines guten Religionsunterrichtes und äußerer Ermunterung zur Sparsamkeit, ferner bei einer vortheilhaften Einwirkung der Fabrikherren auf den Lebenswandel ihrer Gehülfen, sehr Vieles vermag, um den Zustand derselben zu verbessern'.

11 Rau (1854), II, S. 58: 'Auch in der ganzen Classe der Fabrikarbeiter lassen sich viele ungünstige

Factory owners, for example, have the opportunity to do evil in this manner, therefore government must protect their workers from being treated too badly 53 v
and injuriously.[8]

Naturally, it is a major concern of the state that manual workers, who lead a wretched life, yet are a large part of the population and one of the mainstays of society, not be made to suffer even more by the caprice and for the sake of a few rich people. The polity must always try to maintain the general progress of civilization and therefore the state must neither hinder this great development by measures of its own nor tolerate its obstruction by the selfish actions of some individuals, which often may jeopardize the happiness of present and future generations.[9]

As mentioned above, we encounter this problem especially in factories; here the factory owner has the opportunity to further the intellectual and emotional development of many people by gentleness, benevolence, and good treatment 54 r
and thus turn them into good citizens;[10] by treating them roughly and overworking them, he can cause the workers, who are on a very low level any way, utterly to degenerate – to become the very scum of the population. Thus, the so-called proletarians and communists come into existence, as the result of the ill-treatment by the rich, who are now haunted by their spectre.

The factory owners may influence decisively even the physical development of the working class;[11] and for this very reason, the state must pay close attention to life in the factories in order to prevent workers from degenerating physically as a result of their being overworked. Therefore, factory owners are not allowed to let their labourers work more than a certain maximum [in the margin: 15 hours], even if workers were willing to submit to such disastrous treatment, pressed either by necessity or induced by a higher wage; the government prohibits, for example, a 15-hour day in factories[12] since the worker's physical

8 In that part of the Wealth of Nations which deals with the 'duties of the sovereign' Smith does not speak of the maltreatment of workers by their employers, nor does he consider preventive legislation against it, but he castigates the attempts of 'masters' to lower wages in I.viii.12,13.
The next 10 paragraphs mainly follow Rau (1854), II, pp. 52–63, on 'factories'.

9 This paragraph contains the gist of Rau (1854), II, pp. 1–143, on 'industrial policy'. Rau is of the opinion that the branches of manufacturing industry 'get along with each other for the most part'. In other words, they have few 'external effects' on one another, unlike the different branches of agriculture. This makes for freedom of trade as the general principle of industrial policy.

10 Rau (1855), p. 523, considers how masses of 'easily provoked wage labourers' may endanger public safety. He stresses the importance of the workers' moral education by the factory owners.

11 Rau (1854), part II, p. 58 ff. Effects on 'health and morals' of factory workers are mentioned; the copious footnotes summarize numerous reports from England (e.g. Chadwick), France, Belgium etc.

12 This goes beyond Rau (1854), II, p. 54, where it is only argued that the earnings of children

gewisses Maß arbeiten zu lassen [am Rand: 15 Arbeitsstunden], selbst wenn diese durch Not oder höheren Lohn zu dieser ihnen verderblichen Behandlung sich freiwillig veranlaßt fühlen würden, z.B. werden 15 Arbeitsstunden täglich in Fabriken von der Regierung aus verboten,[12] da die physische Kraft und die
54 v Gesundheit des Arbeiters darunter leidet, wenn er eine so große Stundenanzahl am Tag in schwerer Arbeit verbringt, wodurch seine geistige Entwicklung völlig abgestumpft wird und er zu einer Maschine herabsinkt. [Am Rand: Unmündige Kinder!]

Ein noch verderblicheres Übel des Fabrikslebens ist die Zuziehung unmündiger Kinder zur Arbeit; dadurch leidet die körperliche und geistige Entwicklung ganzer Generationen des Arbeiterstandes; denn die schwere Arbeit in so jungen Jahren untergräbt für immer die Gesundheit und hindert ein kräftiges Wachstum; ferners schwindet dadurch die Möglichkeit eines geregelten Schulbesuches und nebst dem Mangel jeder Bildung führt auch der fortwährende Umgang mit den oft verderbten älteren Arbeitern eine völlige moralische Verkommenheit herbei.[13]

Hier ist es die Sache des Staates, im Interesse eines so wichtigen und großen Standes mit Macht aufzutreten, um dadurch das Interesse der Gesamtheit zu wahren.

So wichtig es für den Staat ist, viele und reiche Fabriksbesitzer aufweisen
55 r zu können, die ein Hauptfaktor der allgemeinen Entwicklung und der Wohlhabenheit sind, so ist es dennoch seine Pflicht, bei Eintritt der obenerwähnten Fälle in ihre wirtschaftlichen Bestrebungen einzugreifen und lieber ihren Mehrgewinn zu hindern, um dadurch ein großes, noch allgemeineres Interesse des Staates zu wahren und eine ganze *Bevölkerungsklasse*, auf deren Schultern der Bestand jeder Industrie mitberuht, vor Schadennahme in ihren *wichtigsten Interessen* zu schützen.

Hier bringt der Staat seinem momentanen Vorteil, der unstreitig im Reichtum seiner Bürger liegt, zugunsten der Gerechtigkeit und Menschlichkeit ein Opfer, aus dem aber ein dauernder großer Segen für die Gesamtheit, *und zwar auch für die Volkswirtschaft*, erblüht. [Gemeint ist: 'Hier bringt der Staat seinen … Vorteil … zum Opfer …'. Hrsg.]

Erscheinungen in Bezug auf Gesundheit, Sittlichkeit, Erziehung der Kinder, dürftige Lage und Gefahr der Verarmung wahrnehmen'. Die Fußnoten gehen ausführlich auf englische Berichte (z.B. Chadwick), französische, belgische usw. ein.

12 Rau (1854), II, erwähnt S. 54 nur, daß 'der Verdienst der Kinder eine wohlthätige Vermehrung des Einkommens vieler dürftiger Familien bildet' (meine Hervorhebung), und nennt S. 57 f. in den Fußnoten nur Stundenbeschränkungen für Kinder und Jugendliche, wobei für die zweitgenannten die höchste angegebene Zahl zwölf Stunden ist. Smith (1776), I.viii.44, andererseits spricht von der Überarbeitung der Arbeiter aus Gewinnsucht, insbesondere bei der Akkordarbeit.

13 Alle Argumente finden sich bei Rau, ebenda (insbesondere Gefahren für die Gesundheit und für den Schulbesuch der Kinder) ausführlich dargestellt; weiters Rau (1855), § 398a, wo die Gefahren für die Sittlichkeit besonders hervorgehoben werden. Da Menger stark kürzend zusammenfaßt, sind die Formulierungen von ihm.

strength and health suffer if he spends that number of hours daily at hard labour, thereby having his mental faculties blunted completely and sinking to the state of a machine. [In the margin: Children and minors!] 54 v

An even more disastrous feature of factory life is the employment of young children; this impairs the physical and intellectual development of whole generations of workers, for hard labour at a tender age undermines a person's health permanently and impedes vigorous growth; in addition, regular attendance at school becomes impossible and, apart from the lack of formal education, continued association with often depraved older workers also leads to utter corruption.[13]

Here it is the task of the state to act in the interest of the community as a whole by intervening strongly on behalf of such an important and populous class.

Important as it is to have many wealthy factory owners, as a mainstay of general development and prosperity, the state is nonetheless obliged to intervene in their economic activities in such cases and rather to prevent additional profits from accruing to those factory owners, if this is in the greater, general interest of the state, and to protect the vital interests of a whole class of the population from being harmed, since the existence of industry rests on its shoulders, too. 55 r

In this situation, the state sacrifices some of its present good fortune, which the wealth of its citizens undoubtedly is, in the interest of justice and humanity; from this sacrifice, however, there will be derived a great and lasting benefit to the community and that is to say: to the national economy.

are welcome additional income for very poor families. The work hours discussed in the footnotes pertain to children and juveniles only, the highest number of hours permissible being stated as 12, however, and not 15. Smith (1776), I.viii.44, says of 'workmen': 'Mutual emulation and the desire of greater gain, frequently prompted them to over-work themselves, and to hurt their health by excessive labour'.

13 This recapitulates Rau (1854), II, § 202a, where the effect of child labour on health is considered and the importance of guaranteeing school attendance is treated at length. Cf. also Rau (1855), § 398a (quoted in the passage mentioned above), where the dangers to morality, not only of children, but also of women, are enumerated.

Das egoistische Interesse einzelner kann oft wegen eines momentanen Vorteils zur Ausführung einer Handlung führen, die zwar die Grenzen *der freien Benützung* des Eigentumes nicht überschreitet, aber dennoch für viele, *und selbst*
55 v für den Eigentümer, einen dauernden Schaden herbeiführen kann.[14] In diesem Falle ist es die Sache des Staates, dieses Unheil durch gute Ratschläge oder durch Verordnungen zu verhindern; es ist zwar ein starker Eingriff in die wirtschaftlichen Bestrebungen des einzelnen, der aber nur dort bedingt ist, *wo das durch den Egoismus des einzelnen bedrohte Interesse der Gesamtheit es erfordert*, und daher die schützende Vorsicht der Gesamtheit zur Notwendigkeit wird. [Am Rand: Ausholzung der Wälder]

Es begegnet uns dieses Verhältnis besonders *auch* bei waldwirtschaftlichen Angelegenheiten.

Oft will ein Waldbesitzer im Gebirge, um sich in einer vorübergehenden Verlegenheit Geld zu verschaffen,[15] seine auf Höhen liegenden Wälder ausholzen; daraus entsteht *leicht* ein Schaden auf ewige Zeiten, da die Regengüsse als Gießbäche abfließen und den ganzen Humus herunterschwemmen,[16] Überschwemmungen im Frühjahr, *dagegen Dürre im Sommer* und verschiedene andere *Schädigungen der Landwirtschaft in der Ebene* sind die Folgen einer ähnlichen Waldwirtschaft *auf den Höhen*,[17] *Nachteile überdies, welche* mit der Zeit immer ärger *zu*
56 r werden *pflegen*. Südtirol, Istrien, Dalmatien sind die traurigen Beweise der blinden Habgier der einzelnen und der unaufmerksamen Nachlässigkeit *früherer* Regierungen.

[14] Menger folgt hier (wie unten ersichtlich) Raus Überlegungen zur Waldnutzung. Rau (1854), S. 309 f.: 'Die Waldungen einzelner Staatsbürger dürfen in keinem Falle einer so starken Bevormundung unterworfen werden, als die den Körperschaften angehörenden (Rau hatte davor die mangelnde Motivation und Vorsorge der Verwalter fremden Eigentums bei Gemeinden, Stiftungen, kirchlichem Eigentum usw. angesprochen; Hrsg.), denn bei jenen ist es der Eigenthümer selbst, welcher die Bewirthschaftung vornimmt oder veranstaltet und dieser sollte in der Verfügung über sein Vermögen so wenig gehindert werden, als es mit höheren Rücksichten vereinbar ist ... Dennoch läßt die Aufhebung aller Beschränkungen manche gemeinschädliche Folgen befürchten...'

[15] Rau (1854), S. 309: 'Die Handlungsweise des einzelnen Waldbesitzers, mag sie nun auf Berechnung des in kurzer Frist zu ziehenden Gewinnes an Capital und Zins, oder auf Trägheit und Unwissenheit beruhen, zieht bisweilen den Untergang von Waldungen nach sich'. Interessanterweise geht Menger, wenn der Kronprinz ihn richtig wiedergibt, nicht auf die mögliche 'Trägheit und Unwissenheit' des Waldbesitzers ein. Eine hohe Zeitpräferenz ist ein auf unvollkommenem Kapitalmarkt unausgeglichener Präferenzunterschied, 'Trägheit' hingegen Funktionsuntüchtigkeit der Wirtschafter.

[16] Rau (1854), S. 311 f.: 'Waldungen auf hohen Bergrücken dienen ... zur fortdauernden Anziehung und Festhaltung atmosphärischer Feuchtigkeit, wodurch sie den Bächen und Flüssen fortdauernde Nahrung verschaffen, während von entwaldeten Bergen in einzelnen Zeitpunkten verheerende Gießbäche (!) herabstürzen'. Die Verwendung des nicht alltäglichen Ausdrucks 'Gießbäche' durch den Kronprinzen zeigt einerseits, wie wörtlich Menger Rau folgte, andererseits wieder einmal das wortgetreue Gedächtnis des Schülers.

[17] Rau (1854), S. 312: 'Durch die Zerstörung der Wälder (wird) das Hinabschwemmen des entblößten Bodens, das Überschütten tieferer Grundstücke ... verursacht'.

Because of a momentary advantage, the selfish interests of individuals may often lead to an action that can still cause permanent damage to many, including the owner, although it does not overstep the limits of uninhibited use of property.[14] In this case the state ought to prevent such damage by persuasion 55 v
or by decree; this is a serious intervention in individual economic action, which is justified, however, when the interest of the community is jeopardized by the selfishness of an individual; in this situation, defensive precaution on the part of the community becomes a necessity. [In the margin: Clearing of forests]

We encounter this sort of problem especially also in forestry.

Quite often a forest owner in the mountains who is temporarily short of money[15] will want to clear his high-lying forests; this can easily cause irreparable damage, since the rainfall will then run off in torrents and wash out the humus layer;[16] floods in springtime, droughts in summer, and other kinds of damage to agriculture in the plains result from such deforestation of the mountain sides[17] and tend to worsen over time. The Southern Tyrol, Istria, Dalmatia are sad object lessons of the blind greed of individuals and thoughtless negligence of former governments. 56 r

[14] Here, Menger turns to the treatment of forest conservation policy by Rau (1854), p. 309 ff. Rau is altogether very much concerned with an advantageous ordering of property rights: while the trustees or administrators of corporate forest owners (local communities, foundations and church property) are to be closely supervised by the government so as to guard against malversations, individual forest owners must be regulated as little as possible in their economic activities. Some regulation is necessary, of course, because of 'paramount interest' and in order to guard against 'damage to the public'.

[15] Rau (1854), p. 309, points to the motive of 'short run gain' as a reason for the destruction of forests. He adds that such destruction may also be due to 'indolence and ignorance' of the owner. If the rendering by the Crown Prince is complete, Menger had characteristically suppressed this argument of a proprietor's insufficient knowledge. Note that high time preference (implicitly not equalized to the general rate in a highly imperfect capital market), the one argument given by Menger, is of quite another order than inattentiveness of an economic agent in the care for his property. The first named argument implies only warding off one external diseconomy (effects of deforestation) due to another (imperfection of capital markets).

[16] Rau (1854), p. 311 f., considers the possibility of soil erosion due to the deforestation of 'high mountain ridges' as an important reason for regulation. The danger of erosion was particularly topical for the arid southern parts of Austria (Southern Tyrol, Istria, Dalmatia) mentioned by Menger below. Rau uses an unusual German term for torrents ('Gießbäche'). The identical term used by Rudolf shows, on the one hand, that Menger followed Rau verbatim and, on the other, once more Rudolf's ability to reproduce faithfully the very words of the lecturer.

[17] Rau (1854), p. 312, points to the erosion of the soil in the plains by inundation in consequence of the deforestation of the mountains.

Der Schutz der Wälder ist eine Hauptpflicht des Staates, die durch ihre Bedeutung ihm *das* Eingreifen in die betreffenden wirtschaftlichen Bestrebungen der einzelnen gestattet.[18]

Nur in dieser Weise, wie es in den angeführten Beispielen erwähnt wurde, darf der Staat in die wirtschaftlichen Bestrebungen seiner Bürger eingreifen.

Sonst sei sein erster Grundsatz vollkommene Freiheit des Bürgers in seinen Tätigkeiten, Hilfe, dort wo des einzelnen Kraft zu schwach ist, und Schutz dann, wenn der einzelne seine Interessen verderblich für jene der Gesamtheit ausbreitet.[19] [CM am Rand: *Zur Erreichung seiner wirtschaftlichen Ziele oder zur Verhinderung bedrohlicher Gefahren.*]

Dieses Verfahren wird ein friedliches, natürliches Verhältnis zwischen dem
56 v Staate und seinen Mitgliedern herbeiführen. Durch das Gefühl einer weisen und aufgeklärten Vertretung und Leitung des Staates würden sich die wahren Bürgertugenden, Fleiß, Redlichkeit, und in Gefolge dessen Zunahme der Bildung entwickeln;[20] geschützt durch den mächtigen Arm des Staates, der zum Retter wird in gefährlichen, schwierigen Lagen; im Augenblicke des Glücks aber, zum Schauplatz der freien ungehinderten Bestrebungen eines echten Bürgertums wird sich ein moderner Staat im edelsten Sinne des Wortes entfalten, in dem die Teile in der Gesamtheit keine neben ihnen stehende Macht, sondern jenen Organismus erkennen, dessen Glieder sie sind, und dieser wieder in jenen sich selbst, die *Elemente*, die das Ganze bilden.

Dieser Zustand ist eine Folge eines vollkommenen Vertrauens aller untereinander, das weder durch Bevormundung und Überwachung noch durch Fahrlässigkeit
57 r in Augenblicken der Not von seiten des Staates aus getrübt ist.

[Am Rand: Schluß] Dann wird er als Gesamtheit der Teile deren Interessen in jeder Weise wahren, und diese werden zur Macht des Ganzen, zum allgemeinen Wohle, zu jedem Opfer bereit sein.

Dieser Standpunkt ist ein Ideal, das jeder Staat zu erreichen bestrebt sein muß; ein wichtiger Faktor dazu ist Einflußnahme des Staates auf die Tätigkeiten der einzelnen, durch direkte Eingriffe nur in den seltensten Fällen, sonst aber durch Freiheit der Bürger in ihren wirtschaftlichen Bestrebungen.

Wien, den 21. Februar 1876 Rudolf

18 Das ist die Tendenz der Aussage der auf 31 Seiten vergleichsweise sehr ausführlich dargestellten Aufgaben der Forstpolitik bei Rau (1854); vgl. S. 303–33 ('Waldbau'), siehe insbesondere S. 320 f.

19 Wiederholung der oben (S. 114) gebrachten Argumente nach Rau (1854), S. 7 f.

20 Rau (1854), S. 34 ff., bringt einen Abschnitt über 'Fleiß und Geschicklichkeit der Arbeiter', Eigenschaften, die 'vor Allem (durch) die Befestigung des Rechtszustandes und der gesetzlichen Freiheit im Staate' (S. 34) herbeigeführt werden. Rau zitiert dort sich selbst: vgl. (1855), S. 127 f., wo, genau umgekehrt wie bei Menger, 'fortschreitende gesellige Bildung' (S. 128) die Ursache, nicht die Folge des 'Fleißes' ist.

Protecting forests is among the major duties of the state which, by virtue of their importance, justify government intervention in individual economic activity.[18]

The state may intervene in the citizens' economic activities only in the manner described in the above examples.

Otherwise, its first principle should be: complete freedom for the citizen in his activities, support where individual energy is insufficient, and protective prevention when an individual pursues his interests in a manner detrimental to the community. [CM in the margin: To attain economic ends or to ward off impending dangers.][19]

Observing this principle will bring about a harmonious, natural relationship
between the state and its members. Their awareness that government is represented 56 v
and headed by wise and enlightened men will lead them to develop the true civic virtues of thrift and honesty and consequently to improve their education;[20] defended by the mighty arm of the state to which they turn for help in dangerous and difficult situations; in good times, however, a modern state in the noblest sense of the word will develop as the arena of the unfettered activities of a genuine citizenry; its parts will consider the whole not as an independent entity but as an organism whose members they are, while the organism will see the parts as elements that make up society as a whole.

This situation results from complete mutual trust which the state never spoils
by paternalism and controls or by negligence in times of distress. 57 r

[In the margin: end] Representing its individual parts, the state will defend their interests in every way; in turn, they will be willing to make any sacrifice for the power of the state, for the common good.

This sort of relationship is an ideal every country must strive for; an important prerequisite is for the state to use the right amount of influence on individual activities: usually by leaving citizens free to do as they please in their economic endeavours and only very rarely intervening in a direct way.

Vienna, 21 February 1876 Rudolf

18 This is the message of the long chapter on forest policy in Rau (1854), pp. 303–33.

19 Recapitulation of the general argument (see above, p. 115) of Rau (1854), p. 7 f.

20 See Rau (1854), p. 34 ff., where 'thrift and dexterity' of workers are due to 'legal security and statutory liberties'. Rau here quotes his own work(cf. 1855, pp. 127 f.), where such 'thrift and dexterity' are the consequence, not the cause, of 'education' or 'enlightenment' (or 'association' – the German term 'gesellige Bildung' is somewhat ambiguous).

Politische Ökonomie VIII. 1876 Februar/März

Über den Zustand des Papiergeldes in Österreich–Ungarn und die
1 r **Mittel, ihn zu reformieren I** [1, 2]

Das Papiergeld finden wir in zwei Arten bei uns in Österreich–Ungarn vertreten, nämlich in der Form von Banknoten und Staatsnoten.[3]

Bevor wir zum eigentlichen Gegenstande übergehen, muß bemerkt werden, daß unser Geldwesen durch die vielen bedeutenden Kriege und durch Krisen, sowie Umwälzungen aller Art, welche in den letzten 26 Jahren unseren Staat aus den veralteten, fast mittelalterlichen Formen zu einem modernen Staat im wahrsten Sinne des Wortes gemacht haben, sehr gelitten hat, und in den dringenden Lagen, in denen sich der Staat befand, teils durch Verschulden desselben,
1 v oft aber auch nur in Folge der kritischen Verhältnisse, in einen ungünstigen, ungesunden Zustand verfallen ist.

Wir sind im Wege der Besserung begriffen, und Friede nach außen sowie Ruhe im Innern werden auch die Geldverhältnisse in kürzester Zeit ins richtige Geleise bringen.

Besonders wenn gewisse fördernde Maßregeln ergriffen werden, denen wir jetzt unsere Aufmerksamkeit schenken wollen.

Wie oben erwähnt, haben wir bei uns 2 Arten des Papiergeldes; betrachten wir zuerst die Übelstände, die unseren Banknoten anhaften. Das erste Merkmal
2 r jeder Banknote ist ihre Einlöslichkeit gegen Metall. Sie ist ja eigentlich nur eine Anweisung an die Bank für die Banknotenbesitzer, welche jeden Augenblick

1 In den Heften VIII und IX ist sehr viel geändert und gestrichen. Von diesen beiden Heften wurde eine Reinschrift verfertigt, deren Seiten separat numeriert sind. Sie ist in den in der Liste auf S. 1 unter 16 und 17 verzeichneten Heften enthalten und stammt nicht von Rudolfs oder Mengers Hand, sondern einer dritten, bislang nicht identifizierten. Abgedruckt wird hier diese Reinschrift.

2 Ausnahmsweise folgt dieses Kapitel nicht Smith (1776), der in II.ii.26 sich ganz für das Papiergeld ausspricht – freilich in Unkenntnis der Papiergeldprobleme ab der Französischen Revolution. Da dieses Kapitel ein österreichspezifischer Traktat ist, findet sich hierzu keine Vorlage in einem allgemeinen deutschsprachigen Lehrbuch.

Möglicherweise gehen die vielen Korrekturen eben darauf zurück, daß Menger hier ganz selbständig vortrug und sich daher in potentiell gefährlicher Position befand.

3 Obwohl des spezifisch österreichischen Charakters dieses Abschnitts wegen eine selbständige Behandlung durch Menger anzunehmen ist, konnte er sich in der von ihm verwendeten Lehrbuchliteratur an dem sehr ausführlichen Abschnitt über 'Papiergeld' bei Rau (1855), S. 367–86, orientieren.

Political economy VIII. 1876 February/March

On the State of Paper Money in Austria–Hungary and the Means to Reform It[1, 2] 1 r

In Austria–Hungary paper money takes two forms: bank notes and state notes.[3]

Before we come to our subject proper, we must remark that our currency has suffered greatly from many momentous wars and from crises and from all sorts of profound changes which, within the last 26 years, have turned our realm from its obsolete, almost medieval form into a modern state in the truest sense of the word; in the precarious situations in which the state found itself the currency deteriorated to an unserviceable unsound condition, partly through the government's fault, partly, however, merely as a result of the critical conditions. 1 v

We are now on our way to recovery, and peace abroad and harmony within will very shortly bring our monetary system back to normality.

Especially if certain helpful measures are taken, to which we will now turn our attention.

As mentioned above, we have two kinds of paper money; let us first look at the deficiencies of our bank notes. Convertibility into precious metal is the foremost 2 r

1 In Notebooks VIII and IX a great deal was altered and deleted. A fair copy was made from them, the pages of which are numbered separately. It is neither in Rudolf's nor in Menger's handwriting, but in that of a third person as yet unidentified, and is contained in the Notebooks that are numbered 16 and 17 in the list on p. 1. This fair copy is printed here.

2 This chapter, for once, does not build upon Smith (1776), who is all in favour of paper money. He says in II.ii.26: 'The substitution of paper in the room of gold or silver money, replaces a very expensive instrument of commerce with one much less costly, and sometimes equally convenient'. But he only considers voluntarily accepted bank notes of essentially private banks, no government issue.

As this chapter deals with a specifically Austrian problem it cannot be derived from a general German language textbook.

The many corrections are possibly due to the fact that Menger was here entirely on his own and had to be on his guard.

3 In part the chapter may reflect the extensive treatment of paper money in Rau (1855), pp. 367–86. The division in banknotes and state notes is similar to one in Rau, p. 369 in conjunction with p. 379.

denjenigen Betrag an Metallgeld erhalten, auf welchen die Noten lauten. Durch die Sicherheit der Einlöslichkeit gegen Metall erhält die Banknote ihren Wert und wird dadurch zu einem wichtigen Gegenstand des Verkehres.[4]

Alle diese wichtigen Eigenschaften finden wir bei unseren Banknoten leider nicht.

Unsere Banknoten sind gegen Silber nicht einlöslich; vergebens würden wir zur Bank gehen, um uns unsere Noten in Silber einlösen zu lassen; sie kann uns keines geben, trotzdem es das gute Recht jedes Notenbesitzers ist, diese Summe zu verlangen, welche auf der Note geschrieben steht und dadurch von
2 v der Bank garantiert ist. Daher entspricht unser Banknotenwesen in dem Hauptpunkte nicht, und wird dadurch zu etwas ganz anderem, als es eigentlich sein soll; statt daß die Bank Anweisungen auf Geld gibt, wie es ihre Pflicht ist, gibt sie einfache Papierzettel heraus, welche, da sie gegen kein Silber einlöslich sind, selbst zu einer Art von Geld werden.

Natürlich würden die Leute keine Banknoten von einer Bank annehmen, die in ihrem wesentlichsten Merkmale und in ihrem Zwecke nicht entspricht; deshalb muß ihnen vom Staate, wenn sie überhaupt angenommen werden sollen, der Zwangskurs gegeben werden,[5] der darin besteht, daß die Banknoten, wenn sie auch gegen Silber nicht einlöslich sind, doch im Verkehr angenommen werden müssen und als Geld gelten sollen.

Natürlich liegt darin eine große Willkür und geradezu Gewalttätigkeit gegen
3 r die Bürger, welche gezwungen werden, Banknoten, die sie sonst nicht annehmen würden, gleich wie Metallgeld im Verkehr zu akzeptieren.

Aus den beiden obigen Übelständen ergibt sich noch ein anderes Übel, welches unserem Banknotenwesen anhaftet.

Sind nämlich Noten gegen Metallgeld nicht einlöslich und werden dieselben nur durch den Zwangskurs im Verkehre erhalten, so verlieren sie im Vergleiche zum Metallgelde an Wert, so zwar, daß sie auf eine bestimmte Summe von z.B. 100 fl.Ö.W. [Gulden österreichischer Währung] lautend, doch lange nicht die gleiche Summe in Silbergeld wert sind, und die Besitzer derselben dadurch Schaden nehmen. Diesen Zustand, der eine Folge solcher trauriger Verhältnisse ist, nennt man Disagio.

Alle diese krankhaften Erscheinungen haften unseren Banknoten an, welche dadurch ihrem Zwecke keineswegs entsprechen.

3 v Trotzdem hat diese Art des Papiergeldes im gesunden Zustande ihre volle Berechtigung und wird durch zunehmende Besserung der Verhältnisse langsam

So gibt Rau, S. 369, die Einteilung in 'Privat- und Staatspapiergeld', wobei Banknoten 'die gewöhnlichste Art des Privatpapiergeldes' sind (S. 379).

4 Rau (1855), S. 380 f., behandelt ausschließlich die Einlösbarkeit der Banknoten in Münzen. Daher betonen die folgenden Absätze, daß in Österreich eine solche gerade nicht gilt.

5 Rau, ebenda, S. 375: 'Ein solches Privatgeld, bei welchem der obrigkeitliche Zwang den geschwächten Kredit ersetzt, ist ausgeartet und nimmt die Eigenschaften des Staatspapiergeldes an'.

characteristic of a bank note. Actually, the bank note is just an order to the bank to pay to the bearer, upon presentation, in specie the amount indicated on the note. The value of the bank note derives from the certainty of its conversion into specie, which makes it important for commercial transactions.[4]

Our bank notes do not show any of these important properties, unhappily.

They are not convertible into silver; in vain would we walk to the bank to have our notes redeemed in silver; the bank cannot give it to us although every note bearer is entitled to demand the sum indicated on the note and thereby guaranteed by the bank. Thus, in this major respect our currency is not what it should be and becomes something quite different; instead of issuing orders for 2 v
specie as the bank ought to, it issues simple pieces of paper that become a kind of money themselves, since they cannot be converted into silver.

Naturally, people would not accept bank notes from a bank that lacks a bank's most essential characteristic and purpose; if the bank notes are to be accepted at all, government must make their acceptance obligatory,[5] i.e. bank notes have to be accepted and be valid as money even though they cannot be redeemed in silver.

Naturally this is an act of considerable wilfulness and even compulsion against the citizens, who are forced to accept as specie bank notes they would 3 r
not accept otherwise.

From the two defects mentioned there follows still another one inherent in our paper currency.

For if notes cannot be converted into specie and are kept in circulation only by decree, they lose value relative to specie inasmuch as they may still be denominated, e.g. as 100 florins (Austrian currency), but are far from equal to 100 florins in silver coins; so their owners suffer a loss. This deplorable difference in value is a 'discount' on the bank note.

All these symptoms of disorder are apparent in our bank notes so they do not fulfil their purpose at all.

Nevertheless, if it is sound, this kind of paper money is very useful and will 3 v
eventually serve its purpose as the situation improves. Only then, however, will

4 Rau (1855), p. 380 f., considers only convertibility of banknotes in specie. Presumably for this reason, the following paragraphs emphasize that this is not the case in Austria.

5 This follows Rau, ibid., p. 375.

ihren Zweck erfüllen. Die Nationalbank wird dann aber auch erst jene Aufgaben erfüllen, welche die Banken aller Länder mit geordnetem Geldwesen lange schon durchführen.

Ähnliche Übelstände, wie wir sie bei den österreichischen Banknoten zu beobachten Gelegenheit hatten, können wir auch bei den österreichischen Staatsnoten konstatieren. Eine gesunde Staatsnote bedarf keines Zwangskurses, sie wird von den Bürgern freiwillig so wie Metallgeld angenommen und hat deshalb auch kein Disagio; unsere österreichischen Staatsnoten dagegen werden vom Staate in zu großen Quantitäten ausgegeben und müssen daher, um
4 r überhaupt angenommen zu werden und um im Verkehre zu verbleiben, Zwangskurs erhalten, dadurch sind sie gegen Silbergeld entwertet und haben ein Disagio.

Wir haben somit gesehen, in welch gleich übler Lage sich unsere Banknoten und Staatsnoten befinden; betrachten wir nun die Folgen dieses Zustandes für die allgemeinen Interessen.

Das Geld ist das Mittel, dessen der einzelne so wie der Staat zur Befriedigung seiner Bedürfnisse benötigt; die Bestrebungen beider gehen daher nach Erlangung desselben.

Für beide ist ein geordnetes sicheres Geldwesen die Basis jedes Gedeihens und jeder sicheren wirtschaftlichen Entwicklung; das unsichere dagegen erschreckt den einzelnen Bürger, raubt ihm die Grundlage jeder sicheren Berechnung und erfüllt ihn mit Sorge in Betreff seiner wichtigsten Interessen: Für den Staat aber ist ein ungeordnetes Geldwesen von gleicher Verderblichkeit wie für den einzelnen, denn dasselbe entzieht auch ihm jede Möglichkeit einer sicheren Berechnung in seinem eigenen großen Haushalte, es verlockt ihn, um
4 v momentan sich zu helfen, Maßregeln zu ergreifen, die ihn für die Dauer immer tiefer in die größten Verlegenheiten reißen.

Nur starke Überwindung und Festigkeit den Versuchungen gegenüber werden es Regierungen ermöglichen, sich aus dem Netz der Geldverlegenheiten zu reißen.

Nicht nur der positive Übelstand, welcher aus einem so ungeordneten Geldwesen resultiert, ist aber in Betracht zu ziehen, sondern ebenso auch der moralische Schaden, den diese Verhältnisse dem Ansehen der Regierung bereiten; denn stets wird die Verantwortung solcher übler Zustände auf den Staat zurückfallen. In dringenden Momenten, wo das Staatsschiff schwankt, bemächtigt sich nicht selten der Regierung eine gewaltige Schwäche, die sie verleitet, Mittel zur momentanen Rettung zu ergreifen, welche dauernde Übelstände zur Folge haben.

5 r Folgen nun diesen Mißgriffen ähnliche neue Mißgriffe und daher auch naturgemäß stets größere Verlegenheiten der Regierung, dann sinkt das Ansehen derselben nach außen und das Vertrauen im Innern. Von den Mitgliedern des Staates wird dann Schwäche und Unsicherheit der Regierung weit mehr vorausgesetzt, als es der Fall ist, und wegen der ungünstigen Geldverhältnisse,

the National Bank perform those functions that the banks of all countries with a sound currency have carried out for a long time.

Flaws like those we had occasion to observe in the Austrian bank notes are also apparent in the Austrian state notes. A sound state note need not have its value determined by decree; it is willingly accepted by the people just like specie and therefore does not show a discount; our Austrian state notes, on the contrary, are issued by the government in excessive quantities and in order to be accepted at all and to remain in circulation, they must be made obligatory; consequently, they are depreciated in relation to silver coins, i.e. they show a discount. 4 r

So we realize how our bank notes and our state notes are equally deficient; let us now look at the consequences of this state of affairs for the common good.

Money is the means used by the individual and the state to satisfy their needs; both strive to obtain it.

For both, an orderly and reliable monetary system is the prerequisite for prosperity and secure economic development; insecurity, on the other hand, deters the individual citizen, deprives him of the basis for reliable calculations, and makes him worry about his most vital interests: but a disorderly monetary system is just as injurious for the state as for the individual as it divests the state of all possibilities for reliably calculating its own substantial budget; for the sake of temporary relief, the state is tempted to adopt measures that will eventually get it into ever greater difficulties. 4 v

Only utmost self-restraint and firmness in the face of temptation will help governments to disentangle themselves from the web of financial difficulties.

Not only the material damage caused by an unsound currency, but also the moral disgrace that government incurs, must be taken into account; for it is always the state that will be held responsible for such disorder. In critical moments, when the ship of state is tossed about, government is not infrequently seized by an inordinate weakness and led to take measures that bring immediate relief, but cause lasting problems.

If such mistakes are followed up by similar mistakes and thus naturally by 5 r
ever increasing difficulties for the government, its reputation abroad and confidence in it at home will wane. The citizens will assume that the government is far weaker and less secure than it really is; and as monetary disorder is of the greatest concern to the individual and affects his vital interests, discontent will

die den einzelnen am tiefsten bekümmern und ihn in seinen vitalsten Interessen schädigen, entsteht Unzufriedenheit. Der Handel und Verkehr, die Grundlagen und Haupttriebfeder jeder volkswirtschaftlichen Entwicklung, beruhen nicht zum geringsten Teile auf einem soliden geregelten Geldwesen.

Der schwankende Kurs des Geldes und die Unsicherheit aller Berechnungen werden deshalb das Gedeihen des Staates in seinen Grundfesten erschüttern; der ganze Staat wie der einzelne Bürger wird in seinen Unternehmungen im
5 v Innern wie nach außen überall Mißtrauen und Hemmnisse finden.

Der einzelne wie der ganze Staat werden in allen Erwerbsquellen stets Benachteiligungen erdulden müssen; denn die Summen, die man einnehmen soll, wird man erhalten, aber in entwerteten, im Kurs schwankenden Noten, und daher de facto um vieles weniger, als man zu gewinnen glaubt. Aus diesem Grunde wird der Staat, der ohnedies sich in mißlichen Geldverhältnissen befindet, sein bestimmtes Einkommen, das er eben deshalb am notwendigsten brauchen würde, in Wahrheit in einer geringeren Summe erhalten, was für ihn die Kette der üblen Situation fortsetzt.

Hier ersieht man klar den Fluch, der auf früheren Fehlern ruht, und wie sich diese immer wieder fühlbar machen. Auch raubt diese traurige Lage den Kredit
6 r nach außen, und den Handels- und Gewerbsleuten wird dadurch der Verkehr mit dem Auslande um vieles erschwert.

Der Regierung werden sich im Bedarfsfalle alle auswärtigen Banken und Handelshäuser wohl hüten, große Summen zu leihen, denn sie werden mit Recht fürchten, bei diesem Geschäfte Schaden zu nehmen.

Zahlungen in österreichischem Gelde und österreichische Wechsel werden im Auslande gar nicht[6] oder nur mit großer Mehrzahlung angenommen werden, und mit dem Sinken des Ansehens des Geldes, das unstreitig eine große, wenn nicht die größte Macht ist, sinkt jenes des ganzen Staates; und mit Grund kann deshalb behauptet werden, daß durch ein unsicheres, ungeordnetes Geldwesen
6 v ein wichtiger Lebensnerv des Staates unterbunden wird, da diese Verhältnisse tief in das wirtschaftliche Leben und in dessen Fortschritte eingreifen.

Darum muß besonders dahin gestrebt werden, einen gesunden Zustand des Geldwesens zu erreichen; damit dies aber gelinge, muß man sich vor allem der Gründe, wegen deren unser Papiergeld ungesund ist, bewußt sein.

Betrachten wir zuerst die ungünstigen Umstände, in denen sich unsere Staatsnoten befinden, und den Ursprung dieses Übels.

Die Staatsnote ist jenes Papiergeld, welches der Staat herausgibt, und das nur durch das Recht der Bürger, damit Steuern zu zahlen, zum Range eines Geldes gelangt ist.

6 Wohl etwas übertrieben. Rau (1855), S. 360 (Fußnoten zu § 289), sagt: 'Besteht das Umlaufsmittel eines Landes größtenteils aus einem gegen Münze im Preis gesunkenen Papiergelde, so müssen die auf solches gestellten Wechsel einen niedrigeren Curs haben. In Wien stand im Jan. 1855 das Papiergeld zu 127 gegen 100 Silber'.

ensue. To a large extent, trade and commerce, the pillars and mainspring of all economic development, are founded upon a well-established and orderly monetary system.

Fluctuations in the exchange rate and uncertainty in all calculations will therefore shake the prosperity of the state to its very foundations; in their activities at home and abroad the state as a whole and each individual citizen will encounter distrust and obstacles everywhere. 5 v

Both individuals and the state will always suffer losses in their sources of income; the sums they are to receive will be paid in depreciated notes whose value fluctuates; thus, income is in fact much smaller than expected. For this reason, the state, in financial straits already, will find the actual value of a given revenue that it therefore desperately needs getting smaller, and so the situation goes from bad to worse .

Here we clearly see the curse of past mistakes and how they continue to make themselves felt. This unfortunate situation ruins credit abroad and makes business transactions in foreign countries much more difficult. 6 r

Since they will rightly fear suffering a loss, all foreign banks and merchant-houses will shy from lending large sums of money to the government in need of them.

Payments abroad in Austrian currency and Austrian bills of exchange will not be accepted at all[6] or only with a considerable surcharge; and with the diminishing reputation of the currency – which doubtless is of great, if not the greatest, influence – the reputation of the state as a whole diminishes; therefore, it can reasonably be argued that an uncertain, disorderly currency is a vital deficiency of a state, because it makes itself deeply felt in all of economic life and its progress. 6 v

Therefore we must strive especially for a sound currency, and to do this successfully, we must first of all find out the reasons why our paper money is unsound.

Let us first consider the unfortunate condition of our state notes and its causes.

The state note is the paper money which is issued by government and has acquired the status of money only because citizens are entitled to pay their taxes with it.

6 A somewhat exaggerated remark. Rau (1855), p. 360 (notes to § 289), gives the surcharge for January 1855 in Vienna as 127 in paper against 100 in silver.

An und für sich, und in geringer Quantität in Zirkulation gesetzt, haben die Staatsnoten sich überall für den Verkehr als unschädlich erwiesen und zugleich
7 r den Staatsregierungen ein nützliches Mittel geboten, sich in momentanen Geldverlegenheiten die nötigen Geldsummen zu verschaffen.

Wird nun aber die Staatsnote in für das allgemeine Wohl schädlichen, zu großen Summen ausgegeben, so muß ihr der Staat den Zwangskurs geben, was freilich für ihn momentan sehr vorteilhaft zu sein scheint, aber gegenüber den Notenbesitzern ein willkürliches Verfahren ist; darum folgt aber auch die Entwertung der Staatsnoten. Durch ihr Disagio sind alle ihre Eigentümer benachteiligt, welche, so viel als der Staat auf seine Noten setzen läßt, zu besitzen glauben, de facto aber im Vergleiche zum Silbergeld viel weniger haben.

7 v Nicht nur der einzelne wird aber dadurch benachteiligt, sondern vielleicht noch mehr der Staat, denn diese oben charakterisierten Zustände beurkunden eine gewisse unsichere Lage und zeigen am deutlichsten die Schwäche und Kurzsichtigkeit der Regierung, die durch ein der Gesamtheit zugefügtes Übel sich fortwährend helfen will, und hiedurch die Volkswirtschaft in immer größere Nachteile stürzt.

Als den Hauptgrund also, daß unsere Staatsnoten entwertet sind, müssen wir ihre zu große Anzahl im Verkehre betrachten; der Staat sah sich häufig in mißlichen Lagen genötigt, zu diesem Mittel zu greifen, und leider waren noch nie die Geldverhältnisse so günstig, daß er leicht den Entschluß, diese Übel
8 r wiedergutzumachen, fassen konnte.

In jedem Lande, welches sich eines geregelten Geldwesens erfreut, muß eine bestimmte Umlaufmenge der Staatsnoten fixiert sein, und die Regierung soll es sich dann zum Grundsatze machen, diese Summe unter keinen Umständen durch Mehrausgabe zu überschreiten. Die Staatsnoten haben nur dadurch ihren Wert, daß die Steuerzahlungen mit denselben geleistet werden können, zu diesem Behufe ist eine verhältnismäßig kleine Summe ausreichend, jede Mehrausgabe von Staatsnoten, als zu diesem Behufe nötig ist, wird sicherlich schädliche Folgen nach sich ziehen, da die Staatsnoten dadurch entwerten und der in jedem Falle schädliche Zwangskurs ihnen gegeben werden muß. 100 Millionen Staatsnoten wären beiläufig die Summe, welche für Österreich–Ungarn vollkommen genügend wäre und auch keine schädlichen Folgen nach sich ziehen würde. Leider haben wir aber diese Summe bedeutend überschritten, denn circa 350 Millionen Staatsnoten sind bei uns de facto im Umlaufe.

Um demnach das Disagio der Staatsnoten und ihren Zwangskurs aufheben zu können, müßte der Staat den Entschluß fassen, beiläufig 250 Millionen
8 v dieser Noten einzuziehen und sie vernichten zu lassen; es wäre ein großes Opfer, welches aber gute Früchte tragen würde.

Um diese Reduktion der Staatsnoten aus den laufenden Staatseinnahmen nach und nach durchführen zu können, müßte sich der Staat in sehr geordneten und glücklichen finanziellen Verhältnissen befinden, welche

In themselves, these state notes have everywhere proved harmless when circulated in small quantities, and at the same time, by providing required sums
of money, they have come in handy to governments in short-term financial 7 r
difficulties.

If, however, state notes are issued in excessive quantities detrimental to the common good, the government has to fix their terms of exchange by decree, which may seem quite advantageous at the moment, but for the note bearers it is an arbitrary act; consequently, the state notes are devalued. Through the discount all owners of such notes suffer a loss; they think they own the amount denominated on the state notes, but, in fact, have much less than that sum in silver coins.

It is not only the individual who suffers a loss; the state does, too, perhaps
even more, for the situation described above indicates a certain insecurity and 7 v
most clearly shows up the weakness and shortsightedness of the government that keeps trying to help itself by harming the community, thereby getting the economy into ever greater difficulties.

So we must take the over-abundance of our state notes to be the main cause of their devaluation; in adverse circumstances, the state often felt compelled to adopt this method, and sadly the monetary situation has never since been
favourable enough for the government to decide easily to redress this damage. 8 r

In any country with a well-ordered monetary system, the quantity of state notes in circulation must be fixed, and the government should then resolve not to exceed this quantity under any circumstances by issuing more notes. State notes derive their value only from the fact that they may be used for paying taxes; a fairly small quantity of them is sufficient for this purpose; an issue of notes in excess of this requirement will certainly have harmful consequences, since the notes are thereby devalued and must then have their terms of exchange fixed by decree. 100m [florins in] state notes would be approximately sufficient for Austria–Hungary and would have no negative effects. Alas, we have exceeded this sum by far, as there are about 350m [florins in] state notes in circulation.

In order to revoke the discount on state notes and the terms of exchange fixed by decree, the state would have to decide to withdraw about 250m [florins] of
these notes from circulation and have them destroyed; it would be a great 8 v
sacrifice, but one with good effect.

In order to bring about this reduction gradually – by withdrawing the notes from circulation as they flow in as public revenue – the state would have to find itself in a settled and auspicious financial situation to allow

Politische Ökonomie IX. 1876 März[1]

9 r momentan so bedeutende Verwendungen seines Einkommens zulassen würden; wenn diese günstige Situation aber nicht vorhanden wäre und der Staat, so wie es bei uns der Fall ist, an einem ungesunden Geldwesen leidet, dann müßte die Regierung ein Darlehen aufnehmen, das ebenso groß wäre wie die Summe der einzuziehenden Staatsnoten.

Dasselbe dürfte aber selbstverständlich nicht von der Nationalbank in Anspruch genommen werden, denn sonst würde dieselbe, statt daß ihr durch Einziehung der Staatsnoten geholfen würde, von neuem verletzt und tief erschüttert werden.

Wenn der Staat dieses Mittel ergreift und mit den von verschiedenen großen Handelshäusern oder direkt von der Bevölkerung im Wege öffentlicher Begebung
9 v geliehenen Summen in die Lage versetzt ist, die übermäßig zirkulierenden Staatsnoten einzulösen, und auf diese Weise der Entwertung der Staatsnoten und dem Zwangskurse derselben ein Ende zu machen, dann ist auch zugleich der Schlüssel gefunden, um unsere Nationalbank wieder aufzurichten und ihr zu dem richtigen normalen Zustande der anderen Banken der großen europäischen Staaten zu verhelfen.

Es ist nämlich ein großer, sehr verbreiteter Irrtum, wenn angenommen wird, daß der Zwangskurs der Banknoten und ihr Disagio im Zustande der Nationalbank selbst begründet sind. Jetzt ist dieselbe nicht nur unschuldig an diesen Verhältnissen, sondern sogar vollkommen in Ordnung.

10 r In früheren Zeiten, z.B. in den 50er und 60er Jahren, lag der Grund der schlechten Zustände unserer Banknoten in den sehr großen Darlehen, welche der Staat von der Nationalbank nahm. Dadurch wurde sie nämlich außer Stand gesetzt, die Noten jeweilig gegen Metallgeld einlösen zu können; und da, um die Bank nicht vollständig zugrunde gehen zu lassen, mußte der Staat den Banknoten Zwangskurs geben.

Wegen der großen Verderblichkeit dieses Verfahrens, welches der Bank einen bedeutenden Schaden bereitet, den Notenbesitzern gegenüber aber eine unverantwortliche Willkür ist und ein Leck auf lange Zeiten hinaus dem Geldwesen beibringt, wird gegenwärtig dieses Verfahren auch nicht mehr angewendet.

[1] Vgl. Anmerkung 1 zum vorhergehenden Kapitel, S. 134.

Political economy IX. 1876 March[1]

at once such a momentous allocation of revenue; if the situation were less 9 r
auspicious and the state were to suffer from an unsound currency, as is the case with us, then the government would have to raise a loan amounting to the sum of state notes to be withdrawn.

This loan, of course, must not be put to any use by the National Bank; for then, instead of being helped by the withdrawal of the state notes, the Bank would once more get a jolt and be deeply shaken.

If the state takes these measures and manages to withdraw the excess notes from circulation by borrowing from various big merchants or directly from the population through treasury bonds, it could bring an end to the devaluation of 9 v
state notes and the compulsory terms of exchange; then a way will have been found to put the National Bank back on its feet and help it to acquire the condition that is normal for other banks in the major countries of Europe.

For it is a grave, though very common, mistake to assume that the compulsory terms of exchange and the discount of the bank notes are caused by the condition of the National Bank itself. Not only is the Bank not responsible for the present situation, but it is in perfectly good order.

Formerly, e.g. in the 1850s and 1860s, the deplorable condition of our bank 10 r
notes was caused by the huge sums the state borrowed from the National Bank. These made it impossible for the Bank to convert the notes into specie upon presentation; and in order not to have the Bank altogether ruined, the state had to make the notes obligatory.

This procedure is quite destructive: it causes great damage to the National Bank, represents an act of irresponsible wilfulness with respect to note owners, and amounts to a long-term drain on the monetary system; therefore it is no longer applied today.

1 See note 1 to the previous chapter, p. 135.

10 v Zwar gewährte die Bank auch anläßlich der letzten Erneuerung ihres Privilegiums dem Staate ein unverzinsliches Darlehen von 80 Millionen fl., doch ist dieses Darlehen nicht so groß, daß es den gesunden Zustand der Bank zu alterieren vermöchte.

Darum kann man die gegenwärtigen Übelstände unserer Banknoten nicht in dieser Richtung suchen; der Grund derselben liegt nicht in der Bank selbst, denn ihr Metallschatz ruht in schönster Ordnung in ihren Kellern, auf bessere Zeiten und auf Einlöslichkeit der Noten harrend.

Die Anzahl der Banknoten ist ferner keine zu bedeutende, und in angemessener Zahl verkehren sie in der Monarchie. Mit einem Worte, die Bank ist in geordneten Verhältnissen und wäre jeden Augenblick in der Lage, ihre Noten einzulösen,
11 r doch der Staat hindert sie daran, indem er aus früher schon besprochener Schwäche und Kurzsichtigkeit, teilweise allerdings auch in Fällen dringender Art, seine Untertanen mit Staatsnoten überschwemmt hat.

Die Nationalbank kann unter solchen Verhältnissen in ihrem eigenen Interesse sowie in jenem der gesamten Volkswirtschaft unmöglich die Einlösung der Banknoten gegen Metallgeld beginnen; in kürzester Zeit würden nämlich alle Banknoten aus dem Verkehre verschwinden, denn jeder Notenbesitzer würde sie sich gegen Silber einlösen lassen, um den wirklichen Wert seines Geldes zu erlangen, und alle Schulden würden dann in den entwerteten Staatsnoten gezahlt werden. Der ganze Verkehr würde somit bald lediglich durch die entwerteten Staatsnoten vermittelt werden.

11 v Also nicht in den Banknoten ist der Fehler zu suchen, sondern in den Staatsnoten, und es liegt daher ganz in der Hand des Staates, das Papiergeldwesen in Österreich–Ungarn herzustellen.

Nur eines Entschlusses und eines Opfers bedarf es somit, um gesicherte und gute Geldverhältnisse und hiemit unzählige Vorteile für den Staat herbeizuführen.

Eine große Zahl, beiläufig 250 Millionen Staatsnoten müßten eingezogen und vertilgt werden; dadurch würden die übrigbleibenden im ungefähren Betrag von 100 Millionen Gulden ihr Disagio verlieren und als ein gesundes Papiergeld für gewisse Zahlungen, wie Steuern, von vorteilhafter Wirkung sein; die
12 r Banknoten hingegen könnten dann für Metallgeld einlöslich werden, und die Bank würde endlich, von ihrem ungesunden Zustande befreit, ihre eigentliche Aufgabe erfüllen.

Wenn dies geschehen ist, hätten wir das normale Papiergeldwesen anderer Staaten erreicht, doch nach Erlangung dieses glücklichen Zustandes müßte der Staat, eingedenk der lange dauernden üblen Situationen in dem Geldwesen, vor allem seine Aufmerksamkeit darauf richten, frühere Fehler nicht neuerdings zu wiederholen, z.B. sollte er es sich besonders zum Grundsatze machen, niemals die Nationalbank um ein bedeutendes Darlehen anzugehen, und wäre die Lage des Staates eine noch so kritische, und die Versuchung eine noch so große; diese
12 v Überwindung und der weite Blick der Regierung, der über die momentane

It is true that the Bank accorded the state a loan of 80m florins free of interest 10 v
on the occasion of the last renewal of the Bank's 'Privilege'; but this loan is not so big as to jeopardize the soundness of the Bank.

So the present poor condition of our bank notes must not be ascribed to that; it has not been caused by the Bank, for its hoard of precious metals is just where it should be, namely in the vaults, awaiting better times and convertibility of the notes.

Furthermore, the quantity of bank notes is not excessive, and they circulate in the Monarchy in appropriate numbers. In short, the Bank is in sound condition and could at any moment convert its notes into specie, were it not prevented
by the government that has flooded the country with state notes, partly from 11 r
weakness and shortsightedness as mentioned above, partly, however, because of emergencies.

Under such circumstances, the National Bank – for its own sake as well as that of the economy as a whole – cannot possibly begin to convert bank notes into specie; in no time at all these bank notes would all disappear from circulation: every note owner would have them converted into silver in order to get the full value of his money, yet all debts would be paid in devalued state notes. In other words, all monetary transactions would soon be settled only with devalued state notes.

The fault does not lie with the bank notes then, but rather with the state notes, 11 v
and it is entirely up to the government to put the paper currency of Austria–Hungary on an acceptable footing again.

Resolution and a sacrifice are all that is needed to bring about an orderly and sound monetary system and with it countless advantages to the state.

A large quantity of state notes, about 250m [florins], would have to be withdrawn and destroyed; the rest, about 100m florins, would thereby lose its discount and, as sound paper money, could be usefully employed for certain kinds of payments, e.g. taxes; the bank notes, on the other hand, could then be
made convertible into specie, and at long last the Bank would be rid of its symptoms 12 r
of disorder and fulfil its proper duties.

When this has come to pass, we should have the sort of paper currency that is normal for other countries; but after having attained this satisfactory position, the state, mindful of the long-lasting, deplorable currency situation, would very carefully have to avoid repeating previous mistakes; it should, for example, resolve never to ask the National Bank for any sizeable loan, no matter how desperate the situation and how great the temptation; the sort of self-control and farsightedness on the part of a government that leads it to look beyond a present emergency
to long-term consequences would bear good fruit; nor must government have 12 v

Notlage hinaus auf die späteren Folgen gerichtet ist, würden gute Früchte tragen; auch dürfte der Staat nicht neuerdings zum Mittel der Staatsnoten greifen, um durch Fabrikation eines übergroßen Quantums derselben sich augenblicklich Geld zu verschaffen.

Er müßte sich stets in jeder Lage seiner Geschicke des Grundsatzes bewußt sein, nie mehr als höchstens etwa 100 Millionen Staatsnoten herauszugeben.

Wenn die Regierung diese erwähnten Grundsätze durchführt und selbst die Opfer, welche damit in Verbindung sind, nicht scheut, würde sie bald sich großer Vorteile bewußt werden.

13 r Auf dem geordneten Geldwesen eines Staates beruht ein großer Teil seiner Macht; ein geordnetes Geldwesen trägt wesentlich zur Ruhe, Zufriedenheit und zum Vertrauen im Innern, zum Ansehen, zur Stärke und zum Kredit nach außen bei; hingegen ist ein korrumpiertes Geldwesen, dessen Ursachen tief gewurzelt sind, ein Hauptgrund, um jedes Übel zu einer Katastrophe zu stempeln, und der Faden, der einen Unglücksfall mit dem folgenden verbindet.

Diese traurigen Erfahrungen haben wir leider in bedeutendem Maße in Österreich gemacht, und es ist höchste Zeit, daß die Regierung dafür sorgt, diesen üblen Verhältnissen, die schon teilweise glücklich beseitigt sind, vollends ein Ende zu machen und zur Herstellung eines geordneten Geldwesens, die
13 v Wichtigkeit desselben erkennend, keine Opfer zu scheuen.

[eigenhändig:]

Wien, den 8. März 1876 Rudolf

recourse to state notes again and be able to come into money at a moment's notice by printing an excessive quantity of them.

Under any circumstances, it would have to stick to the principle never to give out more than approximately 100m [florins in] state notes.

If the government observes the aforesaid principles and does not shy away from the consequent sacrifices, it would soon become aware of great advantages.

A sound currency is a major prerequisite of state power; it contributes 13 r
substantially to peace, contentment, and confidence at home, and to prestige, firm standing and credit abroad; on the other hand, a deeply corrupted currency is a major reason why all sorts of misfortune turn into catastrophe, and, at the same time, it is the thread that links one mishap to the next.

Such, in substantial measure, has been our sad experience in Austria, and it is high time for the government to strive to bring to an end once and for all this unhappy situation, which in part has already been remedied; it should shy away from no sacrifice to re-establish a sound currency, knowing how important that 13 v
is.

[in his own hand:]

Vienna, 8 March 1876 Rudolf

Politische Ökonomie X. 1876 März

69 r **Nach welchen Grundsätzen soll der Staat seine Beamten und Diener entlohnen?**
(Zur Lehre vom Arbeitslohne)

Der Arbeitslohn, der für jede Tätigkeit und Verrichtung in allen den vielen verschiedenen Berufen gezahlt wird und eigentlich der Kaufpreis für die geleistete Arbeit ist, wird nicht nach Willkür und Laune der Arbeitgeber und Arbeitnehmer ausgezahlt, sondern er richtet sich nach bestimmten Grundsätzen und Regeln, die über die Grenzen des Standes, des Berufes, des Volkes sowie des Staates hinausgehen und für die menschliche Gesellschaft im großen und ganzen allgemeine Geltung haben.

Im unaufhörlichen Austausch der Fähigkeiten und Kräfte für fixierte Tauschgegenstände sind Unterschiede entstanden,[1] die dem Maße des Geleisteten in bezug auf dessen Lohn, angepaßt sind.

Unzählige Einflüsse spielen mit bei dem schweren Kapitel der gerechten Verteilung des Lohnes für die einzelnen Arbeiten.

Gewisse Haupteinteilungen hat sich der menschliche Geist geschaffen, die,
69 v von den Lebensverhältnissen beeinflußt, die Ausmaße der Löhne regeln; sie bilden alle vereint das Lohngesetz.

Der Staat muß vor allem die Löhne seiner Diener im Sinne dieser Grundsätze bestimmen, er als die Gesamtheit aller Teile, quasi in einer Person zusammengefaßt, soll darauf sehen, daß in jenen Posten, die für das allgemeine Interesse arbeiten, die Entlohnung für die Arbeiten gerecht und nach dem Maße der Leistungen verteilt werde.

Er muß *wünschen*, daß ein gerechtes Lohnverfahren in allen Geschäften seiner Untertanen ausgeübt werde, darum aber ist es vor allem seine Pflicht,

[1] Menger enthält sich jeder Analyse des allgemeinen Lohnniveaus, abgesehen von der Bemerkung, daß die Festsetzung des Lohnes nicht willkürlich erfolgt, sondern nach einem 'Lohngesetz' (siehe unten), das er im weiteren als den Grund für die Lohndifferentiale hinstellt. Kapitel I.vi und I.viii des Wealth of Nations sozusagen überschlagend, gibt Menger sogleich eine Kurzfassung von I.x. Die Wiedergabe von Smith, der ja die angebotsseitigen Ursachen der Lohnunterschiede betont, entspricht in vielem nicht Mengers eigener Grenzproduktivitätstheorie der Entlohnung, welche auf den Beitrag zum Nutzen des Grenzkonsumenten und somit auf die Nachfrage abstellt. Menger steht hier auch in Widerspruch zu Rau, seiner hauptsächlichen deutschen Quelle: Rau behandelt – preistheoretisch – die Bestimmungsgründe des allgemeinen Lohnniveaus, äußert sich aber im Unterschied zu Smith nicht zu Lohnunterschieden.

Political economy X. 1876 March

Principles According to Which the State is to Pay Its Officials and Public Servants 69 r
(On the Theory of Wages)

The wage that is paid for any activity or performance in all the different occupations and is actually the purchasing price for labour performed is not determined by the discretion or inclination of employers and employees, but by certain principles and rules that transcend the boundaries of any single vocation or profession, of a people and of a state and are valid more or less for human society as a whole.

In the never-ending exchange of abilities and energies for tangible items of exchange, differentials[1] have developed that correspond to the relation between the work performed and the wage paid for it.

Innumerable influences contribute to the difficult question of what constitutes a just distribution of wages for the various types of work.

Man has thought up certain main categories that, having regard to practical life, determine the size of wages; collectively, they make up the Law of Wages. 69 v

Above all the state has to fix the wages of public servants with a view to these principles; as the representative of all its subjects, quasi a person, it has to see to it that wages are just and allocated in proportion to individual performance in all positions where people work for the common good.

The state must be interested in a just allocation of wages in all economic activities of its subjects; it is its foremost duty therefore to see to it that those who devote

[1] Menger skips the analysis of the general level of wages – apart from saying that the determination of wages is not arbitrary, but that there is a 'Law of Wages' (see below), which is explained as a theory of wage differentials. Thus, skipping chapters I.vi–viii of the Wealth of Nations, Menger immediately presents an abbreviated version of I.x, 'Of Wages and Profits in the different Employments of Labour and Stock'. Once more, the rendering of Smith, stressing the supply side causes of wage differentials, is much at variance with Menger's own marginal productivity theory of remuneration, stressing the contribution to the utility of the ultimate consumer and thus the demand side.

Menger is also at variance with Rau, his main German source, who treats the forces working on the general level of wages extensively in a price theoretic framework, but – in contrast to Smith – is silent on wage differentials.

darauf zu sehen, daß jene Menschen, die ihre Dienste dem Wohle des Ganzen, dem Staate widmen, auch dafür *entsprechend* entlohnt werden, *das ist*, nach dem Maße ihrer Ausbildung[2] und ihres Wirkungskreises.[3] Vor allem aber muß es eine Sorge jeder weisen Regierung sein, dem Talente und der fleißigen Verwertung *der geistigen Fähigkeiten* zum Besten des Ganzen eine freie Bahn
70 r zur Erlangung der hohen Stellen offen zu lassen.[4] Der Staat kann *nämlich* nicht wie der Private in ein und derselben Stelle die bessere Ausübung besser entlohnen, dafür aber eröffnet er den vorzüglichen *Staatsdienern* eine große Karriere, während der mittelmäßige sich im kleinen Wirkungskreise fortbewegt.

Im großen und ganzen beherrschen mehrere Prinzipien das Lohnsystem, *die man in ihrer Gesamtheit die Theorie vom Arbeitslohn* nennt.[5] Die gewöhnlichsten Arbeiten, die keine weitere Vorbildung erheischen, werden eben nur so viel entlohnt, um den Arbeiter*familien* den Lebensunterhalt zu gewähren.[6] Die höheren *sogenannten qualifizierten* Arbeiten, die schon eine Ausbildung voraussetzen, werden nach dem Maße der Kosten der nötigen Heranbildung *höher bezahlt*,[7] ferners ist die Annehmlichkeit oder Unannehmlichkeit der Arbeit von *Einfluß auf den Arbeitslohn*,[8] und *endlich die größeren oder geringeren Studienanlagen, die zur Ausübung eines Berufes erforderlich sind.*[9]

2 Dies ist der zweite von Smiths 'Hauptgründen' von Lohnunterschieden (I.x.b.1), derjenige, den Smith am ausführlichsten behandelt und der Menger am meisten am Herzen liegt, da er dem Kronprinzen die Grundsätze der Entlohnung der Staatsbeamten erklären will, zu denen er selbst gehörte. Dieser zweite Grund bei Smith sind die Kosten der Ausbildung. Vergleiche hierzu I.x.b.5–9. Smiths Aussagen über die Bezahlung von Juristen und Ärzten (die höheren österreichischen Beamten waren in der überwiegenden Mehrzahl Juristen oder Ärzte) stehen im Widerspruch zu einem der Hauptgedanken der Grenznutzenlehren, die Menger verfocht: Obwohl alle Juristen und Ärzte etwa gleiche Ausbildungskosten haben, sind ihre Einkommen doch sehr verschieden, und zwar je nach der Nachfrage nach ihren Leistungen.

3 Das soll wohl Smiths (1776) viertem Grund für Lohndifferentiale entsprechen (I.x.b.17): dem unterschiedlichen Vertrauen, das in Arbeitskräfte zu setzen ist. Auf österreichische Verhältnisse übertragen bedeutet das in etwa die Position des einzelnen Beamten in der Hierarchie und somit das Ausmaß seiner Verantwortung.

4 Hier wird ein dringendes Anliegen von Smith (1776) angesprochen (vergleiche I.x.c, 'Ungleichheiten, welche durch die europäische Wirtschaftspolitik veranlaßt sind'). Für österreichische Verhältnisse bedeutete das die Forderung, die hohen Beamtenstellen nicht der Aristokratie vorzubehalten – eine Forderung Mengers und später auch des Kronprinzen.

5 Nach Menger die Theorie der Lohndifferentiale.

6 Das ist die Kernaussage von Smith (1776) 'über den Arbeitslohn' (I.viii), z.B. I.viii.15: 'Ein Mensch muß stets von seiner Arbeit leben, und sein Lohn muß wenigstens hinreichend sein, um ihm den Unterhalt zu verschaffen.'

7 Wiederholung des zweiten Hauptgrundes von Smith (1776), I.x.b.5 (siehe oben, Anmerkung 2).

8 Smiths erstem Grund zufolge (I.x.b.2) schwankt der Arbeitslohn, 'je nachdem das Geschäft leicht oder schwer, reinlich oder unreinlich, ehrenvoll oder verachtet ist'.

9 Der Lehrer kommt hier nochmals auf die Ausbildungskosten zu sprechen. Ob Menger Smiths dritten Grund (I.x.b.11), die Beständigkeit oder Unbeständigkeit der Beschäftigung, wegließ? Der Kronprinz erfährt nie etwas über die Probleme der Arbeitslosigkeit, und das am Tiefpunkt der Großen Depression der 1870er Jahre. Menger könnte hier Smiths fünften Grund erwähnt haben (I.x.b.21), daß die Löhne mit der Wahrscheinlichkeit bzw. Unwahrscheinlichkeit des Erfolges in verschiedenen Beschäftigungen variieren, und diese Wahrscheinlichkeit von den

their services to the common good, to the state, are paid wages in proportion to their training[2] and their sphere of activity.[3] Above all, a wise government must see to it that talented people, intent on employing their intellectual faculties for the common good, have unrestricted access to high positions.[4] Unlike a private person in a comparable position, the state cannot pay a higher wage to the person doing the better job, but it can open up a promising career to excellent civil 70 r
servants while leaving mediocre ones within a limited sphere of activities.

On the whole, several principles dominate the system of wages; together, they are called the theory of wages.[5] The simplest sort of labour, for which no training at all is required, will be paid just enough to provide the means of subsistence for working class families.[6] The more advanced and, as it were, highly skilled types of labour require previous training and will be paid more, in proportion to the cost of the necessary training;[7] furthermore, the pleasantness or unpleasantness of the job affects the wage[8] and last of all the greater or lesser talent for training or studies needed to enter a profession or vocation.[9]

2 This is the second of Smith's 'principal circumstances' which cause wage differentials (I.x.b.l), the one that gets the lengthiest treatment and the one closest to Menger's heart as he wishes to explain to the Crown Prince the principles of remuneration of the professional civil service class, to which he himself belonged. This second reason of Smith's is the costliness of training. Smith, I.x.b.5: 'Secondly, the wages of labour vary with the easiness and cheapness, or the difficulty and expence of learning the business'. 6-8 elaborate this point. I.x.b.9 points out: 'Education in the ingenious arts and the liberal professions, is still more tedious and expensive. The pecuniary recompence, therefore ... of lawyers and physicians, ought to be much more liberal: and it is so accordingly'. Austrian civil servants were mainly lawyers (and physicians). Note once more that this is at variance with one of the main thrusts of the 'Marginalist Revolution', one of whose leaders was Menger. The marginalists stressed that, although all lawyers and physicians incur about equal cost in education, their incomes are very different according to the different valuations placed on their services by those who demand them.

3 This probably should stand for Smith's (1776) fourth reason for wage differentials, I.x.b.17, '... the small or great trust which must be reposed in the workmen', meaning in this case the position in the hierarchy or the level of responsibility of the civil servant.

4 This mirrors a great concern of Smith's (1776). See I.x.c, 'Inequalities occasioned by the Policy of Europe', where the author rails against 'restraining the competition in some employments'. (In the Austrian context this meant that higher positions in the civil service should not be reserved to members of the aristocracy – a known concern of Menger and later of the Crown Prince).

5 Which, according to Menger, is the theory of wage differentials.

6 This is the linch pin of Smith (1776), I.viii, 'Of the Wages of Labour'; see, e.g. I.viii.15: 'A man must always live by his work, and his wages must at least be sufficient to maintain him'.

7 Repetition of the second circumstance, ibid. I.x.b.5.

8 Smith's first circumstance, ibid. I.x.b.2: 'Firstly, the wages of labour vary with the ease or hardship, the cleanliness or dirtiness, the honourableness or dishonourableness of employment'.

9 Another repetition of the second circumstance, the cost of training. Menger may have skipped Smith's third reason (ibid. I.x.b.11), wages varying 'with the constancy or inconstancy of employment'. For the Crown Prince is never introduced to the problems of unemployment, and that at the very depth of the great depression of the 1870s. Menger may have mentioned

Der wichtigste dieser Grundsätze ist der ersterwähnte, das *sogenannte* eiserne
70 v Lohngesetz,[10] da es den Hauptgrundsatz jede*r Lohnbestimmung* enthält und sich *auf die* größte und zahlreichste Klasse der Arbeiter *bezieht, ja geradezu eine Existenzfrage derselben betrifft.*

Das oberste Prinzip jeder Entlohnung muß *für den Staat* die Gerechtigkeit und die Unparteilichkeit sein, da, *abgesehen von* der großen Immoralität jeder ungerechten Entlohnung und der damit verbundenen schrankenlosen Willkür, hierdurch die sicherste Basis des Staates, die Achtung seiner Mitglieder vor der Regierung, untergraben wird.

Es ist eine schwere Sache für den Staat, gerecht und klug in der Entlohnung seiner Diener zu verfahren. Leicht ist die Besoldung zu gering und trotz anderen Aneiferungsmitteln verläßt der Staatsdiener seine Stelle *oder stockt der Zufluß neuer tauglicher Kräfte für den Staatsdienst, wenn bei* großer und verantwortungsvoller Arbeit *den Staatsdienern* keine genügenden pekuniären
71 r Vorteile *geboten werden*;[11] doch ebenso leicht verfällt der Staat in den Fehler falscher Großmut; er will seine Diener auf Kosten des allgemeinen Wohles glänzend stellen und *schädigt solcherart* das Volk, für dessen Gedeihen und Wohlfahrt doch alle diese Staatsdiener *wirken sollen*. Der Staat soll gewiß nicht die Dienste seiner Diener verkennen, und soll sich der Mühseligkeit und Opferwilligkeit derselben bewußt sein,[12] doch er soll nicht über *das* Wohlwollen zu ihnen *die Rücksichten der Sparsamkeit vergessen. Mit einem Worte, der Staat soll seine Beamten und Diener weder zu hoch noch zu niedrig, sondern den allgemeinen Lohngesetzen entsprechend bezahlen.*

Der Staatsdienst in was immer für einem Gebiete ist eine Pflicht einzelner Mitglieder des Staates; er ist eine Ehre und eine Auszeichnung,[13] denn das Bewußtsein, dem Vaterlande zu dienen und dadurch für viele Gutes zu tun, seine Kräfte dem allgemeinen Wohle zu widmen, ist ein edles, schönes Gefühl, und daher sind auch die Träger dieser Idee vor jenen in ihrer sozialen Stellung ausgezeichnet, die nur für ihre eigenen Interessen arbeiten.

'Studienanlagen' abhänge. Immerhin wird dieser Grund später, S. 76v f., noch ausgeführt werden. (Vor Mengers Korrektur hatte Rudolf an dieser Stelle nur erwähnt, daß 'natürlich auch die Art der Ausführung' der Arbeit von Einfluß auf den Arbeitslohn sei.)

10 Bemerkenswert ist, daß Menger den Inbegriff der klassischen Theorie, die Subsistenztheorie des Lohnes, hier in der Sprache des revolutionären Sozialisten Lassalle wiedergibt.

11 Diese Formulierung des Gesetzes von Angebot und Nachfrage (Smith (1776), I.vii.7–15) als Bestimmungsgrund der Entlohnung der Staatsbeamten kommt grenznutzentheoretischen Grundsätzen am nächsten.

12 Entlohnung nach Leistung (Smiths erster Grundsatz, I.x.b.2) ist wiederum ein klassischer, nicht ein grenznutzentheoretischer Gedanke, zumindest solange man nicht von 'Leistungslohn' spricht, d.h. der Variation der Anstrengung mit dem Lohn – was Menger auch nirgends tut.

13 Vgl. Smith (1776), I.x.b.2, zur Ehre, die ein Beruf bringt, als Lohnkomponente. Nach Smith sind ehrenvolle Berufe eben dieser Eigenschaft wegen im allgemeinen unterbezahlt.

The most important of these principles is the first one mentioned, the so-called Iron Law of Wages;[10] it embodies the major principle of wage determination 70 v
and concerns the very existence of the largest and most numerous class of labourers.

In paying wages, the state must first and foremost observe the principles of justice and impartiality, for, apart from their great immorality and the unbridled wilfulness implied by them, unjust wages would undermine the firmest foundation of a state, the respect of its members for government.

In remunerating public servants, it is difficult for the state to be just and disinterested. Wages are easily set too low, and in spite of other incentives, public servants may leave their jobs, or the supply of new capable persons for the civil service may slacken, if insufficient monetary rewards are offered for important and responsible work;[11] but the state may just as easily make the mistake of showing inappropriate generosity; it may want to remunerate its servants 71 r
splendidly – at the expense of the common good – which damages the people for whose prosperity and welfare all these public servants should be working. Certainly, the state should not ignore the services of its employees and should be well aware of their efforts[12] and their willingness to make sacrifices, but benevolence should not make it oblivious to considerations of thrift. In a word: the state should pay civil servants and its other employees neither too much nor too little, but according to the general laws of wages.

Civil service in any field of activity is a duty of some members of society; it is an honour and a distinction,[13] since the knowledge that in serving one's country one is serving the interests of many and that one is devoting one's energies to the common good is noble and beautiful, and therefore those who represent this idea are distinguished in their social position from those who work solely for their own private interests.

Smith's fifth circumstance (ibid. I.x.b.21), wages varying 'according to the probability or improbability of success ... in different employments' and that this probability depended on talent. This point will be elaborated on on p. 76v f. (Before Menger's correction, Rudolf had here only mentioned that 'the manner of execution of work' would affect the wage.

10 It is particularly strange that Menger presents the very epitome of classical theory, the subsistence theory of wages, in the catchy German phrasing of the Revolutionary Socialist Ferdinand Lassalle!

11 This statement of the law of supply and demand (Smith (1776), I.vii.7–15) as a determinant of civil service remuneration comes closest to the principles of marginalist economics.

12 Remuneration according to effort (Smith's first circumstance, cf. I.x.b.2) is once again a classical and not a marginalist idea, at least as long as one does not consider 'efficiency wages', i.e. effort varying with wages, which, however, is nowhere suggested by Menger.

13 Smith (1776), I.x.b.2: 'Honour makes a great part of the reward of all honourable professions. In point of pecuniary gain, all things considered, they are generally underrecompensed'.

71 v Nachdem ich die allgemeinsten Grundsätze dargelegt habe, nach welchen die Staatsdiener zu entlohnen sind, übergehe ich nun zur Darstellung der für die einzelnen Kategorien derselben geltenden besonderen Grundsätze.

Auch der Staat hat Diener, welche die untersten Arbeiten verrichten, Diener, deren Heranbildung sehr geringe, vielleicht selbst gar keine Mühe*n und Kosten* verursacht;[14] wie z.B. die Amtsdiener, Postillone, Portiere bei Staatsgebäuden etc. etc. *Diesen Personen gegenüber* muß der Staat sich ganz nach der Lehre vom Arbeitslohne halten, welche bestimmt, daß vollkommen unqualifizierte und gemeine Arbeiter nur eben so viel erhalten, als sie zu ihrer und ihrer Familie *Erhaltung* benötigen *(den sogenannten notwendigen Unterhaltsbedarf)*;[15] es ist ein harter Grundsatz, doch es muß auch in dem Systeme der Arbeitslöhne ein Schema geben, und was für einen Lohn sollte der Arbeitgeber seinen Arbeitern bieten, deren Ausbildung eine kostspielige war und deren Talente hervorragend sind, *wenn er den gänzlich unqualifizierten Arbeitern einen ihren notwendigen Unterhaltsbedarf beträchtlich übersteigenden Lohn zahlen würde?* Bald würde dann das Maß der Löhne jedes Vermögen und alle Kräfte der einzelnen wie
72 r des Staates übersteigen; darum ist es eine eiserne Notwendigkeit, demjenigen Arbeiter, der ohne Bildung und Wissen nur solche Verrichtungen *zu leisten vermag*, die ein jeder in der kürzesten Zeit erlernt, lediglich das Erforderliche für den Lebensunterhalt zu geben.[16]

Nicht unerwähnt möchte ich hier einen Umstand lassen, welcher nicht ohne Einfluß auf die Entlohnung der Staatsdiener ist, nämlich den Ort, an dem der Arbeiter sich befindet; der Staatsdiener in einer kleinen Provinzstadt wird weniger Lohn erhalten als derjenige in derselben Stellung, der in Wien seinen Posten hat; und trotzdem wird ersterer wahrscheinlich *ebensogut, ja vielleicht* besser leben als letzterer, da in einer großen Stadt selbst die bescheidenste Existenz sehr teuer zu stehen kommt.[17]

Der Staat ist verpflichtet, aus Rücksichten der Gerechtigkeit und Billigkeit solche Verhältnisse in Betracht zu ziehen und ihnen Rechnung zu tragen.

Umständlicher und schwieriger schon wird es für den Staat, wenn er die Löhne seiner höheren, *der qualifizierten* Diener gerecht und zweckentsprechend *feststellen* will; *hier hat er sich ziemlich* an das Maß der Ausbildung und der
72 v Vorstudien *zu halten*; je kostspieliger dieselben waren, desto höher muß er auch den Lohn *fest*setzen.[18] Dies muß vor allem als Hauptgrundsatz gelten, denn dieser Vorgang allein *ist* ein gerechter und eifert die Jugend zu höheren Studien an;

14 Einmal mehr Smiths zweiter Grund, I.x.b.5.

15 Wiederum Smith (1776), I.viii.15.

16 Das steht in völligem Widerspruch zu der traditionellen österreichischen Vorstellung vom wohlmeinenden und väterlichen Monarchen, der um der Würde der Monarchie willen und der Dienste wegen, die sie ihm leisten, seinen Beamten mehr bezahlt.

17 Vgl. Smith (1776), I.viii.31, wiewohl er der Meinung ist, daß die Arbeitslöhne von Ort zu Ort größere Unterschiede aufweisen als die Preise der Nahrungsmittel.

18 Nochmals Smiths zweiter Grund, I.x.b.9.

After having laid down the most general principles for the remuneration of public servants, I shall now go on to present the particular principles pertaining to the various categories of them. 71 v

The state, too, has employees who perform the lowest type of work: servants who are trained at very little, perhaps at no effort and cost at all,[14] e.g. ushers, postilions, doormen in public buildings, etc. etc. In remunerating them, the state must strictly observe the theory of wages according to which unqualified and common labourers should receive just as much as they need for their own and their family's upkeep (the so-called minimum necessary for subsistence);[15] it is an austere principle, but there must be a pattern in the system of wages, and what sort of wage should the employer offer to employees whose training has been costly and whose talents are extraordinary if completely untrained employees were to be paid a wage which considerably exceeded the minimum necessary for subsistence? In that case the amount of wages paid would soon exceed the assets and powers of individuals and the state; therefore it is absolutely necessary that a person without training and education who performs only those duties that anybody can learn in no time at all be paid only what he needs to subsist.[16] 72 r

There is a factor not without influence upon the wages of public servants which I should not like to leave unmentioned, namely the locality of a worker; a public servant in a small town in the provinces will be paid less than one in the same position who works in Vienna, and yet he will live at least as comfortably or perhaps even more so than the latter, since in a big city even the most modest life-style is very costly.[17]

For reasons of justice and fairness the state is obliged to attend to such differences and take them into account.

It will be more complicated and more difficult for the state to determine the wages of its higher-ranking, higher-trained public servants in a just and appropriate manner; here it has to go mainly by the amount of training and previous studies; the costlier these were, the higher the wage.[18] That is to be taken as 72 v
the first and foremost principle, for this sort of calculation is the only just one and spurs young people to advanced studies; for wherever diligent training is

14 Once more Smith's (1776) second circumstance, I.x.b.5.

15 Again Smith, ibid. I.viii.15.

16 This is at variance with the generally received Austrian preconception of a benevolent and patriarchal monarch, who pays civil servants more because of the dignity of the monarchy and of their service to him.

17 Cf. Smith (1776), I.viii.31, though he thinks 'the wages of labour vary more from place to place than the price of provisions'.

18 Once more, Smith's second circumstance, ibid. I.x.b.9.

denn wo der fleißigen Ausbildung die Aussicht auf Erfolg geraubt ist, wird dieselbe immer mehr abnehmen und der Staat wird wirklich gebildete und daher tüchtige Diener für seine höheren Stellen entbehren und statt der Laufbahn, die eigentlich dem Verdienste und der Bildung offen stehen soll, wird ein gemeinschädliches Protektionswesen überhandnehmen.

Die Studien, welche zu den verschiedenen Stellen im Staatsdienste benötigt werden, sind sehr unterschiedliche.

Demjenigen, der viele Studienjahre *und somit eine langwierige und kostspielige Ausbildung* hinter sich hat und der daher mit einem reichen Wissen ausgerüstet ist, steht eine weite Bahn zur Erklimmung selbst der höchsten Stellen im Staatsdienste offen; für gewisse Berufe ist eine *längere, für andere eine kürzere*
73 r Reihe von Jahren der Vorbildung notwendig, z.B. für geringere Kanzleibeamte 4 Gymnasialklassen, für etwas höhere 8 Klassen; für *Konzeptsbeamte* und alle weiteren Grade sind die Universitätsstudien eine Bedingung, denn diesen ist die Bahn für die höchsten Stellen offen, welche *Personen von nicht akademischer Bildung* niemals erreichen können. Ebenso geht der Staat auch in den Unterrichtsangelegenheiten vor; zur Stelle eines Volksschullehrers kann leicht jemand gelangen, der *einen Präparandenkurs oder etwa* nur 4 Gymnasial- oder Realschulklassen durchgemacht *hat*, während an den Mittelschulen nur solche angestellt werden, die alle Gymnasialklassen und die Universitätsstudien studiert haben, es ist aber nicht notwendig, daß sie in einem bestimmten Fache das Doktorat erlangt hätten. Bei den Professoren der Hochschulen hingegen wird das Doktorat *und außerdem eine besondere Ausbildung in einer Wissenschaft* verlangt. *Es ist deshalb auch ganz begreiflich, wenn der Staat die Konzeptsbeamten im großen und ganzen höher entlohnt als die höheren und niederen Kanzleibeamten, die Lehrer an Hochschulen höher als jene* an Mittelschulen und diese wieder
73 v höher als jene an Volksschulen. Geradeso wird auch bei Entlohnung der Ärzte vorgegangen. Der Unterarzt, dessen Ausbildung eine viel geringere ist, der keine so schwierigen *und kostspieligen* Studien haben muß, wird auch viel weniger Lohn erhalten als der Oberarzt, der an der medizinischen Fakultät das Doktorat erlangt haben muß und durch kostspielige Studien sich vollkommen auf der Höhe seiner Wissenschaft *erhalten* muß.

Der Staat hat aber die Verpflichtung, bei dem Maße der Entlohnungen seiner Diener *noch manche andere* Verhältnisse zu berücksichtigen. Es gibt Ämter, *deren Träger neben dem* seiner Vorbildung entsprechenden Gehalte vom Staate noch ganz besondere Bezüge gewährt werden müssen.

Es sind dies Summen, die der Staat eigentlich nicht seinem Diener *für dessen*
74 r private *Zwecke* gibt, sondern man kann sagen, er übergibt sie demselben *für die Erfüllung spezieller Staatszwecke und bei manchen Stellen namentlich*, um den Glanz und die Macht *des Staates* zu bezeugen.[19]

19 Vgl. Smith (1776), V.i.h: 'Ausgaben zur Aufrechterhaltung des Ranges des Fürsten'.

deprived of all chances of success, it will decline more and more, and government will lack soundly trained and capable servants in the higher ranks, and instead of careers being open to those with merit and qualifications as would be proper, patronage detrimental to the common good will prevail.

The courses of study required for the various positions in government service are of the most diverse kind.

A person who has studied for many years and thus has had a time-consuming and costly education and who has command over a wealth of knowledge has a good chance of rising even to the highest positions in government service; for some positions more years of training are required, for others fewer; e.g. four years of grammar school for junior clerks and eight years of grammar school 73 r
for senior clerks; for legal clerks and all ranks above those, university training is required, since they may rise to the very highest ranks that people without academic training cannot attain under any circumstances. The same holds true for posts in the field of education; the position of elementary school teacher can easily be filled by a person who has taken a special preparatory course or who has had only four years of training in a grammar or secondary school, while secondary schools will employ only persons who have graduated from a grammar school and have finished a course of studies at a university, although they need not have acquired a doctor's degree in any particular field. For the position of university professor, on the other hand, the doctorate and additional special training in a particular discipline are required. Therefore it is quite reasonable for the state, on the whole, to pay more to legal clerks than to senior and junior clerks, more to university teachers than to secondary school teachers and more to the latter than to teachers in elementary schools. Physicians are remunerated in the same manner. An assistant physician, whose training is much less thorough and 73 v
who may not have taken a difficult and costly course of study, will be paid far less than a supervising physician, who must hold a doctor's degree from a medical faculty and stay fully abreast of the developments in his science through expensive additional study.

The state is obliged, however, to take account of various other factors in the remuneration of its servants. The holders of some offices must be paid extra sums in addition to the salary proportionate to their training.

Actually, such extra sums are not given to a public servant for his private use but rather, as it were, for fulfilling certain government functions and in some 74 r
cases expressly for the purpose of bearing witness to the splendour and the power of the state.[19]

[19] Cf. Smith, ibid. V.i.h, 'Of the Expence of supporting the Dignity of the Sovereign'.

Dies ist z.B. der Fall bei hohen Diplomaten, Ministern des Äußeren oder Ministerpräsidenten und Statthaltern.

Dies sind die höchsten Würdenträger der Beamtenwelt; ihr Rang erfordert eine *gewisse* Prachtentfaltung, da sie, wie es besonders bei den Diplomaten der Fall ist, ihren Staat auch im geselligen Leben vertreten.

Derselbe muß ihnen daher *gewisse Summen zuweisen*, um sich Equipagen zu halten, um Tafeln, Soireen und Bälle *etc.* geben zu können. *In manchen Fällen* reicht zwar auch dieser größere Lohn nicht aus, und *man pflegt daher bis jetzt zumeist* Männer mit eigenem großen Vermögen an diese Posten *zu stellen, obwohl darüber kein Zweifel bestehen kann, daß es am vorteilhaftesten wäre, wenn der Staat auch den Trägern dieser Posten eine vollständig ausreichende Entlohnung bieten und dadurch in die Lage versetzt würde, stets den Tauglichsten für diesen Posten wählen zu können.* Ähnlich ist es auch bei Kavallerieoffizieren der Fall, wo der Staat denselben ein Pferd und die Mittel, es zu erhalten, geben
74 v muß; dann ist dasselbe kein Luxusgegenstand, sondern das wichtigste Merkmal jedes Kavalleristen, seine Waffe, ohne die er seine volle Bedeutung verliert.

Nicht ohne Einfluß auf die Entlohnung der Staatsdiener *ist* auch der Umstand, ob der Staat denselben Naturalbezüge, *namentlich* Naturalwohnungen, gibt; dies ist für ärmere Beamte sowie auch für die Träger der höchsten Stellen eine große Wohltat und Ersparnis. Im entgegengesetzten Falle muß der Staat jenen seiner Diener, denen er nicht in der Lage ist, die Wohnungen in natura zu geben, ein Quartiergeld dem Lohne beifügen, welches ausreicht, sich eine seiner Stellung würdige Behausung zu verschaffen.

Abgesehen vom Soldatenstande, dessen Mitglieder fast alle in Staatsgebäuden wohnen, erhalten *nämlich* auch viele Beamte wie z.B. Statthalter, Bezirkshauptleute, Minister, Gesandte etc. etc. ärarische Gebäude zu ihrem Gebrauche. *In diesem Falle kann nämlich der Staat ihre Barbezüge etwas niedriger stellen als jene anderer gleichhochgestellter Staatsdiener, welche die obigen Vorteile nicht genießen.*

75 r Ebenso wie der *Private bei der* Entlohnung *seiner* Diener muß auch der Staat besondere Rücksicht auf die Annehmlichkeit und Unannehmlichkeit der einzelnen Berufsgeschäfte und auf die damit verbundenen Auszeichnungen nehmen.

Die Annehmlichkeit des Dienstes muß mit in den Lohn gerechnet werden und *wird denselben deshalb etwas verringern*; die Unannehmlichkeit *des Dienstes* vergrößert *dagegen den Lohn*, *weil man* überhaupt *nur zu einem solchen* Menschen für solche Geschäfte zu gewinnen vermag.[20]

So wird z.B. der Staat mit geringerem Lohne Forstleute und Jäger für die Staatsforste gewinnen können, während er zu Gerichtsdienern und Gefängniswärtern gewiß nur durch bessere Bezahlung Leute locken wird.

[20] Smiths erster Grund, I.x.b.2.

This is the case, for example, of senior diplomats, ministers of foreign affairs, or prime ministers and governors.

These are the highest dignitaries among civil servants; their rank calls for a certain display of pomp as they represent their government also in social life, which is especially true of diplomats.

Therefore the state has to furnish them with certain sums: for keeping coaches and for giving dinners, for after dinner parties, for balls, etc. In some cases even this higher remuneration is insufficient, and for this reason it is mostly men of substantial private means who tend to be chosen for these posts although, of course, there can be no doubt that it would be most advantageous if government could pay the holders of these posts quite adequately and thus always be able to select the person best qualified for a position. The same is true of cavalry officers, whom government must provide with a horse and the means for its upkeep; to a cavalry man a horse is not a luxury but his most important attribute, his weapon, without which he loses his full significance. 74 v

Pertinent to the remuneration of civil servants is the question, too, whether the state makes any payments in kind, above all whether it provides housing; this is a great benefit and saving for poorer civil servants as well as for the holders of the highest offices. For those public servants, on the other hand, for whom it cannot provide housing in kind, the state must pay a certain sum for accommodation that is sufficient for acquiring quarters commensurate with the position.

Apart from the military, nearly all of whose members live in state-owned buildings, many civil servants, e.g. governors, district governors, ministers, ambassadors, etc. etc., are also provided with state-owned homes. In these cases, the state can thus keep money wages somewhat lower than for other civil servants in the same ranks, who do not enjoy such advantages.

In paying its servants, the state – just like a private person – must give special attention to the attractiveness or unattractiveness of the various types of work and to the distinctions that should go with them. 75 r

If public service is attractive, this must be reflected in the wage by reducing it somewhat; unattractive public service, on the other hand, will push up the wage as the only way to induce somebody to do the required work.[20]

For example, the state will be able to employ forest rangers and gamekeepers for the state forests at lower pay, while certainly nothing but higher pay will induce people to become ushers in law courts or prison wardens.

20 Smith's first circumstance again, ibid. I.x.b.2.

Auch zum Bezirkshauptmann, der in seinem Bezirke einen fast selbständigen und großen Wirkungskreis hat, wird der Staat viel leichter Aspiranten trotz geringer
75 v Besoldung finden, als zu einer hohen Beamtenstelle im Ministerium, die bei großem Mangel von Selbständigkeit und einer geringen Verschiedenartigkeit der Geschäfte eine stete Abhängigkeit und Überwachung des Chefs und ein vollkommenes Verschwinden der eigenen Persönlichkeit mit sich bringt.

Als einen wesentlichen Faktor, der in allen Angelegenheiten des Staatdienstes und besonders bei der *Bemessung* der Entlohnung eine Rolle spielt, ist die Ehre, die mit einem Amte verbunden ist. [Richtig: 'Ein wesentlicher Faktor … ist die Ehre'; Hrsg.] In den meisten Fällen ist dies ein wichtiges Mittel, bei geringerer Entlohnung doch viele *begabte* junge Leute in den Staatsdienst zu ziehen;[21] es ist die Ehre auch ein Lohn, den vor allen der Staat geben kann, und nur diejenigen erhalten, die ihre Dienste dem allgemeinen Wohle weihen.

76 r Darum hat der Staat nebst der moralischen Verpflichtung auch ein materielles Interesse daran, die Ehre und das Ansehen seines Dienstes zu wahren und aufrechtzuerhalten; denn wo dieser Faktor verloren geht, werden große Summen, die den Staatsschatz schwächen, ausgegeben werden müssen, um *ausgezeichnete* Leute in den Staatsdienst zu ziehen, und dennoch wird dadurch der Staat nicht so gut bedient sein wie dort, wo bei geringerem Lohne das Ehrgefühl seine Diener zur größten Anspannung ihrer Kräfte drängt.

Darum liegt es im höchsten Interesse des Staates, daß der Militär- und Beamtenstand in großem Ansehen stehe und eine *besonders geachtete* soziale Stellung habe; dadurch werden viele gebildete und anständige Leute diese Berufe ergreifen, und der Staat wird mit geringerer Ausgabe bessere und
76 v ehrenwertere Staatsdiener aufweisen können; daher wird er auch verpflichtet sein, alle Angriffe gegen seine Militär- und Beamten-Hierarchie mit starker Hand abzuweisen und nichts zuzulassen, was imstande wäre, diese Berufe in ihrem Ansehen herabzusetzen oder zu entwürdigen; auch soll er denjenigen, der dies versucht, als einen dem Gemeinwohl sowie der Regierung schädlichen Feind betrachten.

Ein großes Interesse des Staates ist es auch, besonders für gewisse Stellen hervorragende Talente zu erhalten, denn es gibt Plätze, deren Wirkungskreis unbedingt Männer mit großer Begabung und vieler Bildung erheischt. Doch um solche zu erlangen, muß der Staat ihnen die Aussicht auf rasches Fortkommen ermöglichen,[22] denn größere Entlohnung der talentierten *Beamten einer bestimmten Rangstufe* als der untalentierten, *ein Verfahren, das* an und für sich kein schlechtes beim privaten Arbeitgeber ist,

[21] Im Heft des Kronprinzen Wiederholung eines schon behandelten Punktes, der sich bei Smith (1776), I.x.b.2, ausdrücklich erwähnt findet.

[22] Smiths fünfter Grund, der vom Kronprinzen zunächst nicht angegeben wurde. I.x.b.21 behandelt die Wahrscheinlichkeit oder Unwahrscheinlichkeit von Erfolg.

The state will also much more easily recruit candidates for the post of a district governor, who, though lowly paid, is quite independent and has a wide range of action in his district, than for a high position in a ministry, where, apart from 75 v
the lack of independence and variety in such a position, the person in it is always dependent on and controlled by a superior and is completely divested of his own personality.

The honour that attaches to an office is an essential factor in all matters of public service and especially in wage determination. In most cases this is an effective means for drawing many talented young people into the civil service in spite of lower pay;[21] honour is a reward in itself that only government can grant and only those who devote their services to the common good can receive.

Apart from its moral obligation the state thus has a material interest in 76 r
preserving and maintaining the honour and the prestige of its civil service; for where these are lost, large sums that drain the treasury will have to be spent in order to attract first-rate people, and yet the state will not be served as well as when – in spite of little pay – their honour leads public servants to exert themselves to the utmost.

It is in the foremost interest of the state that the military and the civil servants be held in high esteem and have an especially distinguished social position; this will cause many educated and respectable people to enter these careers, and the state will have better and more honest public servants at its disposal while spending less on them; it will thereby be obliged to reject firmly any attack on the military 76 v
and on the bureaucratic hierarchy and not permit anything likely to lower the reputation of or degrade these professions; if anyone tries to do so, the state should regard him as an enemy of the common good and of the government.

The state has a major interest also in finding persons with outstanding gifts especially for those positions with a sphere of activity that absolutely requires men with great talent and a very good education. But in order to recruit such people, the state must offer them the chance of quick advancement,[22] for if it paid its talented civil servants better than the untalented ones in the same rank – a policy that in itself is not bad when used by a private employer – it would be reproached for being

21 Repetition in the Notebook of a point already made and explicitly stated by Smith (1776) in I.x.b.2.

22 Smith's fifth circumstance, originally not given by Rudolf. Cf. ibid. I.x.b.21, 'the probability or improbability of success'.

77 r würde dem Staate als Ungerechtigkeit vorgeworfen werden; darum muß dem Talente eine *größere und raschere* Laufbahn offenstehen, während der Untalentierte in seinem beschränkten *Wirkungs*kreise verbleibt.

Dadurch werden viele talentierte Männer in den Staatsdienst gelockt, denn sie sind sich bewußt, daß ihrem Ehrgeize Genugtuung geschehen wird und auch ihr ferneres *materielles Wohl* in ihren eigenen Händen ruht.

Den größten Schaden bereitet sich der Staat selbst durch das Protektionswesen, denn er führt *in das System der Entlohnung seiner Diener* eine unmoralische Willkür und Ungerechtigkeit ein, die Vertrauen und Ansehen raubt, sowie auch dadurch die guten Elemente sich vom Staatsdienste zurückziehen, während die schlechten überhandnehmen. Die Regierung, die eigentlich erhaben über den gemeinen Leidenschaften und Parteigetrieben stehen soll, sinkt dadurch zur Tiefe der Intrigen herab.

77 v Es gibt Anstellungen, zu denen der Staat Männer von besonderer Ehrlichkeit und Rechtlichkeit notwendig braucht. Da oft besonders für Leute *der* unteren Klassen die Versuchung eine sehr große ist und der Staat *für gewisse Stellen* Männer benötigt, in die er sein volles Vertrauen setzen kann, muß er in gewissen Anstellungen die Vertrauenswürdigkeit *besonders* entlohnen.[1]

Das ist z.B. der Fall bei Staatsdienern, die *viel* mit Geld zu tun haben,[2] wie Kassiere und *Verwalter von Staatsvermögen*; bei Beamten, welche große Staatsgeheimnisse erfahren oder selbst bei Ministern, besonders bei Finanzministern, denen ihre Stellung oft die Möglichkeit verschafft, vieles früher zu wissen als das große Publikum, was, wenn sie es geschickt zu benützen verstehen, ihnen große Geldvorteile bieten kann.

Natürlich sind aber solche Handlungen für den Staat von Nachteil, da sie stark
78 r an den Betrug streifen und die Bevölkerung eine Benützung der hohen Stellung zu privativem Vorteil auf Kosten anderer *mit Recht* sehr übelnimmt und leicht in der flüchtigen Beurteilung der Dinge, statt den Verdacht auf den einzelnen zu beschränken, gleich die ganze Regierung verdächtigt.

Für die meisten unbemittelten Menschen ist es eine Hauptsorge und der Grund vieler Bekümmernis, in welcher Weise *sie* ihre alten Tage zubringen *werden*, auch beschäftigt *jeden Familienvater* der Gedanke sehr, wie, im Falle er früh sterben würde, seine Frau und Kinder versorgt *würden*.

1 Smiths vierter Grund, I.x.b.17, das 'größere oder geringere Vertrauen'.

2 Smith (1776), I.x.b.18.

Political economy XI. 1876 March

unjust; therefore the talented person must have the prospect of a greater and 77 r
faster career while the untalented person will remain in his restricted sphere of activities.

In this manner, many gifted men are drawn into the civil service as they are aware that their ambitions will be fulfilled and that their future material well-being rests in their own hands.

The state causes the greatest damage to itself by practising patronage, for this introduces an immoral wilfulness and injustice into the system of remunerating public servants, which destroys the confidence in and the reputation of government and causes the good people to leave public service and the bad sort to take over. The government, which is supposed really to be above common passions and party clamour, thereby sinks to the level of intrigue.

There are positions in which the state urgently needs men of extraordinary 77 v
honesty and integrity. Since especially lower class people are often prone to temptation and since government has to find absolutely trustworthy men for certain positions, it must pay extra for such reliability in these positions.[1]

This is true e.g. for civil servants who handle money,[2] such as cashiers and superintendents of state property; it is also true for civil servants who are informed of major state secrets or even for ministers, especially ministers of finance, whose position enables them to know about matters sooner than the general public – knowledge which can bring substantial monetary advantages if they make clever use of it.

Naturally such actions are detrimental to the state since they come close to
being fraudulent, and the general public rightly and strongly resents the abuse 78 r
of a high position for one's personal advantage at other people's expense; in hasty judgement it easily suspects the government as a whole instead of restricting its suspicions to the single perpetrator.

To most people without material means the question how they will pass their old age presents a major problem causing much worry; every family head is also concerned about how his wife and children would be cared for if he were to die at an early age.

1 Smith's fourth circumstance, ibid. I.x.b.17, variation of pay 'according to the small or great trust which must be reposed in the workmen', now more clearly explained than before.

2 Smith, ibid. I.x.b.18.

Der private Arbeitgeber zahlt oft seinen Bediensteten mehr als der Staat und sie können, so lange sie arbeiten, ein besseres Leben führen. Doch sobald das Alter und die Arbeitsunfähigkeit eintritt, ist der noch so verdiente Arbeiter brotlos vor die Türe gestellt; der Staat aber sichert seinen Dienern für ihre alten Tage eine entsprechende Pension.

Das ist ein kräftiges Mittel, mit dessen Hilfe der Staat manche Männer in seine Dienste lockt und durch welches er sich manche verhältnismäßig geringe
78 v Entlohnung möglich macht; eben dieselbe Wirkung haben auch die Staatsversorgungen der Witwen und Waisen; es sind dies kräftige Magnete, die viele in die Staatsdienste ziehen, denn die Beruhigung, das eigene Alter und die Existenz der Familie gesichert zu wissen, ist den meisten mehr wert als der momentane größere *Arbeitslohn oder Gehalt*, den häufig Privatanstellungen gewähren.

Dagegen ist die willkürliche Verleihung solcher Vorzüge an unverdiente, oft junge Staatsdiener und die unbegründete Bevorzugung einzelner zum Schaden vielleicht verdienterer älterer Diener ein Verfahren, welches das Ansehen der Regierung herabsetzt und manche gute Elemente zum Austritte bewegt, während dadurch schlechtere herangezogen werden.

Grundlose Bevorzugungen der Mitglieder eines und desselben Amtes dagegen
79 r *und* vollkommen unbegründete Entlassungen anderer nähren und vergrößern die Unzufriedenheit, und wo die reinste Gerechtigkeit und gleiche Behandlung aller nicht ganz streng durchgeführt wird, schwindet der gute Geist, und statt seiner treten Intrigen und Protektionswesen ins Leben; dadurch wird der Staat immer schwerer *tüchtige* Leute für seine vielen wichtigen Stellen finden, und er wird zu dem Mittel großen Lohnes greifen müssen, was fühlbar seinen Schatz verkleinern wird.

Darum muß der Staat schon durch die Schule den Patriotismus, das Ehrgefühl und das Bewußtsein, welch schöner Zweck in der Arbeit des einzelnen für das Gesamtwohl liegt, heben und nähren; auf diese Weise zieht er sich seine Jugend heran, die in gereifteren Jahren bereit sein wird, ihre Tätigkeit dem Staate zu widmen. Um aber dann ausgezeichnete Diener aufweisen zu können, muß die
79 v Regierung mit dem Staatsdienste Auszeichnungen und Ehren verbinden *und den Staatsdienern* eine gute soziale Stellung verschaffen, dadurch wird auch das Ehrgefühl und das Ansehen der Staatsdiener geweckt. Durch Pensionen und die früher schon erwähnten Versorgungen muß der Staat denselben eine gesicherte Existenz bis zu ihrem Tode verschaffen und ihre Familie *versorgen.*

Auf diese Weise wird der Staat bei einer geringen Belastung des Staatsschatzes sich einen ehrenwerten, tüchtigen Militär- und Beamtenstand heranbilden, der, getragen von Ehrgefühl und Patriotismus, aufopferungsvoll seine Dienste dem Wohle der Gesamtheit widmet.

17. März 1876 Rudolf

The private employer often pays his employees more than the state does and, as long as they continue to work, private employees can lead a more comfortable life. But as soon as old age and infirmity set in, the worker, no matter how deserving, is sacked and loses his livelihood; the state, on the other hand, pays an appropriate old age pension to its servants.

This is an effective method by which the state attracts a number of men into its employ and by which it can get away with comparatively low wages for a number of posts; state pensions to widows and orphans have just the same effect; 78 v
they act as powerful magnets, drawing many into public service, as most people value the assurance that their old age and their family's livelihood are provided for more highly than the temporarily higher wage or salary often commanded in private employment.

If, on the other hand, such benefits are arbitrarily conferred upon undeserving young public servants and for no good reason some of them are favoured at the expense of older and perhaps more deserving persons, then the government's reputation will be reduced, many good people will leave its service, and worse ones will be attracted.

Unfounded preferences for some office holders and wholly unjustified
dismissals of others feed and increase dissatisfaction and when true justice and 79 r
equal treatment are not quite strictly observed, the productive spirit vanishes, and intrigues and patronage step into its place; thus, the state will have increasing difficulties in finding capable persons for the many important positions to be filled, and it will have to have recourse to high wages – which will noticeably diminish its resources.

Therefore the state must enhance and foster patriotism, self-respect, and an awareness that it is meritorious to work for the common good; in this way, it can have its young people brought up so that, when grown up, they will be prepared to devote their energies to the state. But in order to have excellent public servants, the government has to have honours and distinctions to go with public
service and has to provide its servants with a good social position, thereby boosting 79 v
the self-respect and prestige of public servants. Through pensions and the sort of provisions mentioned above, the state must take on responsibility for their livelihood until their death and provide for their families.

In this manner, the state, while spending only a moderate amount of public resources, will come to have a class of honourable and capable military and civil servants who, borne by self-respect and patriotism, will devote their life's work to the common good.

17 March 1876 Rudolf

80r [Am Rand: begonnen 18. März 1876]

Wovon hängt die Höhe des Zinsfußes bei Staatsanleihen ab? (Zur Lehre vom Kapitalzins)[3]

Der Zinsfuß, zu welchem der Staat seine Darlehen in seinen großen Geschäften erhält, richtet sich nach ähnlichen Prinzipien, wie im kleinen es bei den einzelnen Personen der Fall ist.

Wie in allem und jedem *finden* die guten oder üblen Verhältnisse des Staates sowohl wie des einzelnen auch in der Größe des Zinsfußes, der bei Darlehen erhalten wird, *den Ausdruck. Der Zinsfuß ist solcherart das Spiegelbild aller* privatesten *wirtschaftlichen Einflüsse*,[4] welche sich unwillkürlich in demselben geltend machen.

Wenn der Staat nur die Gesamtheit aller Teile ist, so wird *sein Kredit auch von ihrem Kredit* beherrscht, während diese auch in solchen Angelegenheiten,
80 v wo er als ein Ganzes handelt, bis in die kleinsten Details dominiert werden.

Darum kann man vollkommen mit Recht sagen: Es richte sich der Zinsfuß des einzelnen nach dem des ganzen Landes, und der Ruf der Sicherheit in Geldgeschäften, des Reichtums an Kapitalen *in einem Volke*[5] wird *wiederum* wohltuend *auf den Staatskredit zurückwirken*; natürlich kann man diesen Einfluß des guten oder schlechten Rufes der Gesamtheit[6] nur als einen Charakterzug betrachten, der sich im großen und ganzen über die Geldverhältnisse eines Volkes erstreckt: Im einzelnen spielen die äußeren und inneren Charaktereigenschaften und die *wirtschaftliche* Lage der einzelnen Person die wichtigste Rolle.[7]

Der Zinsfuß hängt daher hauptsächlich von dem landesüblichen Zinsfuß im allgemeinen, und *im besonderen* von dem Kredit und der Vertrauenswürdigkeit desjenigen ab, der das Darlehen nimmt. *Diese Vertrauenswürdigkeit des Kreditwerbers bei den Kapitalisten ist aber umso größer, je gesicherter seine*

3 Menger hält sich in seiner Darstellung der Lohntheorie an Smiths Kapitel I.x, das die Lohndifferentiale behandelt, und nicht an Kapitel I.viii, das sich mit dem Lohnniveau befaßt. Nun kehrt er nochmals zu Smith (1776) zurück und präsentiert I.ix, 'Der Kapitalgewinn', das von Absatz 4 an hauptsächlich den Kapitalzins behandelt. Ebenso wie Menger das Thema der Löhne vom Standpunkt des Staates aus als Frage der angemessenen Entlohnung der Staatsdiener behandelte, diskutiert er nun den Zinssatz unter dem Aspekt der Zinsen, die der Staat für seine Anleihen zu bezahlen hat.

4 Smith (1776) betont, daß hoheitliche Regelungen des Zinssatzes dort, wo sie wirksam waren (in England) sich nach dem Marktzinssatz richteten, nicht umgekehrt (I.ix.5). Das ganze Kapitel dreht sich darum, daß der Zinssatz ein Ausdruck der wirtschaftlichen Lage – des Reichtums oder der Armut – eines Landes sei.

5 Smith (1776), I.ix.13.

6 Smith (1776), I.ix.16, erwähnt als einen Grund für hohe Zinsen die Unsicherheit der Rückzahlung.

7 Rau (1855), S. 281–4, dürfte für diesen und den nächsten Absatz Pate gestanden sein. Rau behandelt die Zinswirkung der Risikounterschiede zwischen verschiedenen Schuldnern und auch die Bedeutung der Rechtssicherheit bzw. -unsicherheit.

[In the margin: begun 18 March 1876] 80 r

What Determines the Rate of Interest for Treasury Loans? (On the Theory of Interest)[3]

The rate of interest at which government can borrow on a large scale is determined by principles similar to those that hold for individuals on a small scale.

As with everything else, many favourable or unfavourable circumstances of the government <u>and</u> the individual are expressed in the rate of interest for loans. Thus, the rate of interest reflects all the most private economic influences[4] that unintentionally show up in it.

If the state is but the sum of its parts, its credit is determined by the credit of the individuals in it, while in matters where the government acts for society as a whole, it dominates its individual components down to the smallest details. 80 v

Therefore it is correct to say: the rate of interest asked of an individual should depend on that of the whole country, and a society's reputation for reliability in financial matters and its abundance of capital[5] will favourably affect the government's credit; naturally, whether the reputation of a country as a whole is good or bad[6] can only be regarded as a very general feature of its financial situation: in individual cases, a person's acquired and innate characteristics and his economic situation are the most important factors.[7]

The rate of interest therefore depends above all on a country's customary rate of interest in general, and also on the credit and trustworthiness of the borrower in particular. For the capitalist lender a borrower's trustworthiness is the greater

3 As Menger has presented the theory of wages in the differential form of Smith (1776), I.x, 'Of Wages…in the different Employments', and not from I.viii, which discusses the wage level, he now backtracks and presents I.ix, 'Of the Profits of Stock', which – from ix.4 onward – treats mainly of interest. Just as wages were treated from the government angle of the appropriate pay of civil servants, so it is here 'the rate of interest at which government can borrow' which is the line of argument chosen.

4 Smith (1776) stresses that 'statutory regulations' of the rate of interest, where they were effective (viz. in England), 'seem to have followed and not to have gone before the market rate of interest' (I.ix.5). The whole chapter belabours the point that the rate of interest is an expression of 'the condition of a country, as to wealth or poverty'.

5 Smith (1776), I.ix.13.

6 Smith (1776), I.ix.16, gives 'the uncertainty of recovering … money' as one reason for high interest.

7 Rau (1855), pp. 281–84, probably inspired this paragraph and the next. Rau stresses the effect of the differential riskiness of different debtors on interest and also the importance of legal security or insecurity.

Geschäfte, je größer sein Kapitalreichtum und die Solidität seines Charakters ist.

81 r Gerade dieselben *Voraussetzungen bedingen nun auch die Kreditfähigkeit* des Staates.[8] Der Zinsfuß wird ein geringer sein, wenn das Land durch Reichtum an Kapitalien *hervorragt und deshalb der Zinsfuß in diesem Lande ganz im allgemeinen ein geringer ist.*[9]

Hierin liegt der Lohn der Sparsamkeit für den Staat, sowohl wie für den einzelnen. Ist die Sparsamkeit groß und werden in der Folge hievon viele Kapitalien angesammelt, so werden nicht nur die einzelnen, sondern auch der Staat bei geringem Zinsfuß Darlehen erhalten und mit geringeren Kosten ihre Unternehmungen durchführen; während hingegen *in einem durch Verschwendung von Kapitalien entblößten Staate, in welchem die Bürger* im Ruf des Leichtsinns stehen, neben dem wirklichen Schaden und dem Mangel, an dem sie durch ihre ungünstigen wirtschaftlichen Verhältnisse *leiden, dieselben* auch noch den fühlbaren Nachteil eines hohen Zinsfußes *empfinden werden*, der ihnen oft viele Unternehmungen unmöglich machen, gewiß aber alles teurer und schwerer erreichen
81 v lassen wird.[10]

In dieser Beziehung haben einen besonderen Einfluß auch häufig wiederkehrende Anleihen des Staates und übermäßig hohe Steuern.[11] *Denn die ersteren vermindern den Kapitalreichtum des Landes,*[12] *während die letzteren die Kapitalansammlung erschweren.*[13] *In beiden Fällen wird der Staat daher eine Erhöhung des Zinsfußes bewirken. Die Höhe des Zinsfußes, zu welchem der Staat Darlehen erhält, hängt ferner bei ihm, gleich wie bei einem Privaten, von dem Rufe seiner Rechtlichkeit und Pünktlichkeit in der Erfüllung seiner Verpflichtungen ab.*

Gleich wie beim einzelnen ist es *deshalb* auch beim Staate eine seiner
82 r hauptsächlichen Verpflichtungen, mit Rechtlichkeit und Genauigkeit in den großen Geldgeschäften vorzugehen und pünktlich *allen seinen Verpflichtungen nachzukommen*[14] und im eigenen und des gesamten Landes größten Vorteil den

[8] Smith (1776), V.iii.2: 'Dieselbe Neigung zum Sparen und Zurücklegen herrschte im Staat wie bei den Untertanen'.

[9] Rau (1855), S. 290: 'Der Zinsfuß ist dagegen niedrig 1) bei hohem Wohlstande, wo das Capital sich beträchtlich schneller vermehrt als die Volksmenge'.

[10] Menger präsentiert – auch hier im Gegensatz zu seiner eigenen subjektiven Wertlehre – eine Kostentheorie des Wertes (vgl. z.B. Smith (1776), I.vii.33, wo ausgesagt wird, daß der natürliche Preis der Waren mit dem 'natürlichen Satze' jedes seiner Bestandteile – Arbeitslohn, Gewinn und Rente – schwanke). Eine Erhöhung des Zinssatzes macht also 'alles teurer'.

[11] Mäßige Steuern sind eine wichtige Voraussetzung für den Wohlstand eines Landes; so Smith (1776), IV.vii.b.20. Holland etwa habe sich durch hohe Steuern 'ruiniert' (V.ii.k.79).

[12] Die Staatsverschuldung vermindert das Kapital, das den 'produktiven Arbeiter' erhalten soll, und somit den Wohlstand eines Landes; so Smith (1776), V.iii.47; sie ist auch Ursache einer Kapitalvernichtung (V.iii.49).

[13] Laut Smith (1776), V.ii.h.14, vermindern hohe Steuern das Kapital.

[14] Möglicherweise orientiert sich Menger hier auch an einer der liberalsten Passagen in dem Lehrbuch seines älteren Kollegen in Wien, Lorenz von Stein (1871), S. 672 ff., über 'Die Verzinsung der Staatsschuld'; hier S. 673: 'Die Finanzverwaltung (muß) die Höhe und den Werth ihres Credits durch ihre Zuverlässigkeit in der wirklichen Erfüllung eingegangener Zinsverpflichtungen sichern'.

the safer his business transactions, the bigger his stock of capital, and the more reliable his personality.

These very same qualities also determine a government's credit.[8] The rate 81 r
of interest on a loan will be low when a country is noted for its abundance of capital and the rate of interest there is generally low therefore.[9]

This is the reward of thriftiness for government as well as for the individual. If thrift is substantial so that capital is accumulated by many people, then not only individuals but also the state will be able to borrow at low rates of interest and will do business at lower cost; if, on the other hand, a country is divested of capital because of its extravagance and if its citizens have a reputation for recklessness, they will suffer actual damage and want because of their unfavourable economic circumstances; in addition, they will feel the disadvantage of a high rate of interest, which will often render many enterprises impossible and certainly
make everything more expensive and harder to come by.[10] 81 v

In this respect, both frequent borrowing by the state and excessive taxes[11] are of special influence. The former diminishes a country's stock of capital[12] while the latter stand in the way of capital accumulation.[13] In both cases, the state causes the rate of interest to go up. Furthermore, the rate of interest at which the state can borrow depends upon its reputation for honesty and promptness in meeting its obligations – just as with a private person.

Just as with the individual, it is therefore one of government's major obligations
to go about its large-scale monetary operations honestly and painstakingly, to 82 r
meet all its obligations promptly,[14] and to maintain the reputation of honesty

[8] Smith (1776), V.iii.2: 'The same disposition to save and to hoard prevailed in the sovereign, as well as in the subjects'.

[9] Rau (1855), p. 290: The rate of interest is low when a country is wealthy, meaning where capital grows considerably more rapidly than population.

[10] Again in contrast to his own subjective value theory Menger presents a cost theory of value (e.g. Smith (1776), I.vii.33, 'The natural price… varies with the natural rate of each of its component parts, of wages, profit, and rent'). Therefore, a higher rate of interest makes 'everything more expensive'.

[11] 'Moderation of … taxes' is an important reason for a country's prosperity, according to Smith (1776), IV.vii.b.20, while 'Holland' has been 'ruined' by 'heavy taxes' (V.ii.k.79); while a 'full complement of riches' is the main reason for low interest rates (I.ix.14).

[12] Public debt reduces the capital which supports 'productive' labour and thus the prosperity of a country, according to Smith (1776), V.iii.47, and causes 'destruction of … capital', according to V.iii.49.

[13] High taxes diminish the stock of capital, according to Smith (1776), V.ii.h.14.

[14] Here, Menger may have in mind a most liberal paragraph in the textbook of his senior colleague at Vienna University, Lorenz von Stein (1871), p. 672 ff., 'The Interest on the Public Debt': 'the treasury has to ensure the amount and the value of what it can borrow by complete reliability in the unflinching payment of interest owed' (p. 673).

Ruf der Ehrlichkeit und der Solidität aufrecht zu erhalten. Diese Prinzipien werden sich dann heilbringend auf das Volk erstrecken, wodurch Blüte der Volkswirtschaft und durch Erleichterung aller Geldgeschäfte allgemeiner Reichtum entstehen wird.

Der Staat hat aber *besonderen Grund, in seiner Geldangelegenheit mit skrupulosester Ehrlichkeit vorzugehen*. Seine Unredlichkeiten ziehen *nämlich* große Folgen nach sich.[15] Auch steht über dem einzelnen das wachsame Gericht, während die Regierung keinen höheren Richter über sich kennt, der *sie zur Erfüllung ihrer Verpflichtungen* anhalten könnte. Doch auch ihren Freveln gegen die Grundsätze der Ehrlichkeit sind durch die aus denselben entstehenden bedeutenden positiven wie moralischen Schäden und die *aus denselben resultierende*
82 v Unzufriedenheit, die häufig selbst Umsturz herbeiführt, Schranken gesetzt; auch muß man den Urteilsspruch der Geschichte als einen wichtigen Faktor bezeichnen, der Monarchen und Regierungen vor mancher schlechten Handlung in großen Staatsangelegenheiten zurückhalt*en soll*.

Die Versündigung gegen die Prinzipien rächt sich bitter, wenn der unordentlichen Wirtschaft ein oder gar mehrere Staatsbankrotte folgen,[16] dann wird der Zinsfuß *bei etwa notwendig werdenden neuen* Staatsdarlehen ungemein steigen und es wird große Mühe kosten, überhaupt *Kredit zu finden*; auch werden solche Zustände herbeigeführt, wenn die Regierung ihre Gläubiger durch ungerechte Vexationen und Schikanen plagt, wie z.B., wenn *die Kupons der Staatsschuld mit hohen Steuern belegt, wenn* die Zahlstellen der Kupons im Auslande aufgehoben werden oder in sonstiger Weise die Einkassierung der Zinsen der Staatsschuld den Gläubigern erschwert wird.

83 r Es gibt auch Fälle, wo der Staat nicht bloß durch eigenes Verschulden, sondern *bisweilen* auch durch den Zwang gewisser Ereignisse genötigt wird, *größere Ausgaben zu machen, als seine Einnahmen betragen, und dadurch nach und nach* in eine üble Finanzlage gerät. Meistens werden in der momentanen Not die Folgen *der übermäßigen Inanspruchnahme des Kredites* nicht berücksichtigt,[17] und so wächst die Kalamität mit dem *steigenden Defizite*, und dadurch wird die Erlangung *neuer Anleihen* immer schwieriger. In Folge einer *solchen* Situation steigt der Zinsfuß bei Staatsanleihen immer mehr, das Defizit *wird ein perpetuierliches*, namentlich, wenn die Steuern ohnedies schon sehr bedeutend sind und große Schulden auf dem bereits geschwächten Staatsschatz lasten.

Wenn leicht vorausgesehen werden kann, daß einem Lande Kriege oder Revolutionen drohen, wird der Zinsfuß auch steigen, denn jeder weiß, daß
83 v ähnliche Ereignisse bedeutende Geldsummen erfordern und verzehren, daß

15 Smith (1776), V.iii.7: 'Handel und Industrie können selten lange in einem Staate blühen, der sich nicht einer geregelten Rechtspflege erfreut'.

16 Den Staatsbankrott als Folge der Staatsverschuldung behandelt Smith in V.iii.60.

17 Vgl. Smith (1776), V.iii.4,5.

and trustworthiness – to its own and the whole country's greatest advantage. The observation of these principles will have beneficial effects upon the people: the economy will flourish, and as all financial transactions become easier, general prosperity will come about.

Government, though, has a special reason for transacting its financial affairs with the most scrupulous honesty. Dishonesty on its part would have momentous consequences.[15] And while the individual has above him the watchful courts of justice, government has no judge to look up to who could impel it to meet its obligations. But then its trespasses against the principles of honesty find their limits in the ensuing substantial damages – material as well as moral – and the consequent dissatisfaction which of itself often leads to revolt; furthermore, the judgement of history must be considered a factor of some weight, supposed to 82 v
keep monarchs and governments from not a few misdeeds with respect to affairs of state.

The violation of principles will be painfully paid for when disorder in economic matters is followed by national bankruptcy once or even several times;[16] then the rate of interest for new treasury loans which may become necessary will go up enormously, and it will be very difficult to find any lenders at all; like situations are brought about if government besets its creditors with unjustified vexation and chicanery as, for example, if the interest paid on treasury bonds is highly taxed, if the offices that are to pay out such interest abroad are closed down, or if the payment of interest on treasury bonds to the creditors is in any other way impeded.

It can also happen that the state has to spend more than its income – not only 83 r
through its own fault but sometimes through force of circumstances – and thus eventually finds itself in financial straits. In an emergency, the consequences of excessive debts are usually not taken into account,[17] and thus the calamity grows with the rising deficit, which makes it increasingly difficult to raise further loans. In consequence, the rate of interest on treasury loans will rise ever higher, and the deficit will be there to stay, especially if the tax burden is quite substantial to start with and the public treasury is already burdened with large debts.

If it can be predicted with some probability that a country will be threatened by war or revolution, the interest rate will also go up, for everyone knows that such occasions call for and use up considerable sums of money and that, 83 v

15 Smith (1776), V.iii.7: 'Commerce and manufactures … can seldom flourish in any state in which there is not a certain degree of confidence in the justice of government'.

16 National bankruptcy due to public debt is treated by Smith (1776), V.iii.60.

17 Cf. Smith (1776), V.iii.4,5.

weiters die Einnahmsquellen der Regierung, die Steuern nämlich, durch das Darniederliegen jeder Arbeit stocken und in Folge aller dieser Gründe die Existenz und die Ordnung eines Staates aufs Spiel gesetzt ist, daher auch die Rückzahlung *und Verzinsung* der Schulden prekär wird.

Ein Staat, welcher vor Ausbruch solcher Gefahren schon durch frühere Mißgriffe oder frühere Unglück*sfälle* und Umwälzungen in ungeordneten Geldverhältnissen sich befindet, riskiert viel durch ähnliche Kämpfe, da er schwerlich in diesem Falle glücklich aus denselben hervorgehen wird. Denn viel Geld und eine berühmte Solidität, auf welche bauend jeder gern *dem Staate Kredit gewährt*, sind Grundfesten des Staates,[18] auf die gestützt er ruhig jeder Gefahr ins Auge sehen kann.

84 r Diesen Standpunkt, den wir noch lange nicht erreicht haben, sollten wir in Österreich zu erreichen streben.

Damit das aber gelinge, müssen wir vor allem bestrebt sein, durch Regelung unseres Papiergeldwesens die Nationalbank auf einen gesunden Standpunkt zu bringen, *durch große Sparsamkeit das dauernde Gleichgewicht zwischen Staatseinnahmen und Staatsausgaben herzustellen*,[19] *durch pünktliche Erfüllung der Verpflichtung den Staatskredit zu heben* und die Steuern womöglich zu erniedrigen; *oder doch durch zweckmäßige Regierungsmaßregeln den Volksreichtum zu erhöhen.*

Dann werden wir in den Ruf eines Staates mit geordneten Finanzen kommen, und im Bedarfsfalle werden wir Geld zu mäßigen *Zinsen* erhalten; dadurch würden wir das Ansehen nach außen und die Zufriedenheit im Inlande steigern.

Wien, den 23. März 1876 Rudolf

18 Smith (1776), V.iii.4: 'Der Mangel an Sparsamkeit im Frieden nötigt zum Schuldenmachen in Kriegszeiten'.

19 In diesem Sinne endet Smith (1776); vgl. V.iii.92.

furthermore, public revenues, i.e. taxes, decline because nobody works; as a consequence the order and very existence of the state are at stake so that repaying and servicing its debts is rendered uncertain.

If, prior to such dangers, the finances of a state have already been in disarray – because of earlier mistakes or misfortunes and upheavals – it runs great risks in a turmoil of this kind and will hardly emerge unscathed. An abundance of money and renowned trustworthiness provide a basis on which anybody would be more than willing to loan to a government and are firm foundations of a state;[18] on this footing, it can calmly face any danger.

In Austria, we have not nearly attained this stage, but should strive to reach 84 r
it.

To this end, we will above all have to strive to put our National Bank in a sound position by straightening out its paper currency, to strike a long-term balance between public revenue and public expenditure by great thrift,[19] to increase the government's credit by promptly meeting liabilities, and – if possible – even to lower taxes or somehow increase the people's wealth by suitable government measures.

Then we will enjoy a good reputation as a country with well-ordered finances, and if necessary we will be able to borrow at moderate rates of interest; in this manner, our reputation abroad and contentment at home would increase.

Vienna, 23 March 1876 Rudolf

18 Smith (1776), V.iii.4: 'The want of parsimony in time of peace, imposes the necessity of contracting debt in time of war'.

19 On this note Smith ends the Wealth of Nations; see Smith (1776), V.iii.92.

Politische Ökonomie XII. 1876 März

85 r **Über die Ursachen der Steigerung des Einkommens von Grund und Boden bei zunehmender Kultur**[1]

In allen modernen Staaten zeigt sich die Tatsache der Steigerung des Einkommens von Grund und Boden durch die Zunahme der Kultur im allgemeinen.[2]

Das Erträgnis der Landgüter wächst von Jahr zu Jahr, und der solideste Besitz, der die Garantie zu stetem Wachstum *seines Wertes und Erträgnisses bietet*, ist unstreitig der Grund und Boden;[3] man sieht die obere Erscheinung in sämtlichen *fortschreitenden* Ländern, besonders in jenen, die noch Gegenden aufweisen können, welche vor nicht geraumer Zeit von den Verkehrsstraßen entfernt in einem unkultivierten Zustand *sich befanden*[4] *und keinen Ertrag abwarfen, durch die Fortschritte der Kultur aber nach und nach immer zu höherem Erträgnis gelangen.* Mit dem Vordringen der Kultur erhalten solche Landstriche einen immer größeren Wert, den der noch zu bebauende Boden oder die großen Waldungen gewähren.

85 v Grundstücke, die z.B. vor 20 Jahren 5000 fl. getragen, tragen jetzt 10–15000 fl.; dies ist besonders der Fall in *jenen* Ländern, wo der Bau von Verkehrsstraßen *rasch* aus dem primitivsten Zustand in den der Kultur *überging*. Eine deutliche Bestätigung, daß das Einkommen von Grund und Boden in stetem Wachstum ist, ist die Tatsache, daß der grundbesitzende Adel *und die Grundbesitzer überhaupt* auf einem *viel* komfortableren Fuße leben als je zuvor; dies findet seine Erklärung darin, daß der Wert der Güter *und das Einkommen aus denselben* durch die zunehmende Kultur im *steten* Wachsen begriffen ist, daher auch der Landwirt jeden Standes *und jeder Vermögenslage* eine Garantie für eine schöne Zukunft *hat* und versichert sein kann, daß seine Einkommensquellen auf der festesten Basis ruhen.[5]

1 Smith (1776), I.xi: 'Die Grundrente'.

2 Smith (1776), I.xi.p.l, bemerkt, daß 'jede Verbesserung in den Verhältnissen der Gesellschaft mittelbar oder unmittelbar die wirkliche Grundrente… erhöht'.

3 Smith (1776), II.iv.17: 'die bessere Sicherheit der Ländereien'.

4 Smith (1776), I.xi.b.5: 'Gute Wege, Kanäle und schiffbare Flüsse ermäßigen die Frachtkosten… und ermuntern den Anbau der entlegenen Gegenden eines Landes'. Der Kronprinz äußert sich dazu weiter unten noch ausführlicher.

5 Diese, typisch Smithsche, Voraussage wurde genau zu der Zeit formuliert, als Europa am Anfang des wahrscheinlich stärksten Grundrentenverfalls überhaupt stand: Durch die Importe aus Übersee wurden die adligen Grundbesitzer ruiniert.

Political economy XII. 1876 March

On the Causes of the Increase of the Rent of Land with Progressive Cultivation[1] 85 r

All modern states witness increases of the rent of land as cultivation is advanced in general.[2]

The returns from agricultural property grow from year to year; and land is unquestionably the most reliable kind of property that guarantees a perpetual increase in value and returns;[3] this phenomenon is to be observed in all advancing countries, especially in those where areas that, until recently, lay far from the roads were as yet uncultivated[4] and yielded no return, but now yield ever larger returns due to progressive cultivation. With the advance of civilization, such stretches of land become increasingly valuable because of their untilled soil or vast tracts of woods.

Parcels of land which may have yielded 5000 florins twenty years ago now 85 v
yield 10–15000 florins; this is especially true of countries that have advanced quickly from the most primitive stage to a civilized one through the construction of roads. Landed aristocrats and real estate owners in general live far more comfortably now than ever before, which clearly proves that the rent of land is ever on the increase; this may be explained by the steadily increasing value of agricultural produce and the income this yields through progressive cultivation; regardless of their social class and financial position, agricultural producers are guaranteed a prosperous future and can be sure that their sources of income rest on the firmest foundation.[5]

1 Smith (1776), I.xi: 'Of the Rent of Land'.

2 Smith (1776), I.xi.p.1, summarizes: 'Every improvement in the circumstances of society tends either directly or indirectly to raise the real rent of land'.

3 Smith (1776), II.iv.17: '... the superior security of land'.

4 Smith (1776), I.xi.b.5: 'Good roads, canals, and navigable rivers by diminishing the expence of carriage' increase rent and 'encourage cultivation of the remote ... country'. The point is dealt with more extensively by the Crown Prince further on.

5 This forecast, very Smithian, was made just when Europe was at the beginning of perhaps the greatest historical slump of rents, due to overseas imports, a slump which ruined the European landed aristocracy.

Besonders fühlbar ist dies für den reicheren Teil des *grundbesitzenden* Adels,
86 r dessen *Einkommen in starker Progression wächst*; die meisten dieser Herren stehen sich trotz der Verteuerung der Lebensmittel heute besser als wie vor 20 Jahren.

Wenden wir aber nun unsere Aufmerksamkeit den Ursachen all dieser Erscheinungen zu. Vor allem müssen wir die zunehmende Dichtigkeit der Bevölkerung als einen wichtigen Grund ansehen, da je mehr Menschen in einem Landstriche wohnen, desto mehr Bodenprodukte zu ihrer Ernährung notwendig sind.[6] Bei zunehmender Kultur, welche viele Existenzen durch Arbeit ermöglicht und auch fremde Arbeitskräfte ins Land zieht, muß absolut mehr Landwirtschaft betrieben werden, deren Produkte durch den großen Absatz um höhere Preise verhandelt werden, *und solcher Art wird das Einkommen der Grundbesitzer gesteigert.*

86 v Als eine Hauptursache der Steigerung des Einkommens von Grund und Boden müssen wir ferner die Verbesserung der Transportmittel bezeichnen. Rascher, sicherer und *vor allem* billiger gelangen die Bodenprodukte an ihren Markt. *In Folge der billigeren Transporte steigt der Preis der Bodenprodukte an dem Produktionsorte, was dem Bodeneigentümer zugute kommt, dessen Einkommen dadurch wesentlich erhöht wird.* Die Verbesserung der Transportmittel ermöglicht daher die fortwährende Steigerung des Bodeneinkommens und die gesicherte Mehrproduktion von Bodenprodukten in ihrem Gefolge; entlegene fruchtbare Gegenden, deren Reichtum bis dahin teils ganz unbenützt war oder wenigstens nicht zur vollkommenen Geltung gelangte, und *ihren* Eigentümern, *welche die Produkte* wegen Mangel an Kommunikationsmitteln nicht verwerten konnten, keinen *oder nur geringen Ertrag* boten, sind jetzt mit jenen Märkten in enge Verbindung gebracht, an denen die Bodenprodukte ihren Wert erhalten und dadurch den Reichtum *des Produktionslandes* erhöhen.[7]

Die Kommunikationsmittel sind unstreitig bedeutende Hebel der Kultur, indem sie den Austausch der Kräfte entlegener Länder ermöglichen und die großen Unterschiede in Bildung und Wohlhabenheit, die zwischen den einzelnen
87 r Landstrichen bestehen, ausgleichen.

Man kann beobachtend verfolgen, wie im Laufe der Zeiten langsam die Kultur und *die Steigerung des Bodenwertes und Ertrages* Hand in Hand mit der Verbesserung der Kommunikationsmittel ging*en*. Zuerst wurden zum Transporte aus den reichen Landstrichen nach den großen Städten Straßen gebaut, welche dann verbessert wurden; neben den Kommunikationen am Lande nahmen auch jene am Wasser bedeutend zu; so zwar, daß jene Güter,

[6] Roscher (1864), § 156, S. 313: 'die steigende Kultur pflegt auf dreierlei Wegen zur Erhöhung der Rente beizutragen'. Weg 1 ist 'das Wachsen der Bevölkerung' in seiner Wirkung auf die agrarische Produktion; Weg 3 hingegen eröffnet sich, wenn sich 'die Bevölkerung mehr und mehr in großen Städten (concentrirt)'.

[7] Smith (1776), I.xi.b.5.

This is especially noticeable in the case of the wealthier part of the landed
aristocracy whose income grows progressively; most of these gentlemen are 86 r
better off today than twenty years ago, in spite of rising food prices.

But let us turn our attention to the causes of these phenomena. Above all, we must regard the increasing density of population as an important cause, for the more people live on a stretch of land, the more agricultural produce is needed to feed them.[6] The advance of civilization provides work and a livelihood for many persons and even attracts manpower from abroad; it also requires a growing agricultural sector whose products will be sold at higher prices due to the greater demand; thus, the incomes of landowners are increased.

As another major cause of increasing income from land we must name 86 v
improvements in transportation. Agricultural products get to the market more quickly, more safely, and above all more cheaply. Cheaper transport means a higher price for agricultural produce at the place of production; this benefits the landowner whose income is noticeably increased thereby. That is to say, the improvements in transport make possible a continual increase of income from land and warrant additional agricultural output; far-off fertile regions have resources that may have been either wholly untapped or at least not fully utilized and may have yielded little or no return to their owners, who could not sell their products because they lacked means of communication; now, these regions are connected with markets where their agricultural produce is sold for what it is worth, and so their wealth increases.[7]

Undoubtedly, the means of communication are significant instruments of
civilization, since they make it possible for distant regions to exchange resources
with each other and level off the big differences in education and wealth that
separate them. 87 r

Looking back over the course of time, we can see how civilization and the increase of land values and yields slowly went hand in hand with improvements in communication. First of all, roads were built – and then improved – to provide transportation from fertile areas to the big cities; not only traffic by land, but also communication by water increased substantially; this was done in such a way that estates adjacent to navigable rivers could progressively utilize their resources; this is why people have always regulated rivers and organized

6 Roscher (1864), § 156, p. 313: 'The advance of civilization will contribute in three ways to an increase in rent' – the first one being the growth of population and its effects on agricultural production, while the concentration of population in the big cities is taken to be the third way.

7 Smith (1776), I.xi.b.5.

welche an schiffbaren Flüssen lagen, stets mehr zur Verwertung ihres Bodenreichtums gelangen; daher wurden von jeher schon Flüsse reguliert und Schiffahrt darauf organisiert; mit zunehmender Kultur begann man auch Kanäle als Wasserstraßen anzulegen,[8] endlich wurden Dampfschiffe erfunden, welche rasch und sicher stromauf- und -abwärts die Waren zu ihren Märkten tragen.

87 v Im selben Maße nahm*en* auch am festen Lande die Fortschritte im Kommunikationswesen zu; zuerst wurden Pferde-Eisenbahnen als die erste Art der Schienenwege erfunden, bald darauf folgte die Errichtung der Lokomotiv-Bahnen, letztere war ein bedeutender Fortschritt und hatte eine sehr glückliche Wirkung auf die Hebung der Landwirtschaft, da nun in der kürzesten Zeit mit den geringsten Mitteln und auf die sicherste Weise die Naturprodukte auch der entferntesten Landgüter nach den großen Marktplätzen gelangen konnten.

Natürlich hatte der schnelle und gute Absatz eine große Produktion zur Folge, und auf die rationellste Weise wird seit dieser Zeit der Feldbau und die Waldwirtschaft betrieben, wodurch von Jahr zu Jahr das Einkommen *aus Grund und Boden* wächst. Alle Landstriche werden so viel es geht ausgenützt,[9] und
88 r die entlegensten *Grundstücke* werden durch die Berührung mit den Eisenbahnen kultiviert und dadurch zu Quellen großen Einkommens.

Auf diese Weise nimmt der *Ertrag* und der Wert der Grundbesitze stetig durch die Fortschritte der Kultur *und insbesondere durch die Verbesserung der Transportmittel* zu.

Durch die Fortschritte der Kultur sinkt ferner der Zinsfuß, ebenso sinken auch die Preise der Maschinen.[10] Beides ist für den Landwirt von großem Vorteile, besonders wenn er es versteht, durch richtigen Vorgang in Betreff der Mittel zur Hebung des Ertrages seiner Güter den Fortschritten der Landwirtschaft zu folgen.

88 v Wie gesagt, die zunehmende Kultur ist der Hebel *zur Steigerung* des Einkommens von Grund und Boden. Das Wachsen der Einwohnerzahl *hat einen großen Bedarf an* Lebensmitteln *und zahlreiche billigere* Arbeitskräfte *zur Folge*; die guten Kommunikationsmittel verbinden die Güter mit den Städten, erleichtern den Verkehr, verbreiten die Zivilisation; die Erfindung praktischer Agrikulturmaschinen macht die kostspieligen Arbeitskräfte der Menschen entbehrlich und fördert die Raschheit in den nötigen Verrichtungen; dies alles sind Folgen der zunehmenden Kultur. Wie klar und einleuchtend ist es nun, welch *großes* wirtschaftliches Interesse die Grundbesitzer *an* den Fortschritten der Zivilisation haben und *wie sich durch diese letztere ihre Einkünfte heben.*

Dies sind nur die privativen, egoistischen Vorteile. Doch welches Bewußtsein
89 r der Mitwirkung am allgemeinen Wohlstand, an der Kultur des Landes und dem

8 Bis hier entspricht die Aufzählung Smith (1776), I.xi.b.5, wo allerdings Kanäle vor schiffbaren Flüssen genannt sind (die historische Abfolge in der Verbesserung der Verkehrswege also umgedreht ist).

9 Eine auf alle Kapitalarten angewendete Maxime von Smith.

10 Vgl. Smith (1776), I.ix.14.

shipping on them; with advancing civilization canals were built for waterborne communication;[8] finally, steamships were invented to carry goods quickly and safely to their markets up and down river.

In like measure, progress in communication by land took place; at first horse- 87 v
drawn rail carriages were invented as an early type of railway; soon after, engine-drawn trains followed, which were a significant step forward and advanced agriculture quite favourably: now produce from even the most remote estates could get to the big markets in the shortest time, at the lowest cost, and in the safest way.

Of course, quick and profitable sales caused a great increase in production, and since that time, agriculture and forestry have been practised in the most economical manner, increasing landed income from year to year. All land is utilized to best effect,[9] and even the remotest tracts of land are cultivated as a consequence of railway development and become sources of large incomes. 88 r

Because of the progress of civilization and especially the improvements in transport the returns from landed property and its value grow continually.

As civilization progresses, the rate of interest and the prices of machinery go down.[10] Both effects greatly benefit the agricultural producer, especially if he knows how to take advantage of agricultural innovations by properly employing them to increase the returns from his property.

In short, a progressing civilization is instrumental in increasing income from 88 v
land. A growing population spells a high demand for foodstuffs and a large increase in cheaper labour; reliable means of communication bring goods to the towns, facilitate transport, and spread civilization; the invention of useful agricultural machinery makes expensive human labour redundant and tends to speed up required steps in production; all these are consequences of advancing civilization. It is clearly obvious then why the landowners should take such great economic interest in the improvements of civilization and how these increase their incomes.

These are only the private and selfish advantages. There is also the awareness
that the efficient cultivation of one's land represents a personal contribution to 89 r
the common good, that is to say, to a country's culture and wealth; it is not

8 Up to here, this corresponds to the enumeration in Smith (1776), I.xi.b.5, although Smith mentions canals before navigable rivers (reversing the historical order of transport improvement).

9 A general maxim of Smith's for all 'capitals'.

10 Cf. Smith (1776), I.ix.14.

Reichtum bietet die gute Bebauung des Grundbesitzes; es ist nicht nur der eigene Vorteil, sondern auch die Pflicht jedes Landwirtes, gleichen Schritt mit den Fortschritten der Kultur zu halten; Zurückbleiben aus veralteten Prinzipien, starres Festhalten an den Gewohnheiten früherer Zeiten führt den eigenen Schaden und einen Nachteil für den Reichtum des Landes herbei. Darum sollen besonders die großen Aristokratenfamilien, die im Besitze ausgedehnter Güter sind, als die hauptsächlichsten Vertreter des Grundbesitzes mit dem guten Beispiel vorangehen; sie sollen die Landwirtschaft nach ihren modernsten Grundsätzen betreiben, um dadurch die Kultur des Landes zu fördern und um nicht hinter anderen Staaten zurückzubleiben. Durch Gründung von
89 v Musterwirtschaften als Muster und Schule für alle Ökonomen wäre ihnen die schönste Gelegenheit geboten, sich um die Kultur des Vaterlandes große Verdienste zu sammeln. Der Adel sollte eingedenk sein seines schönen Berufes, der ihm in diesem Gebiete blüht; da die größten Komplexe in seinen Händen sind, kann er sich durch das Fördern der Landwirtschaft eine segensreiche Zukunft und eine neue Bestimmung gründen, er kann sich einen Ersatz für seine untergegangene Macht und Ausnahmsstellung schaffen. Im Falle des Gegenteiles aber, wenn er die Prinzipien der Reaktion und die Kurzsichtigkeit in politischen Dingen auf die volkswirtschaftlichen Interessen erstreckt, *wird* er seinem eigenen Reichtum schädlich und versündigt sich an dem Fortschritte seines Vaterlandes.[11]

90 r Darum kann nicht genug wiederholt werden, welchen großen Vorteil die genaue Nachfolge der Neuerungen und der Fortschritte in volkswirtschaftlichen Dingen den Grundbesitzern überhaupt und besonders auch der grundbesitzenden Aristokratie bietet.

Wien, 30. März 1876 Rudolf

90 v **Über die Maßregeln, welche bei einer Hungersnot seitens der Regierung zu ergreifen sind (Zur Lehre vom Preise)**[12]

Seitens der großen Fortschritte der Landwirtschaft *und der Kommunikationsmittel insbesondere* sind Hungersnöte seltener geworden.[13]

11 In diesen überdeutlichen Worten an die Adresse des Adels schwingt Smiths Skepsis mit. In III.ii.7 heißt es: "Ein großer Eigentümer ist jedoch selten ein guter Landwirt', weil die gewinnbringende Verbesserung von Grundbesitz nur durch genaues Achten auf kleine Ersparnisse und Gewinne möglich sei und in Reichtum erzogene Personen selten fähig seien, in diesen Dimensionen zu denken.

12 Im großen und ganzen überschlägt Menger Smith (1776), I.vii, 'Der natürliche Preis und der Marktpreis der Waren'. Statt dessen lehrt er die Preistheorie per implicationem anhand einer Fallstudie, die ihm Smith (1776) nahegelegt haben mag: vgl. IV.v.b, wo es in der Hauptsache um das Problem der Nahrungsmittelknappheit bzw. Hungersnöte und die Maßnahmen, die sachunkundige Regierungen dagegen ergreifen, geht. Ganz ähnlich wie Smith behandelt Rau

simply for his own benefit, but also the duty of every agricultural producer to keep pace with the advances of agriculture; he who stays with obsolete principles and stubbornly sticks to past practices hurts himself and impairs the country's wealth. Especially the large aristocratic families who own vast estates and are the principal representatives of the land-owning class should therefore set a good example; they should work the land in the most modern way to improve cultivation and to avoid lagging behind other countries. By founding model farms as standards of reference and as training facilities for all agricultural producers, aristocratic families would have the best opportunity substantially to serve their country's cultural interests. The aristocracy ought to keep in mind its noble vocation in this field; since it owns the largest estates, it can find a rewarding future and 89 v
a new destination by promoting agriculture and can create a substitute for its vanished power and exceptional position. If it should attempt, however, to deal with matters of national economic interest by maintaining reactionary principles and political shortsightedness, it will impair its own wealth and sin against its country's progress.[11]

Therefore it cannot be repeated too often how much landowners in general 90 r
and the landed aristocracy in particular would benefit from promptly adopting innovations and improvements in the economic sphere.

Vienna, 30 March 1876 Rudolf

On the Measures that Government Should Take in Case of Famine (On the Theory of Price)[12] 90 v

Famines have become rarer because of the great advances in agriculture and especially in the means of communication.[13]

11 This strident exhortation to the nobility echoes, without exactly saying so, Smith's scepticism. He says in (1776) III.ii.7: 'It seldom happens, however, that a great proprietor is a great improver ... To improve land with profit, like all other commercial projects, requires an exact attention to small savings and small gains, of which a man born to a great fortune, even though naturally frugal, is very seldom capable.'

12 On the whole, Menger skips Smith (1776), I.vii, 'Of the Natural and Market Price of Commodities'. Instead he teaches price theory implicitly, by a case study suggested by Smith, viz. the 'Digression Concerning the Corn Trade and Corn Laws', IV.v.b, which deals mainly with the problems caused by what Smith calls 'dearths and famines' and the attempts of

Es ist damit eines der schrecklichsten Unglücke, *die* ein Volk treffen *können* und die in den früheren Jahrhunderten häufig wiederkehrende Ereignis*se* war*en*, auf ein Minimum sehr ausnahmsweiser Fälle reduziert worden.

Die bedeutenden Verbesserungen der Kommunikationsmittel machen es einem Staate möglich, durch Einfuhr dem heranbrechenden Elend ganz vorzubeugen oder es wenigstens sehr zu mindern;[14] besonders sind jene Staaten geschützt vor ähnlichen Ereignissen, die neben der Landwirtschaft auch
91 r bedeutende Quellen der Wohlhabenheit in ihrer Industrie besitzen. Länder wie Rußland, Polen und teilweise Österreich, die ihren Reichtum fast ausschließlich in der Fruchtbarkeit ihres Bodens finden, also *Agrikultur*staaten sind, können von großen Hungersnöten, die sich auf den größten Teil des Landes erstrecken, noch immer zu leiden haben. Wie gesagt, nur große Hungersnöte sind auch in unseren Tagen zu befürchten, wo das ganze Land keine eigenen Hilfsquellen aufzufinden vermag und sich an das Ausland wenden muß.

Partielle, welche in einer Gegend infolge lokaler Übel ausbrechen und über die Grenzen dieses Landstriches hinaus sich nicht erstrecken, können heutzutage schwerlich einen gefährlichen Charakter annehmen, da infolge der Eisenbahnen und der vielerlei Kommunikationsmittel diese Ereignisse durch den Zuschub an Lebensmitteln aus den anstoßenden Bezirken im Keime schon erstickt werden.

Die Hungersnöte, die jetzt entstehen, finden stets ihren Grund in schlechten Ernten.

91 v In den meisten Fällen kann einem reichen Lande eine mißratene Ernte noch keinen so beträchtlichen Schaden zufügen, daß daraus eine Hungersnot entsteht, doch mehrere schlechte Ernten rasch nacheinander können die Ursachen solcher Katastrophen sein.

Jede Hungersnot ist ein sehr großes Unglück für ein Land, einesteils erzeugt sie Krankheiten, die die Folge des großen Elends sind und den Tod vieler Menschen herbeiführen, anderenteils stocken die Fortschritte der Kultur und Bildung, an deren Stelle Rohheit und Verbrechen aller Art, die Folgen der gräßlichen Dürftigkeit, treten, auch wird der Staat, dessen Pflicht es ist, durch alle möglichen Mittel dem Unglücke vorzubeugen, sich in Kosten stürzen und durch große Ankäufe im Auslande den Staatsschatz leeren. Der allgemeine Reichtum des Landes wird tief erschüttert, trotzdem die wohlhabenden Stände *weniger* unter dem Druck solcher Kalamitäten leiden; leider sind es stets die ärmeren Klassen der
92 r Bevölkerung, deren Leben ohnedies in mühseliger Arbeit, unter steter Entbehrung

(1854) Getreidehandel und Hungersnöte (S. 271 ff.). Menger stützt sich offensichtlich sowohl auf Rau wie auf Smith.

13 Rau, (1854), S. 271, sagt: 'Die Gefahr öfterer Theuerungen wird durch die Manchfaltigkeit der angebauten Nahrungsmittel, die gute Betreibung des Feldbaues und die heutige Leichtigkeit der Versendung vermindert'.

14 Smith (1776), IV.v.b.39: Hier wird der Freihandel zwischen den Staaten eines Erdteils als beste Abhilfe bei einer Mißernte bzw. als bestes Mittel zur Verhütung einer Hungersnot angepriesen.

Thus, one of the most terrible scourges that may befall a people and that recurred frequently in past centuries, has been reduced to a minimum, occurring only exceptionally.

Because of significant improvements in communication, a country can nowadays ward off or at least greatly alleviate impending misery by imports;[14] in particular, those countries that have substantial sources of wealth in their industry in addition to agriculture are safe from this kind of event. Countries like Russia, Poland, and – in part – Austria that are agricultural countries whose wealth stems 91 r almost exclusively from their fertile soils may still have to suffer from major famines if they hit the greater part of the country. As mentioned above, today only major famines are to be feared, those that make it impossible for an entire country to furnish the means of relief and require it to seek help abroad.

Regional [famines] that break out in an area in consequence of local shortages and do not extend beyond the confines of the region nowadays can hardly become dangerous, for because of railways and various other means of communication such occurrences are suppressed in an incipient stage, since foodstuffs can be sent from adjacent areas.

The famines that break out nowadays are invariably caused by poor harvests.

In most cases, a poor harvest cannot damage a rich country enough for a famine 91 v to result, but a series of poor harvests in quick succession may cause disaster.

Any famine is a terrible misfortune for a country; on the one hand, it brings about diseases as a consequence of the great misery and they cause numerous deaths; on the other hand, the progress of civilization and education is impeded, and they are replaced by brutishness and all kinds of crimes, resulting from the dismal shortages; the state, whose duty it is to prevent disaster by whatever means available, will go to substantial expenses and will empty the treasury by large purchases abroad. The country's overall prosperity is profoundly shaken, although the wealthy classes suffer less from such calamities; sadly, it is always 92 r

unenlightened government policy in respect of these. In a similar vein, Rau (1854), I, treats grain trade and famines (p. 271 ff.). Menger evidently draws both on Rau and on Smith.

13 Rau (1854), p. 271 (§ 139, second sentence).

14 Smith (1776), IV.v.b.39: '... as among the different provinces of a great empire the freedom of the inland trade appears, both from reason and experience, not only the best palliative of a dearth, but the most effective preventative of a famine; so would the freedom of the exportation and importation trade be among the different states into which a great continent was divided. The larger the continent, the easier the communication through all the different parts of it, both by land and water, the less would any one particular part of it ever be exposed to either of these calamities'.

freudlos vergeht, die auch bei Hungersnöten am empfindlichsten getroffen werden. Bei Mangel an Lebensmitteln steigen *die* Preise *derselben,*[15] die Stadtbevölkerung kann sie nicht erschwingen und der Landmann, den zunächst dieses Elend trifft, hat keine Früchte seiner mühseligen Arbeit. Der Hungertod oder die qualvollste Existenz steht ihnen bevor. Darum ist es eine der heiligsten Pflichten der Regierung und jedes einzelnen, *in Fällen der Hungersnot* nach Kräften zur Besserung der Lage der ärmeren *Klassen* zu arbeiten.

Die Regierung, die in keinem Falle in volkswirtschaftliche Dinge viel eingreifen kann, wird auch bei Hungersnöten Schwierigkeiten finden, die ihren Bestrebungen im Wege stehen und dieselben bedeutend einschränken.[16]

Vor allem soll sie erforschen, ob die Volkswirtschaft in der Lage ist, sich selbst zu helfen, was in jedem Falle das beste wäre.[17]

92 v Meistens geschieht dies auch, indem Maßregeln von allen Seiten ergriffen werden, die vom Gesetz der Notwendigkeit in diesen Lagen diktiert werden; sicher wird diese Abhilfe die zweckmäßigste sein, die naturgemäß aus dem Charakter der Situation, in dem das Volk sich befindet, folgt.

Wenn sich *nicht* Getreide *in ausreichender Menge* im Lande befindet *und infolge hievon Hungersnot eintritt, wird* selbstverständlich der Export dieses *ohnehin nicht ausreichenden Getreides* durch sehr hohe Getreidepreise unmöglich gemacht. Dagegen *wird in Folge der hohen Preise im Lande, wo die Hungersnot besteht aus den* Nachbarstaaten Getreide importiert *werden.*[18] *Ferner werden alle* privaten Unternehmen *von selbst sich veranlaßt finden*, die Branntweinbrennerei *still stehen zu lassen*[19] oder *den Betrieb* wenigstens auf ein Minimum zu reduzieren, damit das Getreide, welches dabei verbraucht *werden würde*, lieber zur Broterzeugung benützt wird.

15 Smith (1776), I.vii.9.

16 Smith (1776), IV.v.b.7; Rau (1854), S. 277, sagt: 'Die Regierung ist außer Stande, die Preise der Dinge zu beherrschen und einzelne Classen von Gewerbetreibenden ... vor Verlusten zu bewahren. .. Von Seite der Staatsgewalt kann also nur darauf hingewirkt werden, daß jene natürlichen Heilmittel beschleunigt ... werden'.

17 Vgl. Smith (1776), IV.v.b.7.

18 Die zwei erwähnten Wirkungen werden von Smith (1776) – da selbstverständlich – nicht ausdrücklich behandelt, sondern in seiner langen Darstellung des Ein- und Ausfuhrhandels aufgrund der Korngesetze unterstellt. Siehe IV.v.b.35–53.

19 Die Auswirkung auf die Branntweinbrennerei erwähnt Smith (1776) nicht.

the poorer classes of the population, who lead a joyless life of hard work and constant deprivation anyway, who are hit hardest by famines. When there is a shortage of foodstuffs, their prices rise,[15] townspeople cannot pay them, and the agricultural producer, who is hit first by this calamity, does not reap the fruit of his toil. Death from starvation or at least a most miserable existence lie in wait for them. Therefore it is one of the most sacred obligations of the state and every individual in it to do their utmost to help alleviate the lot of the poorer classes in cases of famine.

During famines the government, which cannot intervene much in economic matters anyway, will also run into difficulties that thwart and considerably constrain its efforts.[16]

Above all, the government should find out if the economy can help itself – which would be much the best thing in any case.[17]

Usually this is what happens when such measures as are dictated by necessity 92 v
in this sort of situation are taken on all sides; certainly those relief measures that follow naturally from the sort of situation in which the people find themselves will be most expedient.

If grain is not available in the country in sufficient quantities and famine ensues, exporting this already insufficient grain is rendered impossible by very high prices, of course. Conversely, because of the high grain prices a country hit by famine will import grain from neighbouring countries.[18] In addition, all private enterprises will, on their own, stop distilling brandy[19] or at least reduce this business to a minimum so that the grain can preferably be used for baking bread rather than being used up in distilleries.

15 Smith (1776), I.vii.9: '... exorbitant price of the necessaries... in a famine'.

16 Smith (1776), IV.v.b.7: 'The inconveniences of a real scarcity cannot be remedied; they can only be palliated'; and 'the best palliative' is the 'unrestrained freedom of the corn trade'. Rau (1854), p. 277, says that government is unable 'to keep prices in check' and must seek 'natural remedies'.

17 Cf. Smith (1776), IV.v.b.7.

18 The two effects mentioned are not expressly stated by Smith (1776) – as, of course, self-evident – but suggested by his long treatment of exportation and importation according to the corn laws; cf. IV.v.b.35–53.

19 The effect on distilling is not mentioned by Smith.

Politische Ökonomie XIII. 1876 April

93 r Auch bei der Viehfütterung wird *in Fällen großen Mangels an Nahrungsmitteln* auf diese Weise vorgegangen und werden den Haustieren statt Getreide *und sonstigen zur Menschennahrung tauglichen Gegenständen* in solchen Zeiten *auch ohne staatlichen Auftrag* andere Dinge als Nahrung gegeben werden.[1]

Alle diese Maßregeln werden somit nicht durch Verordnungen der Regierung, sondern durch sich selbst, durch den Zwang der Notwendigkeit von jedem einzelnen Ökonomen einzeln ins Leben gerufen.[2]

Ferners wird in solchen Tagen der Not und der Entbehrung gewiß Mäßigkeit und Sparsamkeit im Genusse der wertvollen Lebensmittel angewendet werden. Das arme Volk wird ohnedies durch den einfachen Zwang *der Teuerung und* des Nichtvorhandenseins zum mäßigen Verbrauche gedrängt werden; dieses braucht es sich nicht eigens vorzunehmen; doch die höheren Stände, welche im Überflusse dahinleben, sollen in solchen Momenten, *auch wenn sie hiezu nicht recht unmittelbar genötigt sind, mit den Nahrungsmitteln* sparen, um dem
93 v Volke *von dem Nahrungsmittelvorrate möglichst wenig* zu entziehen; da kommt der Augenblick, wo der reiche Adel seine wahre *Humanität* zeigen könnte und der Hof mit dem guten Beispiel vorangehen sollte; dann würde diese Mäßigkeit in allen Schichten der Bevölkerung befolgt werden, und die ärmsten Klassen hätten mehr Aussicht, dem Hungertode zu entrinnen.

Das Landvolk aber müßte ebenfalls durch sparsamen Gebrauch des Getreides vorsichtig vorgehen, z.B. bei der Aussaat *soll in Zeiten großen Getreidemangels* mit der größten Aufmerksamkeit jede Verschwendung verhütet werden,[3] um eben nur den notwendigsten Bedarf an Körnern zu verwenden; auch dieses Mittel wird der Landmann aus eigenem Antrieb verwenden; denn er fühlt vielleicht am meisten den schweren Schlag einer Hungersnot.

94 r Alle diese bis jetzt erwähnten Maßregeln sind *ein Ausfluß* des *individuellen Egoismus*,[4] es sind die aus der Natur folgenden Wege, welche die Volkswirtschaft dem Volke von selbst zu befolgen vorschreibt.

Wenden wir aber jetzt unsere Aufmerksamkeit jenen Maßregeln zu, welche die *Regierung* bei Hungersnöten zu ergreifen versucht, und in wie weit dies

[1] Auch dieser Effekt ist bei Smith (1776) nicht erwähnt.
[2] Ein für Smith (1776) typischer Gedanke.
[3] Rau (1854), S. 274, spricht ausdrücklich davon, daß die Regierung Maßnahmen ergreifen möge, um die Bauern von dieser Notwendigkeit zu überzeugen.
[4] Die positiven sozialen Auswirkungen des Eigennutzes sind bekanntlich der Kerngedanke von Smith (1776); siehe z.B. I.ii.

Political economy XIII. 1876 April

In cases of a major food shortage cattle feeding, too, will be handled in like manner, and in such times, even without government intervention, domestic animals will be fed other substances than grain and other edibles that are fit for humans.[1] 93 r

All these measures then are not implemented by government decree, but rather autonomously and individually by every single agricultural producer because of the force of circumstance.[2]

Furthermore, in times of misery and deprivation, moderation and economy will certainly govern the consumption of valuable foodstuffs. The poor are induced to restrict their consumption anyway because of sheer dearth and the lack of food; they need not make any explicit, special resolutions; but at such times the upper classes that live in abundance should economize their food consumption, even if they are not immediately forced to do so, in order to impinge as little as possible upon the common people's food supplies; the moment would be at hand for the rich aristocracy to show a truly humane attitude, and the Court 93 v
should set a good example; such moderation would then be copied in all strata of society, and the poorest classes would have more of a chance to escape starvation.

The peasants, too, would have to economize carefully on their consumption of grain; for example, when grain is very scarce, any wastefulness in sowing should scrupulously be avoided[3] so that only a minimum of grain is used; this measure, too, though, will be adopted by the agricultural producer of his own accord, because he may be the one to feel the calamity of famine more acutely than anybody else.

All measures mentioned so far reflect individual self-interest;[4] they are paths 94 r
that open up naturally; the national economy makes people follow them on their own.

Let us now turn our attention to those measures that government attempts to take during famines and see when this is admissible. It is very difficult for

1 This effect is not mentioned by Smith, either.

2 A typically Smithian notion.

3 Rau (1854), p. 274, mentions this explicitly as a measure to be taken by means of moral suasion on the part of government.

4 The social beneficence of self-interest is, of course, the central notion of Smith (1776); see, e.g., I.ii.

zulässig ist. Es ist sehr schwer für dieselbe, in volkswirtschaftliche Dinge, besonders in solche, die oft enge mit den privativsten Interessen der einzelnen Bürger zusammenhängen, einzugreifen.

Die Schwerfälligkeit von Befehlen und Ordonanzen erzeugt oft eben die entgegengesetzte Wirkung von dem, was sie anstreben sollten.[5] Zum Beispiel werden gewiß Vorschriften, die niedere Getreidepreise anordnen, erfolglos
94 v bleiben, denn es ist eine zu natürliche Sache, daß im Falle des Getreidemangels dasselbe teurer wird; und sicher bliebe der Preis der gleiche, trotz Anordnungen der Regierung, nur würde man eine Hintergehung des Gesetzes erzielen und vielleicht eine Erhöhung der Preise hinter dem Rücken der Behörden, es ginge vielleicht so wie mit den Wuchergesetzen.[6]

Ferners wäre ein eigenes Gebot gegen den Export von Getreide vollkommen unnütz, da die Volkswirtschaft in diesem Punkte, wie wir schon früher gesehen haben, sich selbst helfen muß; es ist kaum anders denkbar, als daß die Ausfuhr *bei einer Hungersnot* augenblicklich aufhört, denn der Mangel im Inlande verhindert den Export des wenigen, welches noch vorhanden ist. Darum wäre es in so einem Falle *meist* unnütz, eigene Gebote zu erlassen, und zwecklose Gesetze der Regierung sind immer schädlich. Nur in *dem Falle* des Fortexportes des Getreides ins Ausland, und wenn ein deutlicher Schaden damit verbunden
95 r wäre, könnte die Regierung durch *Exportverbote* die Ausfuhr mit Macht verhindern; doch nur die dringende[7] und gefährliche Situation kann einen derartigen Eingriff in die Rechte der einzelnen Bürger rechtfertigen [CM am Rand: *Nach größeren Mißernten im Auslande und Überschüssen der Ernte im Inlande*]; denn in den meisten Fällen ist ein großer Schaden *für den einzelnen Landwirt* mit solchen Geboten verbunden. Dies *gilt* besonders in jenen Staaten, deren vorzüglichste Einnahmsquelle die Landwirtschaft ist, und deren große Strecken angebauten Landes doch noch im Falle einer *Mißernte* vor vollkommenem Mangel schützen; ist nun diese Kalamität weit verbreitet über mehrere Staaten und auch über solche, die *verhältnismäßig* wenig Feldbau selbst in guten Jahren betreiben, dann wird das Getreide aus dem Agrarstaate um hohe Preise exportiert
95 v werden können, und es würde eine große Benachteiligung einzelner zur Folge haben, wenn der Staat durch strikte Verbote den Export zu verhindern sucht.[8]

5 Um diesen Nachweis geht es Smith (1776) in IV.v.b.

6 Ihre problematische Wirkung erörtert Smith (1776) in I.ix. Ebenda, Absatz 9, ist die Rede von 'sicheren und leichten Mitteln, das Gesetz zu umgehen'.

7 Mit seinem Zugeständnis, bei Fehlernten wären Exportverbote für Korn sinnvoll, widerspricht Menger der Argumentation sowohl von Smith (1776) wie insbesondere von Rau (1854), S. 272. Dort heißt es nämlich: 'Die fast in allen Ländern zur Zeit der Theuerung eingeführten Korn-Ausfuhrverbote (Sperren) hatten nicht die erhofften Wirkungen'. Hingegen meint Rau: 'Das Verbot des Branntweinbrennens aus Getreide ... könnte nur in dringenden Nothfällen gerechtfertigt werden'. Das ungefähre Gegenteil wird freilich von Menger im folgenden herausgearbeitet. Es handelt sich wohl um einen Konflikt zwischen kurz- und langfristig sinnvollen Maßnahmen, den Rudolf vielleicht nicht sehr glücklich wiedergibt.

8 Hier handelt es sich um eine auf spezifisch österreichische Verhältnisse eingehende Stelle, wohl um eine Reminiszenz des Jahres 1867, als allein Österreich keine Fehlernte hatte, während

government to intervene in economic matters, especially when the most private interests of individual citizens are involved.

The cumbersomeness of rules and decrees often produces an effect contrary to what had been intended.[5] For example, decrees that fix low prices of grain will certainly be ineffective, for it is only too natural that grain should become dearer in times of a grain shortage and, in spite of government orders, the price 94 v
certainly would not change; people would simply circumvent the law and would raise the price behind the authorities' back; it might be the same as with the usury laws.[6]

Furthermore, a decree that explicitly prohibits the export of grain would be quite useless, since, as we have seen already, in this respect the national economy must help itself; it is hard to imagine otherwise than that exports would stop immediately in case of famine, since the shortage at home prevents the export of the little that is left. Explicit regulation would therefore be mostly useless, and ineffective laws of a government are invariably harmful. Only if grain continued to be exported and if this caused noticeable damage, could the government prevent exports by enforcing export bans, but only a true emergency situation[7] can justify 95 r
this sort of interference with the rights of individual citizens [CM in the margin: after major bad harvests abroad and over-abundant harvests at home], as in most instances such regulation spells substantial damage to the individual agricultural producer. This is particularly true of countries whose major source of income is agriculture and where large stretches of cultivated land ward off scarcity even in the case of a very poor harvest; if such a calamity is widespread and occurs in several countries, including those having comparatively little tillage even in good years, then the grain from the agricultural country could be exported at high prices, and it would be a striking discrimination against some individuals if the state attempted to prevent exports by strictly prohibiting them.[8] True, this 95 v
boon to agricultural producers and individual grain merchants has the disadvantage of taking foodstuffs out of the country; yet foreign currency comes in as a result;

5 This is the main thrust of the argument of Smith (1776) in IV.v.b.

6 Their problematical effect is discussed by Smith (1776) in I.ix. In I.ix.9 'safe and easy methods of evading the law' are mentioned.

7 Menger's suggestion to stop the export of grain in times of dearth goes against the spirit of Smith as well as of Rau. Rau (1854), p. 272, says explicitly that a ban on corn exports has often proved ineffective but finds a ban on distilling justified in an 'emergency situation'. More or less the opposite position is taken by Menger in the argument following. Perhaps the Crown Prince muddled up what had been pointed out, which may have been the contrast between short-run expediency and long-run best interest.

8 These remarks concern the particular situation of Austria as still a more agricultural than manufacturing country. In particular, Austria had the good fortune in 1867 to experience a good harvest while the whole of Western Europe had a bad one, which made for very high revenues from grain exports in Austria.

Es ist wahr, daß dieser Vorteil *der Landwirte und* einzelner Getreidehändler den Nachteil mit sich bringt, daß dem Inlande Lebensmittel entzogen werden, doch fremdes Geld kommt dadurch in den Staat herein, und ferners könnte die Verweigerung der Ausfuhr von Lebensmitteln nach den fremden Staaten, die im höchsten Elende darben, daselbst *Gegenmaßregeln* hervorrufen. Es könnte z.B. für lange Zeit die Ausfuhr von Produkten, die das Inland entbehrt, vom Nachbarstaate verwehrt werden, oder im Falle einer neuen Hungersnot würden die anderen Länder ebenfalls den Getreideexport verbieten und dadurch das Elend ungemein steigern.

Darum ist es gewiß zweckmäßiger, wenn die Regierung den Bürgern ihr Wohl
96 r anheimstellt;[9] und sie wird dabei gewiß am besten fahren, denn nie wird der einzelne im Momente der Gefahr und der Entbehrung Maßregeln ergreifen, die ihm seine wertvollen Lebensmittel zersplittern und verschwenden. Der gewöhnlichste, einfachste Menschenverstand muß ihn instinktiv zur Sparsamkeit führen und zwingt ihn, jene Mittel zu Hilfe zu nehmen, die ihm einen mäßigen Verbrauch der Viktualien, und zwar nur zum Zweck der Ernährung des Menschen, mit Außerachtlassung aller anderen Verwendungen vorzeichnen.

Aus diesem Grunde müssen wir es *im großen und ganzen* als unnütz erklären,[10] wenn die Regierung sich bevormundend und dadurch nur störend in dem Erlaß von kleinlichen Geboten ergeht, wie z.B. in Verordnungen gegen das Brennen von Branntwein aus Getreide und Kartoffeln; in der jetzigen Zeit wird eine ähnliche
96 v Maßregel *nur selten* Nutzen bieten, denn wo die eigene Vernunft, die Bildung und der eigene Wille der Männer nichts nützt, werden der Buchstabe und die Mittel, die den Beamten zu Gebote stehen, in der jetzigen Zeit gar nichts helfen; ferners ist es auch vollkommen undurchführbar, die genaue Vollstreckung ähnlicher Gebote zu überwachen, da sie tief in das Privatleben der einzelnen eingreifen und es unmöglich wäre, jeden Bürger so genau zu überwachen. Dies ist besonders der Fall im Betreff des sparsamen Verbrauches des Getreides bei der Aussaat und bei der Verzehrung als Brot. Beides wird durch die eiserne Notwendigkeit und durch die einfachste Vernunft dem einzelnen diktiert; wollte der Staat dies nun *zwangsweise* herbeiführen, so müßte er rein jedem Bürger einen Beamten zuteilen, der ihn auf Schritt und Tritt beobachten würde, was mit einigen Schwierigkeiten verbunden wäre.

97 r In dieser Art und Weise kann und darf also die Regierung ihren Eifer zur Beseitigung eines solchen Übels nicht kundgeben; ihre Aufgabe ist in diesem wie in jedem Falle nur der Schutz des Bürgers, dort, wo seine Mittel nicht ausreichen, seine Lage zu bessern *oder sich vor Gefahren zu schützen.* Darum soll bei

diese ganz Westeuropa traf, so daß Österreich außergewöhnliche Exporterlöse im Getreidehandel erzielte.

9 Smith (1776) passim, z.B. IV.ii.9.

10 Dieser Absatz ist repetitiv, gibt jedoch, neben Smith, den Grundgedanken von Rau (1854), S. 271 ff., wieder, daß mangelndes ökonomisches Verständnis 'zur Empfehlung verschiedener Zwangsmittel geführt (habe), die ihre Bestimmung nothwendig verfehlen mußten' (S. 272).

furthermore, a ban on foodstuff exports to foreign countries in utter misery might invite retaliatory measures. For example, the neighbouring countries could for a long time suspend the export of products that the first country needs badly, or in case of another famine the other countries would stop their grain exports, too, thereby increasing the misery enormously.

Therefore it is certainly more expedient if the government leaves the citizens' well-being to themselves;[9] and it will surely get the best results, since in times 96 r
of danger and deprivation the individual will never take steps that would scatter and waste his valuable foodstuffs. The most ordinary, simplest common sense must lead a person instinctively to economize and forces him to adopt measures that restrict moderate consumption of foodstuffs to the feeding of humans only, disregarding all other possible uses.

For this reason it would seem useless on the whole[10] if the government were to pass petty regulations in a paternalistic and annoying manner, e.g. decrees against the distilling of brandy from grain and potatoes; nowadays a regulation like that will rarely prove useful, for when an individual's reason, education, and will power are of no avail, the letter of the law and the instruments wielded 96 v
by civil servants will be of no use at all nowadays; furthermore, it is quite impossible to guarantee exact compliance with such decrees, since they deeply impinge upon the individual's private sphere, and not everybody could possibly be put under such close surveillance. This is especially true for the thrifty consumption of grain for sowing and for bread. In both cases, thrift is forced upon the individual by iron necessity and common sense; if the state were to attempt to bring this about by force it would actually have to assign to every citizen a bureaucrat to watch over him – a procedure certainly not without its difficulties.

In short, this is not the way in which the government could or should 97 r
demonstrate its eagerness to remedy such a deplorable situation; here as everywhere, the government is only obliged to protect the citizen whenever his own means are insufficient to improve his situation or to ward off danger. Therefore government should resort to large-scale imports of grain from abroad only in extreme cases; but even then it would have to take care not to cut off private speculation that can also bring large amounts of foodstuffs into the country.[11]

9 Smith (1776) passim, e.g. IV.ii.9.
10 Explicitly Rau (1854), p. 272.

Hungersnöten die Regierung Getreideeinkäufe in großem Maßstabe im Auslande *nur in den äußersten Fällen* bewerkstelligen, aber *selbst* da vorsichtig vorgehen, um die Privatspekulationen, durch welche ebenfalls viele Lebensmittel ins Land kommen, nicht unmöglich zu machen.[11] Ferners soll sie, wenn sie vor einer Hungersnot dieselbe durch Eintritt der Ereignisse, die sie herbeiführen, voraus*sieht*, schon früher den Einkauf der Lebensmittel beginnen und durch
97 v Verbreitung populärer Schriften alle Landwirte auf die Gefahr gefaßt machen.[12] Durch diese Aufrufe soll teils die Vorsicht und der Fleiß der einzelnen Bürger angespornt werden, teils aber auch der Gemeinsinn und die Opferwilligkeit aller Mitglieder des bedrohten Landes gehoben werden. Die Regierung soll ihnen bezeigen, wie wenig sie in diesem Momente helfen kann, und soll den Bürger auf sich selbst anweisen, ihn lehrend, daß er in seiner eigenen Kraft, in seinem Mute und in seinem Gemeinsinn seine eigene und der Gesamtheit festeste Stütze findet.

Eine weise Regierung, humane und opferwillige höhere Stände und ein kräftiges Volk werden auch der ärgsten Hungersnot entschlossen trotzen und sie rasch zu beseitigen wissen.

Rudolf

[11] Smith (1776) IV.v.b.41.

[12] Rau (1854), S. 273, sagt: 'demnach bleiben vorzüglich folgende Maaßregeln übrig: 1) Zeitige Einziehung genauer Nachrichten über die Ergebnisse der Ernte... 2) Ist das Bedürfniß der Einfuhr außer Zweifel, so ist es nöthig, das Fehlende bald, wo möglich noch vor dem Winter, auf die wohlfeilste Weise anzukaufen.... Es ist am einfachsten, wenn dieß durch Getreidehändler auf eigene Rechnung geschieht. Ist aber die Gefahr dringend', dann mögen Regierungskäufe stattfinden.

If events lead it to expect a famine, the government should furthermore begin buying foodstuffs sooner and alert all agricultural producers to the impending danger with informative brochures in plain language.[12] On the one hand, such appeals should foster prudence and diligence in the individual citizen and, on the other, they should boost the communal spirit and the willingness to make sacrifices in every citizen of the endangered country. Government should show how little it can do in such moments and should leave the citizen to his own 97 v
devices, instructing him that he will find his and the country's firmest support in his own resilience, courage, and communal spirit.

A wise government, humane upper classes that are willing to make sacrifices, and a sturdy populace will resolutely withstand even the worst famine and find ways to overcome it quickly.

Rudolf

11 Smith (1776), IV.v.b.41.

12 Rau (1854), p. 273, suggests that government collect exact information on harvests; if that shows that grain has to be imported, this should be done at the earliest possible time – by grain merchants at their own risk; only in cases of emergency should the government step in as purchaser.

Finanzwissenschaft. Über Steuern I 1876

1 r **Über die direkten und indirekten Steuern**[1]

Der Staat, der die Gesamtheit aller Bürger ist und, als Person gedacht, die Interessen der einzelnen dort vertritt, wo die *Vertretung außerhalb* der Machtsphäre *der einzelnen* liegt, braucht zur Erreichung dieser Zwecke bedeutende Mittel.

Der Staat, der nur in immer seltener werdenden Ausnahmefällen eine *beträchtliche Einnahme*quelle im eigenen Besitze findet,[2] muß in dem Reichtum der Gesamtheit das Mittel zur Erfüllung seiner *Zwecke suchen und* verschafft sich dieselben *durch Steuern.*[3] So schön nun auch der Gedanke einer *gerechten* Besteuerung[4] erscheint, so schwer ist es praktisch, richtig bemessene Steuern
1 v aufzuerlegen; *ein Ziel, das indes um seiner unvergleichlichen Wichtigkeit willen von keinem Staate außer acht gelassen werden darf.*

Wo die Steuern nur für ihr Ziel, das ein allgemeines ist, bemessen sind, wird nur der Ungebildete und Kurzsichtige gegen dieselben sich tadelnd erheben; doch in jenen Fällen, in denen der Mißbrauch und das Ungeschick der Lenker des Staatsschiffes in Verwendung des anvertrauten allgemeinen Gutes der Grund oft lang dauernder *finanzieller* Verlegenheiten und daher auch des Bedürfnisses höherer Steuern ist, da wird Unzufriedenheit berechtigt und das Streben, mit allen Kräften nach Besserung des Zustandes hinzuwirken, am Platze sein. Aus diesen Gründen wies die eiserne Notwendigkeit bald *auf ein Besteuerungssystem* hin, *das* den Zweck hat, mit Gerechtigkeit die einzelnen nach Maß ihrer Mittel zu treffen[5] und gewisse Arten der Steuern in bessere Formen zu kleiden.

2 r Vor allem müßte man bestrebt sein, statt eines Systems, das jedem ohne Berücksichtigung seiner Mittel dieselben Lasten auferlegt, eine proportionierte Besteuerung nach dem Maße des Einkommens[6] einzuführen; denn der Endzweck

[1] Smith (1776), V.ii; freilich werden hier nicht die Worte 'direkt' und 'indirekt' gebraucht.
[2] Smith (1776), V.ii.a.
[3] Smith (1776), V.ii.b.
[4] Smith (1776), V.ii.b.2–7. Es werden hier nicht alle vier Besteuerungsgrundsätze von Smith behandelt.
[5] Smiths erster Grundsatz: Besteuerung im Verhältnis zu den individuellen Fähigkeiten bzw. im Verhältnis zu den Erträgen derselben; vgl. V.ii.b.3.
[6] Neben Smith zog Menger vermutlich auch Rau (1859) heran, ein sehr viel verwendetes Lehrbuch. Auf S. 384 spricht sich der Autor für die Besteuerung proportional zum Einkommen aus (das entsprechende Wort bei Smith heißt revenue).

Public finance. On taxes I 1876

On Direct and Indirect Taxes[1] 1 r

The state, which is the sum total of all citizens and – conceived of as a person – represents the individuals' interests where it is not within their power to do so themselves, requires substantial resources to accomplish its ends.

Only in increasingly rare, exceptional cases does government possess considerable sources of income;[2] it must look to the wealth of the community for the means to accomplish its ends and acquires these through taxation.[3] The idea of just taxation may be very noble,[4] but in practice it is very difficult to impose the appropriate rates – a goal which, because of its incomparable importance, no government must neglect. 1 v

Only the uneducated and shortsighted person will find fault with taxes that are apportioned only with a view to their general purpose; but in cases where the navigators of the ship of state misuse and bungle the common good entrusted to them and thereby cause protracted financial difficulties and thus the need for higher taxes, dissatisfaction will be justified and the attempt to improve the situation by any means will be fitting. For these reasons, iron necessity soon pointed to a system of taxation that has individuals contribute in proportion to their means[5] and finds more expedient forms for certain kinds of taxes.

Above all, one should strive to introduce proportional taxation, i.e. taxation 2 r
in proportion to a person's income,[6] instead of a system that imposes equal tax burdens on everyone without regard to a person's means; it is the ultimate purpose of all taxes to achieve the great ends of government, and everybody who is to enjoy their fruits should contribute as best he can; if practicable, it would

1 Smith (1776), V.ii. Smith, however, does not use the German terms 'direct' and 'indirect' taxes.
2 Cf. Smith (1776), V.ii.a.
3 Smith (1776), V.ii.b.
4 Smith (1776), V.ii.b.2–7. Not all of the four tax maxims of Smith are presented, however.
5 Smith's first tax maxim, viz. taxation 'in proportion to their respective abilities; that is in proportion to the revenue which they respectively enjoy'; cf. (1776) V.ii.b.3.
6 Rau (1859), a very well known textbook, is probably used by Menger in addition to Smith. Rau, p. 384, pleads for taxation proportioned to income (Smith, of course, says 'revenue').

aller Steuern sind die großen Zwecke des Staates, und zu ihrer Durchführung soll jeder, der ihre Früchte genießt, nach seinen Kräften mitwirken; daher wäre es, wenn durchführbar, gewiß am zweckmäßigsten, das reine Einkommen aller Bürger *proportionell* zu treffen, *jedoch* mit Berücksichtigung des Umstandes, daß den ärmsten Klassen eine bestimmte, ihnen zum Leben unbedingt notwendige Summe,[7] das Existenzminimum, gelassen werde; die *besitzlosen* Staatsbürger
6 v sind zuvorderst berechtigt, von der Gesamtheit den Schutz zu fordern, den sie sich selbst nicht gewähren können.[8] Der Staat, zu dessen gewichtigsten Interessen es gehört, die Verbreitung allgemeiner Wohlhabenheit, so weit dies möglich ist, zu fördern und zu unterstützen, wird zunächst trachten, die Steuern aller, in der Grenze der Möglichkeit und besonders die der armen Klassen zu verringern.

In jenen traurigen Lebensverhältnissen, in denen der einzelne und oft ganze Familien nicht einmal in der Lage sind, von dem in schwerer Arbeit erworbenen Lohn einen Teil zurückzulegen, da die ganze Summe für die Befriedigung der notwendigsten Bedürfnisse zur Fortfristung eines kümmerlichen Lebens verwendet wird, da kann der Staat unmöglich seine oft wackersten, arbeitsfähigsten Mitglieder durch Steuern vollkommen vernichten, und selbst dort, wo der
(7 r) Beginn eines unbedeutenden, vom Lohne zurückgelegten Kapitals sich zeigt, kann der Staat diese Summe nicht besteuern, denn dieser geringe Schaden, den er dadurch erleidet, wiegt nicht den großen Vorteil auf, der ihm aus der Sparsamkeit seiner Arbeiterklasse, aus dem Beginne kleiner Kapitalisten erblüht. In diesen Männern, wenn sie zu einer gewissen Wohlhabenheit gereift sind, muß jeder Staat seine Stärke erkennen, denn sie sind in der bittersten Not, im Kampf ums Dasein gestählt worden.[9]

Das Existenzminimum muß ihnen der Staat gewähren; doch sie vollkommen von der Abgabe von Steuern zu befreien, hieße eine ganze Bevölkerungsklasse, die heutzutage ebenso wie jeder Reiche die Vorzüge eines geordneten Staatswesens genießt, von der Erhaltung desselben ausschließen, wodurch sie in den Augen vieler das Recht, ihre Rechte zu fordern und auszuüben, verlieren würden.[10]

Die wohlhabenden Bürger müßten aber durch die progressive Besteuerung
2 v ihres reinen Einkommens getroffen werden; dies würde bestimmt als das richtigste und zweckmäßigste *System* sich in jedem Falle beurkunden; durch genaue Kenntnis des Einkommens aller Bürger wäre der allgemeine Reichtum des Staates bekannt und ein gerechter Vorgang bei der Besteuerung leicht durchführbar.

7 Rau (1859), S. 381, betont für den Fall der 'Armen', daß 'die Steuern (nicht) die Befriedigung der dringendsten Bedürfnisse hindern (dürfen)'.

8 Besteuerung entsprechend den relativen Interessen an dem gemeinsamen Vermögenswert; Smith (1776) V.ii.b.3. Siehe auch V.ii.c.6, wo gefordert wird, daß die Reichen mehr als proportional zu ihrem Einkommen zu den öffentlichen Ausgaben beitragen sollten.

9 Smith (1776) hält Steuern auf den Arbeitslohn für 'töricht und verderblich' (V.ii.i.5), behandelt sie aber im übrigen ausnahmsweise anders als Menger, weil er der Meinung ist, daß sie zur Gänze rückgewälzt werden.

10 Smith (1776), V.ii.g.11.

certainly be best therefore to have the net incomes of all citizens taxed proportionately, taking care, however, that the poorest classes be left with a sum sufficient to provide the minimum of subsistence;[7] above all, the unpropertied citizens are entitled to demand from the community the protection that they 6 v
cannot provide for themselves.[8] The major interest of the state is to foster and support the spread of general prosperity, as best it can, so it should first of all attempt to lower all taxes as far as possible, particularly those of the poor.

In those grievous circumstances when a person and often entire families are not in a position to save even part of the wages earned by hard labour because the whole sum is required for satisfying the most elementary needs and maintaining a miserable existence, the state cannot possibly ruin its most upright and industrious members by taxes, and even where there is an incipient, as yet insignificant stock of capital saved from wages, the state cannot tax this sum, since the small amount of revenue it foregoes is not commensurate with the 7 r
great advantage that it gains from the thrift of its labouring class, from incipient small capitalists. Once those men have acquired a certain prosperity, they must be considered strong support for any state because they have been steeled by the bitterest misery and by their struggle for existence.[9]

Government has to leave them the minimum of subsistence; however, to exempt them altogether from paying taxes would mean excluding an entire class of the population from contributing towards the maintenance of a well-ordered political system whose advantages they enjoy like any wealthy person; in the eyes of many, this class would thereby lose its claim to demand and exercise its own rights.[10]

Affluent citizens, however, would have to be charged by progressive taxation of their net incomes; this would definitely prove to be the best and most 2 v
expedient system in any case; exact information on the income of all citizens would mean that the general wealth of the state were also known, and that taxation could be carried out in a just manner.

7 Rau (1859), p. 381.

8 Taxation according to 'their respective interests in the (management of the joint) estate'; Smith (1776), V.ii.b.3. See also V.ii.c.6, where it is said that 'the rich should contribute to the publick expence, not only in proportion to their revenue, but something more than in that proportion'.

9 Smith thinks taxes on wages 'absurd and destructive' (V.ii.i.5), but otherwise, for once, treats them differently than Menger, thinking they are going to be shifted backward completely.

10 Smith (1776), V.ii.g.ll: '... every tax...is to the person who pays it a badge, not of slavery, but of liberty'.

Doch, wie gar vieles, so ist auch diese Art der Besteuerung, trotz ihres erhabenen und sittlichen Wesens, das sie im Gebiete der Theorie an sich trägt, praktisch undurchführbar; sie gehört unter jene Systeme, die erst dann in Wirksamkeit treten werden, wenn die Menschen sich vollkommen in ihrem ursprünglichsten Charakter ändern, und alle wie eine Familie nur im Streben nach Veredelung *und Förderung der öffentlichen Wohlfahrt* dahin leben werden.

Betrachten wir *zunächst* die positiven Hindernisse, die der Durchführung der Besteuerung des reinen Einkommens[11] *unter den gegenwärtigen Verhältnissen* im Wege stehen.

3 r Die meisten Bürger brauchen zu ihren Unternehmungen für ihre Kräfte bedeutende Mittel, die durch die Steuerlast geschwächt werden und schwer gleich zu ersetzen sind; sie suchen sich daher durch Verschweigen ihres reinen Einkommens oder durch Vorschützen bedeutender Schulden und durch andere ähnliche Mittel den ihre*m Einkommen* angemessenen Steuern zu entziehen.[12]

Es gelingt ihnen auch, denn wo nicht das Einkommen im Lohne besteht, den der Staat seinen Dienern entrichtet, wird es fast undurchführbar sein, die richtige Größe des Einkommens *der einzelnen Bürger* zu erfahren.

Ein Heer von Beamten müßte aufgestellt werden, um die vielartigen Geschäfte und Unternehmungen zu überwachen,[13] und eben diese Schwierigkeiten würden
3 v die Steuerlast nur vermehren. Schwere Ungerechtigkeiten durch zu gelinde Besteuerung einzelner und durch allzu hohe anderer wären die Folgen der Unkenntnis des reinen Einkommens, welche auch für die meisten Stände kaum zu ändern wäre.[14]

Dies gilt besonders für die reicheren Klassen der Bevölkerung.

Bei den *nicht besitzenden Klassen würde wiederum* die Besteuerung des reinen Einkommens zur Übervorteilung *des Staates* und zum Streben, sich *den direkten Steuern* zu entziehen, führen. Oft sind *nämlich* gewisse Klassen der Bevölkerung gar nicht *geeignet*, direkte Steuern zu entrichten,

a *weil sie die direkten Steuern,*[15] *die doch in $^{1}/_{4}$-jährigen Raten bezahlt werden müssen, nicht zurückzulegen vermögen;*

b *weil sie sich den direkten Steuern leicht zu entziehen vermögen.*

(4 v)

11 Rau (1859), S. 385, betont: 'Nur das reine Einkommen … sollte von den Steuern getroffen werden' (wird wiederholt geäußert). Der nächste Absatz entspricht der Begründung bei Rau.

12 Rau (1859), S. 413 f.

13 Rau (1859), S. 416, behandelt die Kosten der Steuereinhebung. 'Man kann in Deutschland die Kosten ungefähr auf 1/10 – 1/8 der Einnahmen anschlagen'!

14 Der Absatz verbindet Smiths (1776) Steuermaximen 2 und 4, Sicherheit und Kostengünstigkeit der Steuern: V.ii.b.4 und 6.

15 Rau (1859), S. 425, führt die von Smith noch nicht verwendete Einteilung in direkte und indirekte Steuern ein, die Menger offenbar nicht genügend deutlich erklärt hatte. Nach Rau sind direkte Steuern ihrer Intention nach nicht zu überwälzen.

But, as with so many things, this sort of taxation, too, is impracticable in spite of its theoretically noble and moral character; it is one of those systems that will become effective only if and when men change their innate character profoundly and live as one family, striving only to improve and advance the common good.

Let us first look at the actual handicaps that, under present conditions, prevent the taxing of net income.[11]

For their undertakings, most citizens need sums that are quite large in relation 3 r
to their earning power; these sums will be diminished by the tax burden and will hardly be replaced at once; therefore people will try to evade being taxed in proportion to their income either by concealing their net income, by pleading heavy debts, or by other such methods.[12]

In that, they are successful, too; for whenever income is not a wage or salary that the state pays to public servants, it will be almost impossible to know the true income of the individual citizens.

An army of officials would be needed to watch over the various transactions and enterprises,[13] and the very difficulty of this would only increase the tax
burden. Marked injustices due to taxing some too lightly and others too heavily 3 v
would follow from such ignorance about net income; for most social classes hardly anything could be done to alter this ignorance, either.[14]

That is above all true for the wealthier classes.

In the unpropertied classes, on the other hand, taxing net income would lead to cheating the government and to an attempt to evade direct taxes. For in many instances, certain social classes are not well-suited to pay direct taxes,

a because they cannot save the amount of their direct taxes[15] that must be paid quarterly;

b because they can easily evade direct taxation.

(4 v)

[11] Rau (1859), p. 385 (and passim) stresses the need to tax only 'net income'.

[12] This paragraph and the next follow Rau (1859), p. 413 f.

[13] According to Rau (1859), p. 416, the cost of tax collection in Germany amounts to $^1/_{10}$–$^1/_8$ of the sums collected.

[14] This paragraph combines, but also modifies, Smith's maxims 2 and 4 on taxation, the certainty of taxes and their cheapness in collection. Under the latter heading Smith deplores 'a great number of (tax) officers'; cf. (1776) V.ii.b.4 and 6.

[15] Rau (1859), p. 425, introduces the division into direct and indirect taxes, not yet known to Smith and evidently not fully explained by Menger. According to Rau, it is the intention of the government that direct taxes should not be shifted.

Die großen Schwierigkeiten, die der Durchführung im Wege stehen, sind *also die geringe Stabilität und geringe Wirtschaftlichkeit* einiger Schichten des Volkes *einerseits* und die schwer erfahrbaren Einkommensverhältnisse *vieler der besitzenden Klassen andererseits*; gewisse Stände, welche ihr Einkommen und ihren gesamten Lebensunterhalt als Lohn für Dienste, welche sie dem Staate leisten, erhalten, werden bei der Besteuerung leicht zu treffen sein, da der Staat als Geber ihres Einkommens dasselbe genau kennt; doch alle anderen Berufszweige, die nicht im Dienste des Staates als solchen bestehen, werden
5 r ziemlich schwer durch Steuern richtig zu erreichen sein.

Darum wurden für alle anderen Staatsbürger *zwei Arten der Steuern eingeführt:*

1. *die Ertragssteuer*
2. *die Verzehrungssteuer.*[16]

[CM am Rand: *nur Ausführung, was das für Steuern sind!*]

Von großer und bis jetzt unübertroffener Zweckmäßigkeit ist die Ertragsteuer für die Grund- und Hausbesitzer,[17] die Unternehmer aller Art und für die Besitzer von Geldkapitalien; dadurch wird weder das Brutto- noch das reine Einkommen, welches die Eigentümer oft selbst nicht kennen, besteuert, sondern der Ertrag jeder das Vermögen bildenden Sache; (CM am Rand: *Dieser Ertrag ist zwar wesentlich verschieden von dem reinen Einkommen der Hausbesitzer etc. Aber die Finanzverwaltung schließt folgendermaßen: ist der Ertrag nur einmal festgestellt, so wird ihn auch jemand als Einkommen beziehen, und sie trifft solcherart annähernd das Einkommen durch Besteuerung des Ertrages*); auf diese Weise *kann der Staat* den positiven Verhältnissen gemäß, nicht aber schablonenhaft besteuern und wird eigene Benachteiligung meidend durch die Ertragsteuer den Vermögensstock seiner Bürger schonen.

Bei der Haussteuer wird jetzt z.B. auf folgende Weise vorgegangen: bei
5 v Zinshäusern erfährt man den Zins, den die einzelnen Parteien zahlen, und weiß dadurch den Ertrag des Hauses. Nun müssen noch die Reparaturkosten *abgezogen* werden, und vom Übrigbleibenden *berechnet* man die Steuer;[18] bei einem Gebäude aber, das vom Besitzer selbst bewohnt wird, ohne daß er Parteien darin unterbringt, mißt man den *Miet*wert durch Vergleich mit nebenstehenden ganz

16 Die Einteilung folgt Rau, jedoch nicht genau auch seiner Ausdrucksweise. Rau (1859) teilt im Hauptstück über 'Eintheilung der Steuern' S. 423 ein in Besteuerung nach den 'Vermögensumstände(n) oder (der) Steuerfähigkeit jedes Einzelnen' einerseits, die er Schatzungen nennt; und nach 'Verwendungen des Vermögens' oder den 'Ausgaben' andererseits, die er 'Aufwandssteuern' oder auch 'Verbrauchs-, Verzehrungs- oder Consumtionssteuern' nennt. Die 'Verzehrungssteuer' ist dabei der steuertechnische Ausdruck in Österreich.

17 Smith (1776), V.ii.e.6,7, hält eine Proportionalsteuer auf Häuser für eine der besten Arten von Steuern, die sich zugleich (so V.ii.e.8) 'mit hinreichender Genauigkeit ermitteln' läßt.

18 In der Detaildarstellung folgt der ganze Paragraph genau einer stark gekürzten Fassung von Rau (1859). Hier zuerst S. 82 f.

So the big obstacles in the way of effective taxation are the lack of stability and of economy in some classes of society and the difficulty of ascertaining the income situation of many members of the propertied classes; those groups that receive their income and all their means of subsistence as wages for public service will be easy to tax because the government pays out such income and knows the precise amount; but for all other trades and professions that are not in the service of government, levying taxes in appropriate amounts will be rather hard. 5 r

Therefore, two kinds of taxes were introduced for all other citizens:

1 the revenue tax
2 the purchase tax.[16]
[CM in the margin: only explain what sort of taxes these are!]

The revenue tax for owners of real estate,[17] entrepreneurs of all sorts, and for the owners of financial assets is highly expedient, in fact unsurpassed so far; neither gross nor net income, which the owners often do not know themselves, are taxed, but rather the return on capital [CM in the margin: this return differs essentially from the net income of real estate owners, etc. But the tax authorities figure as follows: once revenue is calculated, somebody is bound to receive it as income; taxing of revenue amounts approximately to taxing pertinent income]; in this manner, the state can levy taxes with a view to the actual situation and not just routinely; it will avoid disadvantages to itself and by the revenue tax protect its citizens' stock of capital.

The tax on housing, for example, is now implemented in the following way. In apartment houses the rent that the individual parties pay is known so the returns 5 v
on the house are known. Then the repair costs are deducted and the tax is calculated on the rest;[18] in case of a building that the owner himself uses without letting any part of it, the rental value is calculated by comparing it to similar apartment houses in the neighbourhood,[19] and the respective taxes are levied; where no such comparison is possible, as is often the case e.g. with houses in

16 This division is Rau's. Rau (1859), p. 423, speaks of taxation a) according to wealth or 'taxability' (Rau uses the word 'assessment'), and b) according to 'uses of wealth' or expenditure (which he calls expenditure or consumption tax).

17 Smith (1776), V.ii.e.6,7, thinks a proportionate tax on houses one of the best sorts of taxes and also (V.ii.e.8) one where the tax base can be 'ascertained with sufficient accuracy'.

18 This paragraph corresponds to an abbreviated version of Rau (1859), p. 82 f.

19 Rau (1859), p. 86 ff. Rau elaborates on the opportunity cost aspects of this taxation.

ähnlichen Zinshäusern[19] und hebt nun die gleichen Steuern ein; dort wo aber selbst der Vergleich fehlt, wie es z.B. bei Landhäusern oft der Fall ist, da wird nach Anzahl der Zimmer besteuert, was man die Hausklassensteuer[20] nennt.[21]

Bei Grund und Boden wird die Besteuerung nach der Größe des Besitzes, seiner Qualität *und den bestehenden Preisverhältnissen für die Bodenprodukte, also in letzter Linie gleichfalls nach dem Ertrage*, durchgeführt.[22]

Die schwierigste Aufgabe ist für den Staat, mit richtigen Steuern den Kapitalisten zu treffen, der ohne Nebenerwerb bloß von den *Zinsen* seines Kapitals lebt;[23] denn am schwersten ist es bei ihm, den wirklichen Stand seines *Einkommens* zu erfahren.[24] [CM am Rand: *Wie tut dies der Staat?*]

6 r [CM am Rand: *Durchzuführen*:
Die Ertragsteuern sind bei den besitzlosen Klassen nicht durchführbar. Warum? Einkommensteuern wie wir sehen, auch nicht durchführbar. Folglich Verzehrungsteuern. Warum eben diese? Aus 2 Hauptgründen:
1. Geringe Stabilität der nicht besitzenden Klassen;
2. Unfähigkeit der letzteren, große Steuern aber zu bezahlen.]

7 r [CM am Rand: *Weshalb nennt man gewisse Steuern indirekte?*] Diesem Verhältnisse wird am zweckmäßigsten durch die indirekten Steuern abgeholfen,
7 v welche so eingerichtet sind, daß bei einem bestimmten Genusse eine Steuer gezahlt wird,[25] die im Mehrbetrage der Kosten, nicht aber in einer vom Staate direkt geforderten Steuer besteht;[26] auf diese Weise ist niemand, solange er sich im Lande befindet, von der Mitwirkung bei der Steuerzahlung enthoben; der arme Teil der Bevölkerung aber *in die Lage versetzt, Beiträge an den Staatslasten zu gewähren.* [CM am Rand: *Hier darstellen: die besonderen Vorteile der indirekten Steuern. Siehe*: 2 Seiten weiter unten (d.h. Anfang 8v, Hrsg.)]

So groß die Vorteile der indirekten Steuern besonders *mit Rücksicht auf die nicht besitzenden* Volksklassen sind, so müssen sie dennoch *nur als eine subsidiäre Art*[27] der Besteuerung gelten, denn genauer wird das Einkommen,

[19] Rau (1859), S. 86ff. (Rau arbeitet jedoch weit stärker den Opportunitätskostencharakter dieser Besteuerung heraus).

[20] Rau (1859), S. 88 f. Rau spricht ausdrücklich von 'jede Classe' der Gebäude. Ausführlich Stein (1871), II, S. 111 ff. zur 'Gebäude-Classensteuer'.

[21] Der Absatz entspricht auch Smith (1776), V.ii.e.8. Typischerweise wählt Menger eine von Smith behandelte Thematik aus und folgt in der Detailausarbeitung derselben Rau.

[22] Rau (1859), II, S. 44: Die 'Preise (von Ländereien) stehen im Allgemeinen in dem nämlichen Verhältniß zu einander, wie der Reinertrag der Grundstücke'.

[23] Menger folgt hier Rau (1859), II, S. 129 ('Die Empfänger solcher Zinsrenten pflegt man vorzugsweise Capitalisten zu nennen, weil sie großenteils ohne Beschäftigung von ihren Renten leben') und S. 140 ('Die Ausführung der Zinssteuer ist darum schwierig, weil es an offen vorliegenden Kennzeichen der Zinsforderungen gebricht').

[24] Ebenso Smith (1776), V.ii.f.3–7.

[25] Gleiche Argumentation bei Smith (1776), V.ii.k.l.

[26] Dieser schwer verständliche Satz beruht vermutlich auf einer verkürzten Darstellung durch den Kronprinzen. Menger sagte wohl, Smith folgend, daß die Konsumbesteuerung von

the countryside, houses are taxed according to the number of rooms; this is called the tax on housing according to classification.[20, 21]

Land is taxed according to the size of a property, its quality, and the prevailing prices for the land's produce, that is to say: in the last resort also according to revenue.[22]

The greatest problem for the state is the adequate taxation of the capitalist who lives on the interest of his capital without any other source of income;[23] to find out his true income is altogether the most difficult matter.[24] [CM in the margin: How does the state go about it?]

[CM in the margin: Elaborate: 6 r

Revenue taxes cannot be levied on the unpropertied classes. Why? Income taxes as we see are not practicable either. As a consequence, purchase taxes. Why these particularly? For two main reasons:

1 little stability in unpropertied classes;
2 incapable of paying taxes in large sums.]

[CM in the margin: Why are certain taxes called indirect taxes?] This state 7 r
of affairs is best remedied by way of indirect taxes that are designed so as to
have a tax levied on certain acts of consumption;[25] the tax is added to the cost 7 v
but does not immediately appear as government tax;[26] in this way, nobody is exempt from taxation as long as he remains in the country, and even the poor are able to contribute to the public revenue. [CM in the margin: Describe here: Special advantages of indirect taxes. See: 2 pages lower down (i.e. 8v; ed.)]

However great the advantages of indirect taxes, especially with respect to the unpropertied classes, they must nevertheless be considered a subsidiary form of taxation;[27] for direct taxes are the more exact form of taxing income, or revenue

20 Rau (1859), p. 88 f.

21 See also Smith (1776), V.ii.e.8: typically – as here – Menger uses passages found in Smith and then relies on Rau for details.

22 Rau (1859), II, p. 44.

23 Both in stating this difficulty and in the use of the term 'capitalist' (in a narrow, pre-Marxian sense a rentier living on the interest on financial capital) Menger follows Rau (1859), II, p. 140 f. and p. 129.

24 Smith (1776), V.ii.f.3–7, is equally sceptical about taxation of interest and points out (as the first difference with respect to the taxation of rent on land) that 'the whole amount of the capital stock which he possesses is almost always a secret' (V.ii.f.5).

25 Smith (1776), V.ii.k.l, argues in the same way.

26 This cryptic sentence, reflecting a likely remark of Menger's evidently not fully understood by the pupil and reproduced in a garbled manner, becomes clear when we know that Smith thought taxes on necessities only increased the cost of labour (i.e. were shifted into higher wages).

27 Menger follows Rau (1859), II, p. 191.

oder vielmehr der Ertrag, durch die direkten Steuern getroffen, und der Staat wird durch dieselben mit bedeutend geringeren Einhebungskosten größere
8 r Summen *sich zu verschaffen* in der Lage sein; seinen *Bedarf* zu allgemeinen Zwecken wird er sich, so weit es möglich ist, durch die direkten Steuern verschaffen, während er *zu den indirekten Steuern nur deshalb greift, um den nicht besitzenden Teil der Bevölkerung zur Steuerleistung herbeizuziehen.*

8 v Da die *Steuern der Bevölkerung Opfer auferlegen* und selbst die patriotischsten Gefühle durch *eine allzu* große Steuerlast bedeutend abgekühlt werden, muß es ein *hauptsächliches Bestreben* der Regierungen sein, dieses notwendige Übel schon aus egoistischen Gründen so viel als möglich zu mildern[28] oder doch wenigstens in bessere Formen zu kleiden; diesen letzten Zweck erfüllen in ihrem engeren Kreise die indirekten Steuern.

Ferner müssen wir die Unmöglichkeit, sich der Steuerzahlung zu entziehen, als einen großen Vorteil dieser Besteuerungsart bezeichnen. Den direkten Steuern suchen manche durch Verbergen auszuweichen; manche sind auch wirklich nicht in der Lage, die geringste Steuerzahlung zu leisten, alle

notwendigen Gütern nicht von den Arbeitern getragen werde, sondern vielmehr die Arbeitskosten (die Löhne) erhöhe.

27 Menger folgt in dieser Sichtweise der indirekten Steuern Rau (1859), II, S. 191.

28 Entspricht Smiths (1776) vierter Steuermaxime (V.ii.b.6). Daß bei Konsumsteuern 'die Kosten der Erhebung und Überwachung immer um einige Procente größer sind, als bei den Schatzungen' begründet Rau (1859), II, S. 189 f. eingehend. Smith sagt dasselbe von Luxussteuern, vgl. V.ii.k.60 ff.

rather; the state can raise larger sums of money at considerably lower collection costs; as far as possible, it will satisfy its general needs by levying direct taxes, while resorting to indirect taxes only to make the unpropertied classes of the population contribute to tax revenue. 8 r

Taxes mean sacrifices on the people's part, and even the most patriotic spirits are considerably dampened by an excessive tax burden; therefore it must be a major concern of governments to minimize this necessary evil, if simply for selfish reasons, or at least to dress it up more becomingly;[28] this last-mentioned goal is achieved by indirect taxes in their restricted area of application. 8 v

Furthermore, we must consider the impossibility of tax evasion as a great advantage of this form of taxation. Some people try to get around direct taxes by hiding; others are truly in no position to pay even the smallest amount of taxes, but

[28] Smith's fourth tax maxim: taxes which can be raised cheaply; for, above, it is said that direct taxes are raised more cheaply; cf. (1776) V.ii.b.6. That consumption taxes are more costly to levy is argued at length by Rau (1859), II, p. 189 f. Smith argues this point only – but very forcefully so – for taxes on luxury consumption: V.ii.k.60 ff.

9 r diese Personen können sich den indirekten Steuern, von deren Existenz sie *oft* keine Ahnung haben,[1] solange sie im Lande sind, unmöglich entziehen; während eines Genusses werden sie ausgezahlt, und bei jedem Glas Bier oder Wein, bei jeder Speise, welche, wo immer im Lande gekauft wird, *bezieht* der Staat eine *Steuer*; auch wird ihre Last weniger empfunden[2] und durch die Gelegenheit, bei welcher sie entrichtet werden, verlieren diese den Charakter der Steuer, und der Zahlende vergißt sie in der Annehmlichkeit des Genusses; sie werden weniger empfunden, denn nur um ein Geringes sind die Preise erhöht, und das allfällige Ärgernis wendet sich meistens, besonders bei den ungebildeteren Klassen, vom Staate ab, gegen die eigentlichen Steuereinheber wie Wirte, Kaufleute etc. etc.; die Zahlung kann von jedem, der auch die geringsten Ansprüche an das Leben stellt, nicht verweigert werden, denn in vielen Fällen bliebe ihm nur das Mittel, dem notwendigsten Genusse *zu entsagen*, übrig, falls er dieser Art der Besteuerung ausweichen wollte.

9 v Die direkten Steuern sind im allgemeinen die richtige Besteuerungsart für die besitzenden Klassen, die im größeren Genusse des Lebens an dasselbe bedeutendere Anforderungen stellen, daher auch für das Allgemeine mehr zu leisten in der Lage sind; während für die *nicht besitzenden* Klassen der Bevölkerung, deren Leben *zumeist* eine Kette von Arbeit und Mühseligkeit ist, die indirekten Steuern als zweckmäßiger zu bezeichnen sind; denn ohne eine bestimmte Summe von ihrem ohnedies unbedeutenden Einkommen zu zahlen, wirken sie dennoch für die Interessen des allgemeinen Wohles mit und sichern sich dadurch, *auch ohne direkte Steuer zu bezahlen*, im Prinzipe den Vollgenuß der staatsbürgerlichen Rechte.

Diese Art der Besteuerung, wo die direkten Steuern neben den indirekten zweckmäßig angebracht sind, führt *nicht vollständig*, aber annähernd noch am nächsten zum Ziele der vollkommen gerechten Besteuerung aller nach ihrem *reinen Einkommen*.

Beide Besteuerungsarten haben ihre Schattenseiten, meistens wird der Staat
10 r nicht das *vollständig* erreichen, was er eigentlich erlangen *will. Die Kombination beider führt indes zumeist zu einem annähernd richtigen System.*[3] Was bei den

[1] Rau (1859), II, S. 187: '..bisweilen bezahlt, ohne daß der Steuerpflichtige es weiß'.

[2] Rau, ebenda: 'Directe Zahlungen in die Staatscasse erregen mehr unangenehme Empfindungen'.

[3] Rau (1859), II, S. 191: Beide Steuerarten sind zu erheben, 'um durch die Verbindung beider Gattungen die unvermeidlichen Fehler und Nachtheile einer jeden zu verringern'.

Public finance. On taxes II 1876

as long as they are in the country, all these people cannot evade the indirect 9 r
taxes, of the existence of which they often have no idea;[1] they are levied in the course of enjoying oneself. The state receives a tax for every glass of beer or wine, every plate of food bought anywhere in the country; the burden is felt less pressingly,[2] and because of the occasions on which these sums are paid, they lose the character of a tax, and the person who pays them forgets about them because consumption is so pleasant; they are felt less acutely, because prices are raised only a little, and especially among the less educated classes any annoyance is attributed to the actual tax collectors, e.g. innkeepers, merchants, etc. etc. and not to the state; nobody who wishes to get ever so little out of life can refuse payment, for in many cases he could do nothing but refrain from vitally necessary consumption, if he wanted to get around this kind of taxation.

Direct taxes are, on the whole, the proper kind of taxation for the propertied 9 v
classes who, enjoying life more, make greater claims upon it and are therefore capable of contributing more to the common good; on the other hand, indirect taxes are more expedient for the unpropertied classes of society whose life is mostly a concatenation of work and hardships; for without paying a certain sum of their inconsiderable income in direct taxes they nevertheless contribute to the common good and thereby secure for themselves their full rights as citizens, in principle, even without paying direct taxes.

This manner of taxation, namely having direct taxes suitably parallel to indirect ones, does not mean that the goal of a perfectly just system, where everyone is taxed according to his net income, is fully achieved; still it comes closest to that.

Both kinds of taxes have their negative aspects; in most cases, the state will
not get completely what it actually wants. The combination of both, however, 10 r
in most instances creates a more or less effective system.[3] If a rich man sometimes pays too little by way of direct taxes, this is often made up for by

1 Rau (1859), II, p. 187.
2 Rau, ibid.
3 In this, Menger follows the argument of Rau (1859), II, p. 191.

direkten Steuern vielleicht manchmal von einem Reichen *zu wenig geleistet* wird, das ersetzt häufig die indirekte Steuer; auch ist es besser, wenn der Staat hin und wieder einen kleinen Schaden erleidet, als wenn Überanstrengung *der Steuerkraft* den Volkswohlstand gefährdet.

Wir haben mithin die Vorteile der beiden Besteuerungsarten besprochen, es fehlt uns nur noch die Erwähnung jener Gegenstände, welche sich am zweckmäßigsten zur indirekten Besteuerung eignen; dies ist eine wichtige und schwierige Sache, denn leicht verliert man dabei das eigentliche Ziel dieser Steuerart aus den Augen, nämlich die Beteiligung der *nicht besitzenden* Bevölkerung am Tragen der Steuerlast; daher müssen Gegenstände besteuert werden, welche eben *vorwiegend* von diesen Volksklassen gebraucht werden; denn *einerseits werden* jene Dinge welche *hauptsächlich von den wohlhabenden Klassen konsumiert werden und deshalb* einen geringen Absatz finden, dem Staate nicht den Vorteil
10 v bedeutender *Einkünfte* bieten und bloß die Schattenseite jeder Besteuerung, ein Hemmnis der Industrie zu sein,[4] aufweisen; *und andererseits* sollen jene Produkte, die nur von den reichen Klassen der Bevölkerung benützt werden, nicht zum Gegenstand indirekter Besteuerung dienen, denn die wohlhabenden Bürger werden ohnedies *am zweckmäßigsten durch direkte Steuern zur Behebung der Staatslasten herangezogen*; auch *übt* die Regierung *durch die indirekten Steuern leicht* einen großen Einfluß auf die wichtigsten Verhältnisse der einzelnen *aus und kann leicht verleitet werden, denselben* zur Erziehung und vermeintlichen Verbesserung des Volkes zu benützen; *aber abgesehen davon*, daß sie kein Recht dazu hat, und dadurch leicht in den Fehler der Eingriffe in die wirtschaftlichen und privativen Verhältnisse der einzelnen Bürger verfällt, kann sie auch manchem blühenden Zweige der heimischen Industrie hiedurch schädlich werden, wie dies der Fall bei *den meisten* Luxussteuern ist.

Am besten dienen *allgemein gebräuchliche Lebensmittel* und
11 r Genußgegenstände,[5] die im momentanen Gebrauche aufgehen, zur indirekten Besteuerung, wie Bier, Wein, Branntwein, Zucker, etc. etc. oder als Regalgüter: Tabak, Salz, Zündhölzer etc. etc. [Am Rand: allgemeinste Gebrauch]

Daher ist das Prinzip indirekter Besteuerung, wenn es auf Luxusgegenstände oder gar auf *das Einkommen der besitzenden* Klassen gerichtet ist, einesteils ein Eingriff in die eigensten Rechte der einzelnen Bürger, anderesteils eine neue Belastung jener Teile der Bevölkerung, die durch die direkten Steuern ohnedies genügend hart getroffen werden.

11 v Wo *der Ertrag des Vermögens* schon besteuert wird, ist die indirekte Besteuerung des Vermögensstockes ein ungerechtfertigter Druck, der dem

4 Besonders hervorgehoben von Smith (1776), V.ii.k.63.

5 Rau (1859), II, S. 195: 'die Aufwandssteuern sollen ihrer Bestimmung nach auf die entbehrlichen Ausgaben für Genußmittel fallen'; auf S. 211 heißt es, üblich seien Steuern auf 'einige allgemein zum Genuß dienende Nahrungsmittel'. Bis auf Zündhölzer werden alle genannten Güter dann gesperrt gedruckt in den §§ 433–42 erwähnt.

indirect taxes; furthermore, it is better to have the state suffer a little loss now and then than to have excessive taxation jeopardize national wealth.

So we have discussed the advantages of both kinds of taxation; it remains only to mention the objects that best lend themselves to indirect taxation; this is an important and difficult subject for it is easy to lose sight of the true end of this kind of taxation, namely to have the unpropertied classes share the tax burden; therefore objects that are mostly used by these classes of the population must be taxed; for on the one hand, things that are chiefly consumed by the propertied classes and for this reason are sold only in small quantities will not furnish government with the advantage of substantial revenue and taxing them will instead have the negative effect of obstructing their production;[4] on the other hand, those products that are used only by the wealthy classes of the population 10 v
should not be taxed indirectly, for the wealthy are made to help carry the government's burden most expediently through direct taxes anyway; using indirect taxation, government can also easily and substantially influence the most important relationships in the lives of individuals and may easily be tempted to use this influence to educate and presumably improve the people; but apart from the fact that it is not entitled to do that and therefore can easily do wrong by interfering with the economic and the private spheres of individual citizens, the government can also harm many flourishing branches of domestic industry, as happens with most taxes on luxury goods.

Commonly used foodstuffs and such items of pleasure[5] as are consumed at once, e.g. beer, wine, brandy, sugar, etc. etc., or goods on which government 11 r
has a monopoly, e.g. tobacco, salt, matches, etc. etc., are best suited for indirect taxation. [In the margin: most common use]

Thus, the principle of indirect taxation when applied to luxuries or to the income of the propertied classes infringes on the personal rights of individual citizens and is also an additional burden on those parts of the population that are already sufficiently hard hit by direct taxes.

If the returns on capital are taxed already, the indirect taxation of the stock 11 v
of capital is an unjustified burden, which runs counter to the purpose of a just tax and weakens the community.

4 Smith (1776), V.ii.k.63, explains: 'Such taxes necessarily occasion some destruction or discouragement to certain branches of industry'.

5 Recommendation and exact wording of Rau (1859), II, p. 195, together with p. 211. The following paragraphs mention (as easily visible chapter headings) taxes on all the commodities named, except matches. The enumeration of Rau is rendered nearly completely, the exception being meat.

Zweck einer gerechten Steuer widersprechend zu einer Schwächung der Gesamtheit erniedrigt.

In keinem anderen Gebiete kann die Regierung auf so klare Weise *ihre Gerechtigkeit beurkunden* als wie durch das System ihrer Besteuerung und die *energische rücksichtslose* Durchführung desselben.

Die Lenker des Staates, die von dem Vertrauen der Gesamtheit zu den Verfechtern jener allgemeinen Interessen berufen sind, welche *der einzelne zu*
12 r *vertreten* nicht in der Lage ist, *haben indes die dem Staate nötigen Mittel sich nicht nur auf die zweckmäßigste Art zu verschaffen, sondern dieselben auch auf die der Gesamtheit nützlichste Art zu verwenden. Sie* wirtschaften mit dem Reichtum vieler, die ihn vertrauend den Staatslenkern übergaben, in der Hoffnung, die Früchte gemeinsam zu ernten. Darum muß der Zweck, zu welchem Steuern verwendet werden, ein für das Allgemeine nützlicher sein, und hierin liegt die edelste Aufgabe jener, die damit betraut sind, denn sie erfordert eine hohe Auffassung des allgemeinen Wohles und *große Intelligenz und* Gewissenhaftigkeit.

Möglichst geringe Steuern, und diese für *Zwecke der inneren Politik, namentlich zur* Hebung des Volksreichtums verwendet, sind für die Gesamtheit am zweckmäßigsten; denn jene Macht nach außen, die durch das Erschöpfen des inneren Reichtums erreicht wird, ist eigentlich *zumeist* Schwäche und *wird* meistens *auch nur von* dem selbstischen Ehrgeiz einzelner *angestrebt.*

Dort, wo der Volksreichtum am größten, die Bildung am verbreitetsten, der einzelne frei und zufrieden ist, wird auch der Staat, als Person gedacht, am mächtigsten sein, denn er hat am besten sich seinem erhabenen Zwecke genähert; da hören auch die Steuern auf, eine Last zu sein, und werden zu Mitteln, das Wohl der Teile und dadurch die Kraft des Ganzen zu heben.

Rudolf
Ischl, den 11. August 1876

Nowhere can the government prove its fairness as clearly as by its tax system and by the resolute and impartial implementation of it.

Statesmen have been entrusted by the confidence of the community with promoting those common interests that the individual is unable to pursue by himself; they should not only procure in the most expedient manner the resources 12 r
that the state needs, but should also spend them in such a way as to provide the greatest benefit to the community. They employ the wealth of many, who entrusted it to them hoping to enjoy the fruits in common. The end for which tax revenue is used therefore must profit the community as a whole; here lies the noblest task of those who have been entrusted with it, since discharging it requires a clear understanding of the common good as well as great intelligence and scrupulousness.

The lowest possible taxes, levied for purposes of domestic policies, particularly for increasing general wealth, are most expedient for the community; for any power displayed abroad that is achieved by exhausting domestic wealth actually reflects a weakness, and in most cases it is only selfish ambition that aspires to it.

Wherever the community's wealth is greatest, general education highest, and the individual free and satisfied, the state, conceived of as a person, will be most powerful and will come closest to its noble end; here, taxes will no longer be considered a burden, but will become the means for improving the welfare of individuals and strengthening the whole community.

Rudolf
Ischl, 11 August 1876

Samples of Rudolf's original text

The following selected passages show Rudolf's text before Menger changed it. The page-numbers given refer to the Notebook-pages indicated in the margins.

p.42r (to p.42v):
Die Bedürfnisse sind freilich sehr verschieden, doch selbst der Reichste könnte nicht allen seinen Wünschen Rechnung tragen. Zur Befriedigung derselben sind Mittel nötig und daher sucht ein jeder, der sie nicht hat, sie zu erlangen, und derjenige, der solche besitzt, sie zu vergrößern.
Dieser Prozeß erfordert Arbeit, Ausnützung der natürlichen wie der künstlichen Erwerbsquellen, und stete Schaffung neuer, dadurch wird er zum Motor der Kultur.
(The next two paragraphs remained unchanged while the subsequent text read:)
Durch diesen Vorgang entwickelt sich auch langsam ein dauernder Vermögensstock, der dann im steten Zunehmen begriffen ist, und die Gründung von Unternehmungen aller Art ermöglicht; je mehr wirtschaftliche Menschen, je mehr größere Vermögen und Unternehmungen in einem Staate sind, desto bedeutender ist die allgemeine Beschäftigung der ärmeren Klassen, und daher auch die größere Verbreitung der Wohlhabenheit.
Aus diesem ersieht man, wie die Tätigkeit des einzelnen fühlbar aufs Ganze wirkt, und jeder Staatsbürger fördernd oder schadend durch seine wirtschaftlichen Bestrebungen Einfluß nehmen kann; das ist die Wichtigkeit für das gesamte Interesse, doch auch für den einzelnen Bürger selbst ist es natürlich von höchstem Werte, wenn er sich und den Seinigen durch Fleiß und richtige Wirtschaft ein gesichertes, für die Verhältnisse bedeutendes Einkommen verschaffen kann, welches dann, durch glückliche Verwertung, zum allgemeinen Wohle zunehmen wird. Man kann also sagen, …

p.48r, new par.:
Bei den Handelsverhältnissen tritt uns derselbe Fall der unbedingten Hilfe der Regierung entgegen; der Industrielle ist bestrebt, seine Waren in fremde Länder zu exportieren, wodurch er sowohl wie der Staat Nutzen hat, denn durch Handel und Verkehr kommt das Geld aus dem Auslande herein; doch der einzelne Bürger kann unmöglich seinen Produkten in einem fremden Staat Einlaß verschaffen, er als ein Sandkorn dieses Riesenberges des gesamten Volkes verschwindet in

diesen großen Interessen, hier muß die Gesamtheit zum Wohle der Teile wirken, und die einzelnen Staaten müssen in diesem Falle wie Personen untereinander ihre Interessen verhandeln; da werden Handelsverträge geschlossen, welche die Handelsinteressen der einzelnen ermöglichen und dadurch die Blüte des Staates in einem der wesentlichsten Punkte fördern.

p.69v, 2nd par.:
Er muß darauf sehen, daß ein gerechtes Lohnverfahren in allen Geschäften seiner Untertanen ausgeübt werde, darum aber ist es vor allem seine Pflicht, daß jene Menschen, die ihre Dienste dem Wohle des Ganzen, dem Staate widmen, auch dafür gut entlohnt werden, daß sie nach dem Maße ihrer Ausbildung und ihres Wirkungskreises ihren Lohn bemessen erhalten; und vor allem aber muß es eine Sorge jeder weisen Regierung sein, dem Talente und der fleißigen Verwertung zum Besten des Ganzen, der geistigen Fähigkeiten eine freie Bahn zur Erlangung der hohen Stellen offen zu lassen. Der Staat kann nicht wie der Private in ein und derselben Stelle die bessere Ausübung besser entlohnen, dafür aber eröffnet er dem vorzüglichen eine große Karriere, während der mittelmäßige sich im kleinen Wirkungskreise fortbewegt.

p.70v, new par.:
Das wichtigste Prinzip jeder Entlohnung muß die Gerechtigkeit und die Unparteilichkeit sein, für den einzelnen, indem es von ihm vernachlässigt seinen eigenen Schaden herbeiführt, für den Staat aber vor allem, da es neben der großen Immoralität jeder ungerechten Entlohnung ... Willkür, die sicherste Basis ... untergräbt.

p. 71v, new par.:
Auch der Staat hat Diener, welche die untersten Arbeiten verrichten und deren Heranbildung sehr geringe, vielleicht selbst gar keine Mühe kostet; wie z.B. die Amtsdiener, Postillone, Portiere bei Staatsgebäuden etc. etc; in diesen Fällen muß der Staat sich ganz nach der Lehre vom Arbeitslohne halten, welche bestimmt, daß vollkommen unqualifizierte und gemeine Arbeiter nur eben so viel erhalten, als sie zu ihrer und ihrer Familie Ernährung benötigen; es ist ein harter Grundsatz, der oft viel Elend und Mangel nach sich zieht, doch es muß auch in dem Systeme der Arbeitslöhne ein Schema geben, und was sollte der Arbeitgeber jenen Arbeitern geben, deren Ausbildung eine sehr kostspielige war und deren Talente hervorragend sind? Bald würde dann dies Maß der Löhne jedes Vermögen und alle Kräfte der einzelnen wie des Staates übersteigen; darum ist es eine eiserne Notwendigkeit, demjenigen Arbeiter, der ohne Bildung und Wissen nur solche Verrichtungen kann, die ein jeder in der kürzesten Zeit erlernt, nur das Erforderliche für den kümmerlichsten Lebensunterhalt zu geben.

Ein anderer Einfluß beherrscht noch die Masse der Entlohnung, nämlich der Ort, an dem der Arbeiter sich befindet; …

p.75r:
Die Annehmlichkeit des Dienstes muß mit in den Lohn gerechnet werden und denselben verkleinern, die Unannehmlichkeit vergrößert ihn, um überhaupt Menschen zu dem Geschäfte zu ziehen.
In den kleineren Verhältnissen wird z.B. der Staat mit geringerem Lohne Forstleute und Jäger für die Staatsforste anstellen können, während er zu Gerichtsdienern und Gefängniswärtern gewiß nur durch gute Bezahlung Leute locken wird.

p.80r, par. 2, 3:
Wie in allem und jedem zeigen sich die guten oder üblen Verhältnisse des Staates sowohl wie des einzelnen auch in der Größe des Zinsfußes, der bei Darlehen erhalten wird. Es ist dies ein Spiegel aller privativsten Gründe, welche sich unwillkürlich in die äußeren Angelegenheiten hereinmengen, sie bedeutend beeinflussend.
Wenn der Staat nur die Gesamtheit aller Teile ist, wird er auch von ihren Charaktereigenschaften und persönlichsten Geldverhältnissen beherrscht, während diese auch von jenem in solchen Angelegenheiten, wo er als Ganzes handelt, bis in die kleinsten Details dominiert werden.

p.80v, 2nd par.:
Der Zinsfuß hängt daher hauptsächlich von dem landesüblichen Zinsfuß im allgemeinen und von dem Kredit und der Vertrauenswürdigkeit desjenigen ab, der das Darlehen nimmt; diese besteht für den Leihenden in gesicherten Geschäften, in Kapital-Reichtum, und Solidität des Charakters; gerade dieselben Eigenschaften aufzuweisen, bedarf der Staat, wenn er große Darlehen benötigt. Gerade dieselben Eigenschaften muß nun auch der Staat aufweisen, wenn er große Darlehen benötigt. Der Zinsfuß wird ein geringer sein, wenn das Land bekannt ist in betreff seines Reichtums an Kapitalien, und daher auch im Rufe eines soliden, sicheren Geldwesens steht, was eine Folge der Sparsamkeit und des Sinnes für Ordnung der einzelnen Staatsbürger ist.
Hierin liegt der Lohn eines vorsichtigen und geordneten Vorganges in Geldsachen für den Staat, sowohl wie für den einzelnen. Bei geringem Zinsfuß werden sie ihre Darlehen erhalten und mit geringen Kosten ihre Unternehmungen durchführen; während hingegen der im Geldwesen ungeordnete Staat und der im Rufe des Leichtsinns stehende Bürger neben dem wirklichen Schaden und dem Mangel, an dem sie durch ihre ungünstigen wirtschaftlichen Verhältnisse darben, auch noch den fühlbaren Nachteil eines großen Zinsfußes haben, der ihnen oft vieles unmöglich macht, gewiß aber alles teuerer und schwerer erreichen läßt.

Besonders wichtig ist dies für den Staat, denn geordnete Geldzustände sind Hauptversicherungen seiner Existenz, während ungeordnete Unzufriedenheit erzeugen, da er durch dieselben gezwungen wird, zum Mittel großer Steuern und häufiger Anlehen zu greifen; diese zwei letzterwähnten Mittel, die er nur in den dringendsten Lagen ergreifen soll, sind die sprechendsten Beweise ungeordneten Geldwesens und rauben ihm am meisten den Kredit bei allen, die ihm durch Darlehen helfen wollen.
Vor allem soll aber die Regierung ihre Liebe zur Rechtlichkeit und den Drang nach Erfüllung ihrer Verpflichtungen durch das Streben beweisen, niemandem große Summen schuldig zu bleiben, und die großmöglichste Aufmerksamkeit in ihren Geldgeschäften anwenden.

p.82v, new par.:
Wenn der unordentlichen Wirtschaft ein oder gar mehrere Staatsbankrotte folgen, dann wird der Zinsfuß bei den Staatsdarlehen ungemein steigen und es wird große Mühe kosten, überhaupt Gelegenheit Geld zu leihen zu nehmen zu finden; auch werden solche Zustände...

p.84r, new par.:
Damit das aber gelinge, müssen wir vor allem bestrebt sein, durch Regelung unseres Papiergeldwesens, die Nationalbank auf einen gesunden Standpunkt zu bringen, dann die alten Schulden auszubezahlen und die Steuern womöglich zu erniedrigen; dann werden wir in den Ruf eines Staates mit geordneten Finanzen kommen, und im Bedarfsfalle werden wir Geld zu mäßigen Summen erhalten; dadurch ...

p.85v, par.3:
(*Rudolf's original version was grammatically correct, while the latter part of the altered first sentence is not logical*) Grundstücke, die z.B. vor 20 Jahren 5000 fl. getragen, tragen jetzt 10–15 000 fl.; dies ist besonders der Fall in den Ländern, wo der Bau von Verkehrsstraßen in der raschesten Zeit aus dem primitivsten Zustand in den der Kultur verhalf. Ein deutliches Zeichen der Bestätigung dieser Tatsache, daß das Einkommen des Grund und Bodens in stetem Wachstum ist, ist die Tatsache, daß der grundbesitzende Adel jetzt auf einem komfortableren Fuße lebt als je zuvor; dies findet seine Erklärung darin, daß der Wert der Güter durch die zunehmende Kultur ebenfalls im Wachsen begriffen ist, daher erhält auch der Landwirt jeden Standes und Reichtums eine Garantie für eine schöne Zukunft und kann versichert sein, daß seine Einkommensquellen auf der festesten Basis ruhen.

p.86r, new par.:
... da je mehr Menschen in einem Landstriche wohnen, desto mehr Bodenprodukte sind daselbst zu ihrer Ernährung notwendig und die große Dichtigkeit der

Bevölkerung in einem Lande ist die Folge der zunehmenden Kultur, welche viele Existenzen durch Arbeit ermöglicht und auch fremde Arbeitskräfte ins Land zieht; aus diesem Grunde also muß absolut mehr Landwirtschaft betrieben werden, deren Produkte durch den großen Absatz um höhere Preise verhandelt werden.

p.88v, 1st sentence:
Wie gesagt, die zunehmende Kultur ist der Hebel des Einkommens, den Grund und Boden liefert, das Wachsen der Einwohnerzahl erfordert mehr Lebensmittel, stellt mehr Arbeitskräfte zur Verfügung, die guten Kommunikationsmittel...

p.94r, 1st sentence:
Alle diese bis jetzt erwähnten Maßregeln sind die Mittel, mit deren Hilfe der einzelne sich aus der ärgsten Not zu helfen sucht, es sind die aus der Natur folgenden Wege, ...

p.lv, last sentence:
Aus diesen Gründen wies die eiserne Notwendigkeit bald nach Veränderungen im Besteuerungssystem hin, die den Zweck hatten, mit Gerechtigkeit die einzelnen nach Maß ihrer Mittel zu treffen und wo es zulässig war, den Ärmsten zu schützen und gewisse Arten der Steuern in bessere Formen zu kleiden.

p. 3v, from new par.:
Dies gilt besonders für die reicheren Klassen der Bevölkerung.

Bei den ärmeren könnte das Streben nach Besteuerung des reinen Einkommens zu einer für ihre so bescheidenen Verhältnisse viel zu drückenden Last einerseits werden, andererseits würde es eine Übervorteilung und ein Streben, sich dem Gesetze zu entziehen, dem armen Volke aufdrängen, welches die übelsten Früchte tragen würde; oft sind auch gewisse Klassen der Bevölkerung gar nicht in der Lage, direkte Steuern zu entrichten; dies aber richtig zu erfahren, wo die Grenze der Zahlungsfähigkeit sich befindet, und welches Maß des Einkommens als ein Existenzminimum zu gelten hat, ist ein schwieriges Problem der Besteuerung; ferner wäre auch das Mittel der Entziehung der Staatsbürgerpflichten durch Umherziehen in verschiedenen Gegenden zu nahe an die Hand gelegt, was Unsicherheit im Staate und besitzloses, vagabundierendes Proletariat vermehren würde.

References

Blaug, Mark (1985), *Economic Theory in Retrospect*, 4th ed., Cambridge.

Cantillon, Richard, 'Essay on the Nature of Trade in General,' around 1730, published as: 'Essai sur la nature du commerce en général', London (?) 1755; in German as: 'Versuch über die Natur des Handels im allgemeinen', F.A. Hayek (ed.), *Sammlung sozialwissenschaftlicher Meister*, 25, Jena 1931.

Clark, J.C.D. (1985), *English Society 1688–1832. Ideology, social structure and political practice during the ancien regime*, Cambridge.

Good, David F. (1984), *The Economic Rise of the Habsburg Empire 1750–1914*, Berkeley; in German 1986 as: *Der wirtschaftliche Aufstieg des Habsburgerreiches 1750–1914*, Vienna.

Habermas, Jürgen (1962), *Strukturwandel der Öffentlichkeit*, Neuwied (5th edn 1971).

Hamann, Brigitte (1978), *Rudolf. Kronprinz und Rebell*, Vienna.

Hayek, Friedrich A. (1944), *The Road to Serfdom*, London and Chicago.

Hayek, Friedrich A. (1988), *The Fatal Conceit – The Errors of Socialism*, London and New York.

Hermann, Friedrich B.W. (1832), *Staatswirthschaftliche Untersuchungen*, Munich (2nd edn 1870).

Hildebrand, Bruno (1848), *Die Nationalökonomie der Gegenwart und Zukunft*, Frankfurt am Main.

Hufeland, Gottlieb (1807), *Neue Grundlegung der Staatswirthschaftskunst, durch Prüfung und Berichtigung ihrer Hauptbegriffe von Gut, Werth, Preis, Geld und Volksvermögen mit ununterbrochener Rücksicht auf die bisherigen Systeme*, Giessen and Wetzlar.

Jevons, William S. (1871), *The Theory of Political Economy*, London.

Marx, Karl (1867/1987), *Das Kapital. Kritik der politischen Ökonomie*, Marx-Engels-Gesamtausgabe,vol. 23, Berlin; English: *Capital*, New York 1987.

März, Eduard (1968), *Österreichische Industrie- und Bankpolitik in der Zeit Franz Josephs I.*, Vienna.

Menger, Carl (1871), *Grundsätze der Volkswirthschaftslehre*, Vienna. (Facsimile edition in Carl Menger, *Gesammelte Werke* (F.A. Hayek, ed.), vol. I, Tübingen 1968).

Menger, Carl (1884), *Die Irrthümer des Historismus in der deutschen National-Oekonomie*, Vienna. (Facsimile edition in Carl Menger, *Gesammelte Werke* (F.A. Hayek, ed.), vol. III, Tübingen 1970).

Menger, Carl (1891), 'Die Social-Theorien der classischen National-Oekonomie und die moderne Wirthschaftspolitik', *Neue Freie Presse* 6.,8.,Jan.1891, Vienna. (Reprinted in Carl Menger, *Gesammelte Werke* (F.A. Hayek, ed.), vol. III, Tübingen 1970).

Menger; Carl (1976), *Principles of Economics*, translated by James Dingwall and Bert F. Hoselitz, with an introduction by F.A. Hayek, New York and London.

Mischler, Peter (1857), *Handbuch der National-Oekonomie. Part I: Grundsätze der National-Oekonomie; Part II: Entstehung des National-Reichthums und Lehre vom natürlichen Reichthum der Länder*, Vienna.

Rau, Karl Heinrich (1854), *Grundsätze der Volkswirthschaftspolitik*, Heidelberg (4th edition; first published in 1828 as *G. d. V.pflege*).

Rau, Karl Heinrich (1855), *Grundsätze der Volkswirthschaftslehre*, Heidelberg (6th edition; first published in 1826).

Rau, Karl Heinrich (1859), *Grundsätze der Finanzwissenschaft*, Heidelberg (4th edition; first published in 1832 and 1837).

Ricardo, David (1970), *On the Principles of Political Economy and Taxation* (1817, 3rd edn 1821), vol. I of *The Works and Correspondence of David Ricardo*, (ed. P. Sraffa), Cambridge.

Riedel, A.F. (1838), *Nationalöconomie oder Volkswirthschaft*, vol. I, Berlin.

Robbins, Lionel (1952), *The Theory of Economic Policy in English Classical Political Economy*, London (1965).

Roscher, Wilhelm (1864), *Grundlagen der Nationalökonomie*, Stuttgart (5th edition; first published 1854).

Roscher, Wilhelm (1874), *Geschichte der National-Oekonomik*, Munich.

Schäffle, Albert E.F. (1867), *Das gesellschaftliche System der menschlichen Wirthschaft*, Tübingen.

Schüller, Richard (1895), *Die klassische Nationalökonomie und ihre Gegner*, Berlin.

Smith, Adam (1776), *An Inquiry into the Nature and Causes of the Wealth of Nations*, Glasgow edition by R.H. Campbell and A.S. Skinner, Oxford 1976. German edition used: *Untersuchung über das Wesen und die Ursachen des Volkswohlstandes*, translated by F. Stöpel, Berlin 1878.

Stein, Lorenz von (1858), *Lehrbuch der Volkswirthschaft*, Vienna.

Stigler, George (1972), 'Smith's travels on the ship of state', *History of Political Economy*, 4, pp. 265–77.

Streissler, Erich (1990a), 'The influence of German economics on the work of Menger and Marshall' in: *Carl Menger and his legacy in economics* (Bruce J. Caldwell, ed.), Durham, N.C., and London, pp. 31–68.

Streissler, Erich (1990b), 'Carl Menger, der deutsche Nationalökonom' in: *Studien zur Entwicklung der Ökonomischen Theorie X* (Bertram Schefold, ed.), Schriften des Vereins für Socialpolitik, N.S. 115/X, Berlin, pp. 153–81.

Viner, Jacob (1927),'Adam Smith and Laissez Faire', *Journal of Political Economy*, 35, pp. 198–232.

Index